# organizing identity

*Culture, Representation and Identities* is dedicated to a particular understanding of 'cultural studies' as an inherently interdisciplinary project critically concerned with the analysis of meaning. The series focuses attention on the importance of the contemporary 'cultural turn' in forgiving a radical re-think of the centrality of 'the cultural' and the articulation between the material and the symbolic in social analysis. One aspect of this shift is the expansion of 'cultural' to a much wider, more inclusive range of institutions and pratices, including those conventionally termed 'economic' and 'political'.

**Paul du Gay** is at the faculty of Social Sciences at The Open University.
**Stuart Hall** is Emeritus Professor at The Open University and Visiting Professor at Goldsmiths College, the University of London.

Books in the series:

*Representing Black Britain*
*Black and Asian Images on Television*
Sarita Malik

*Cultural Economy*
*Cultural Analysis and Commercial Life*
Edited by paul du Gay and Michael Pryke

*Advertising Cultures*
*Gender, Commerce, Creativity*
Sean Nixon

*Advertising*
*A Cultural Economy*
Liz McFall

*Organizing Identity*
Paul du Gay

# organizing identity:

## persons and organizations 'after theory'

## paul du gay

SAGE Publications
Los Angeles • London • New Delhi • Singapore

SAGE Publications Ltd
1 Oliver's Yard
55 City Road
London EC1Y 1SP

SAGE Publications Inc.
2455 Teller Road
Thousand Oaks, California 91320

SAGE Publications India Pvt Ltd
B 1/I 1 Mohan Cooperative Industrial Area
Mathura Road, New Delhi 110 044
India

SAGE Publications Asia-Pacific Pte Ltd
33 Pekin Street #02-01
Far East Square
Singapore 048763

**British Library Cataloguing in Publication data**

A catalogue record for this book is available from the British Library

ISBN 978-1-4129-0011-9
ISBN 978-1-4129-0012-6

**Library of Congress Control Number: 2006927008**

Typeset by C&M Digitals (P) Ltd., Chennai, India
Printed in Great Britain by Athenaeum Press, Gateshead
Printed on paper from sustainable resources

In memory of REdG

In memory of Pedro

# contents

# acknowledgements

The list of contributors to this book is too long to include in full; however I would particularly like to thank the following organizations and individuals.

The John Lewis Partnership, and especially their Archivist, Judith Faraday, for facilitating access to the partnership archives and for helping me find my way around them. Thanks also to Sophie Taysom for providing research assistance on the 'Self-Service' project.

The Sociology Program at the Research School of Social Sciences at the Australian National University for providing a Fellowship that enabled me to get this book started. Special thanks to Judy Wajcman for inviting and looking after me, and to fellow-visitors Ann-Jorun Berg and Robert Van Krieken for their intellectual companionship.

The Department of Organization and Industrial Sociology at the Copenhagen Business School for allocating a Visiting Professorship that allowed me the opportunity to try out some of the ideas contained in this book in a doctoral seminar on Identity. Thanks in particular to the postgraduates who participated in the seminar and to Ann Westenholz, Torben Elgaard Jensen and Susse Georg for their encouragement and support.

The Centre for Critical Theory at the University of the West of England for offering me a Visiting Chair from 2002 to 2005. Thanks to my friend and colleague Anthony Elliott for his unstinting support, and to Ajit Nayak and Anthony Beckett for their interest and enthusiasm.

The Economic and Social Research Council in the form of their Centre for Research on Socio-Cultural Change (CReSC) for enabling me to take a generous period of study leave that enabled this book to be completed. I am especially grateful to the Directors of the Centre, Mike Savage, Tony Bennett and Karel Williams.

I am deeply grateful to friends and scholars who discussed ideas with me, allowed me to plunder theirs and offered much needed guidance or support. I would especially like to thank: Frances Bonner, John Clarke, Franck Cochoy, Gill Court, Liz McFall, Angela McRobbie, Danny Miller, Sean Nixon, Mike Pryke, Alan Scott, Andy Sturdy, Charlie Turner and Margie Wetherell.

I owe a particular debt to Richard Chapman, Stuart Hall, Ian Hunter, David Saunders and Marilyn Strathern whose work has motivated this book in ways they are probably not aware of and may even find a little odd. A special debt is owed to Hall, Hunter and Saunders who have been constant and indispensable sources of ideas, dialogue and guidance. Needless to say, neither they nor any other person mentioned here is to blame for the failings this book undoubtedly possesses.

Special thanks to Julia Hall, my editor at Sage, who commissioned the book and has maintained a belief in its eventual appearance that often eluded me.

Finally, I would like to thank Jessica Evans and Ella du Gay who have lived with and contributed to this book in one form or another over a number of years.

Portions of this book draw on published and unpublished papers:

Chapter 3 incorporates arguments from 'Which is the "Self" in "Self-Interest"', which first appeared in *The Sociological Review*, 53(3)(2005): 391–411.

Chapter 4 develops arguments first aired in 'Self-Service: retail, shopping and personhood', in *Consumption, Markets and Culture*, 7(2)(2004): 149–64.

Chapter 6 is a revised version of 'The Tyranny of the Epochal: change, epochalism and organizational reform', which appeared in *Organization*, 10(4)(2003): 663–84.

Arguments contained in Chapter 7 first appeared in 'A Common Power to Keep Them All in Awe: a comment on governance', *Cultural Values*, 6(1)(2002): 11–27.

# introduction: 'identity' after 'the moment of theory'

It's hard to alter the course of our destinies once they're underway, if we don't know they're our destinies.

(Javier Marias, *Dark Back of Time*)

Is the end nigh? After many years at the top of the intellectual hit parade, are 'Identity', 'Identification' and their conceptual fellow-travellers slipping down the charts? They've had a good run, no one could deny it. Those whose academic careers (this author included) and publishing profits have been built upon them can attest to this. But has 'Identity' run out of steam?

At first sight this may seem an absurd question. After all, in many disciplinary fields 'Identity' work is thriving. Management studies would be a good example. But can something be simultaneously expanding its empire and losing its explanatory power? I want to suggest that in the case of 'Identity', indeed it can. Moreover, I want to argue that the reason for this lies at the door of what has come to be known as 'the moment of theory'. For the destiny of 'Identity' and 'the moment of theory', I wish to argue, are inextricably linked.[1]

So what exactly is this 'moment of theory' and what has it got to do with 'Identity'? As Ian Hunter (2006) has recently suggested, 'the moment of theory' refers to a series of intellectual-cultural developments taking place within the universities of central and western Europe and their colonial offshoots. Although this moment has a number of distinctive historical precedents, it can be appropriately represented as emerging during the 1960s and continuing into the present. According to Hunter (2006), 'the moment of theory' can be said to signal 'the surfacing of theoretical reflection or philosophical reflection within a variety of disciplines which were thereby recast as "empiricist" or "pre-theoretical"'. What exactly does this mean?

Well, unlike natural scientific theories, Hunter (2006) argues, the theory that emerged in the humanities and social sciences in the 1960s was not defined by its object, as it arose in disciplines with quite divergent objects. Furthermore, the types of theory deployed differed in many important respects. It is therefore understandable that one might balk at the very term 'moment of theory', given the diversity that it is meant to muster into something more uniform. If it is neither a distinctive theory in the singular nor a particular object that frames 'the moment of theory', then what exactly does the term mean? For Hunter (2006), the answer to this conundrum lies with the shared intellectual deportment or attitude that the various constituent developments exhibit, albeit to different degrees. That being so, 'the moment of theory' is characterized by a scepticism not only towards empirical experience, but also towards a priori formalism – which it regards as foreclosing a higher level experiential immediacy – and hence cultivates openness to breakthrough phenomena of various kinds. Stanley Fish (1994: 251), without endorsing it, calls this attitude/deportment 'indeterminate negativity'. Roberto Unger (1986) (with definite endorsement) prefers the phrase 'negative capability'. Hunter (2006) also argues that this attitude is characteristic of a particular kind of intellectual persona, and that providing an account of this persona and the exercises associated with its formation, is central to reflection on 'the moment of theory'.

We can get a clearer grasp of this attitude if we turn briefly to the question of 'Identity' that has figured so large in 'the moment of theory' and whose own destiny is so inextricably bound up with it. In post-structuralist lines of thought, for instance, identity is assumed to arise from the manner in which a fixated consciousness exists by disavowing and repressing its 'other'. As Hunter (2006) suggests, it is this repression/occlusion 'that gives the "other", as self-manifesting being, the capacity to break through its disavowal and throw fragile identity into the flux of becoming. … [T]he notion that identity is the temporary fixing of consciousness by the occlusion of the transcendental phenomenon – the phenomenon whose ruptural appearance calls forth a higher and more fluid form of self – is endemic in poststructuralist thought'. We see this, for instance, in the practice of Derridean deconstructive hermeneutics, where the affirmative meaning of a text is taken to be the product of its repression or marginalization of contradictory or subversive meanings; while the recovery of these through deconstructive reading is taken to be the undoing of positive meaning. Following Hunter's lead once more, we can suggest that the figure of 'the other', together with the whole architecture of occlusion and transcendence (breakthrough), is part and parcel of a practice of self-problematization and self-transformation – a spiritual exercise, in Hadot's words (1992) – through which an individual learns to inhabit a post-structuralist persona. And this persona is not without its attractions. It appears to offer its practitioners a distinct muscle of the spirit or mind whose exercise allows it to float free of the boundaries and lines of demarcation that shape consciousness – those boundaries and demarcations that disavow the other – and thus to remain forever unsettled. Unpindownable. How amazing is that!? Pretty, as Latour suggests:

Do you see now why it feels so good to be a critical mind? Why critique, this most ambiguous *pharmakon*, has become such a potent euphoric drug? You are always right! When naive believers are clinging forcefully to their objects, claiming to do things because of their gods, their poetry, their cherished objects, you can turn all of these attachments into so many fetishes and humiliate all the believers by showing that it is nothing but their own projection, that you, yes you alone, can see. But as soon as naive believers are thus inflated by some belief in their own importance, in their own projective capacity, you strike them by a second uppercut and humiliate them again, this time by showing that, whatever they think, their behaviour is entirely determined by the action of powerful causalities coming from objective reality they don't see, but that you, yes you, the never sleeping critic, alone can see. Isn't this fabulous? Isn't it really worth going to graduate school to study critique? (2004: 239)

For Latour, as for Hunter, this critical persona clearly has some purchase, and not just in the social sciences and humanities. For both authors, the power of post-structuralism and its 'identity' work is proportional to the allure of the persona it allows one to occupy. Its prestige and reach should not be underestimated. This has recently extended into what many would see as more vocational areas of academe (not that it didn't permeate some of the more powerful of these early on in its march through the academy: the Critical Legal Studies Movement (CLS), lest we forget, is nearly 30 years old. See Saunders (2005), for a detailed discussion of CLS and 'the moment of theory').

Nonetheless, the recent emergence of a 'critical management studies' movement tells us something about the dynamics of 'the moment of theory', and thus of the intellectual time–space of 'Identity'. In management studies, the feeling of marginality among critical academics is rife, and the opportunity for theoretical vengeance on the more 'instrumental' or vocational aspects of the disciplinary area therefore enormous. The theoretical persona – post-structuralist, deconstructive, whatever – clearly appears attractive to those whose pedagogic bread and butter is often represented by themselves and by other 'critical' intellectuals as less than spiritually uplifting: 'strategy', 'human resource management' (HRM), 'marketing'. If 'Identity' work follows where theory leads, then when 'the moment of theory' reaches its final frontiers – management, sports science and home economics – and beds down, it is no surprise to find a flourishing of 'identity' work accompanying it. Where (anti-foundational) theory (and the critical hope it expresses) is still a (relative) novelty – often related to the degree of vocational, practical or otherwise 'worldly' purposes of the field it enters – theoretical identity work flourishes. Where that novelty has worn off, frequently where theory first gained a foothold – in the humanities and social sciences, say – we find 'Identity' and 'difference', and the predictable chain of theoretical signifiers running out of steam.

I want to suggest, then, that the upsurge of interest in Identity is inextricably linked to 'the moment of theory', and if that moment is passing then we can expect 'Identity' to begin to lose its foothold in the upper echelons of academe too. However, this demise is unlikely to indicate any diminution in the significance of the positive phenomena to which Identity has been theoretically attached. Theoretical identity, as it were, might be running out of steam, but that does not signal a lessening in the practical import of debates – in politics, management, sociology, history – which invoke identity as a descriptive, as opposed to distinctively theoretical, term. Rather, such 'Identity' work has tended to be occluded by the very problematization that has made theoretical Identity work such a 'big issue' in the social sciences and humanities. In the social sciences, for instance, theoretical 'Identity' is frequently bound up with something called 'social constructionism'. And social constructionism, as Fish (1995) and Hacking (1999) in their rather different ways have shown, has often ended up as an all-purpose, across the board formula, and, as such, has frequently evacuated that which it purports to analyse of any of its determinate or positive content.

How so? Well, the social constructionist formula often takes takes two forms. First, and most frequently, it is deployed as critique: 'Aha! You may think your agenda, project, object, self is somehow obvious, free-standing, natural, but actually it is socially constructed!' The post-structuralist capacity to treat identity as arising only from the manner in which it represses its other is regularly deployed in this move, to chide an object, agenda, project, person for its failure to understand and/or encompass the symbolic (or actual) violence it does to that which it represses in order to be itself. This is a powerful move, as the quote from Latour on p. 3 suggests; it can destabilize, undermine, induce feelings of guilt and all the sorts of affects that the critical mindset wishes to bring about. But really, why? What exactly does this achieve? Well, a frequently stated aim is precisely to indicate that the existence or character of something is not determined by the nature of things. It is neither natural nor inevitable. Not only this, and here is the second move, once its 'constructed' character is revealed, it can be re-imagined and/or radically transformed. In other words, once you have shown that something is socially constructed – as opposed to obvious, there, natural, whatever – you are by dint of this insight, it is argued, better able to revise that thing, or turn it into something altogether different, something more radical, open, less exclusionary, perhaps. You can offer to return to it – as the otherwise fulsomely 'anti-social' constructivists Callon and Muneisa (2005) have recently suggested doing to the market – a politics its current theorization emits, represses, marginalizes and occludes.

These moves raise a number of questions, though. First, do we actually learn anything positive about that which is subject to this theoretical exercise? Or is it the case that the social constructionist move is precisely designed to take away self-evidence from that which forms its object? Secondly, given that the same moves can be made on anything – robots, death, corporations, fish – what exactly is the status of the critical claim being made? Thirdly, why does deployment of the mantra 'socially constructed' – whether post-structuralist or deconstructive, for example – give you any sort of advantage in the practice of revising something, compared with those who do not buy into the social constructionist programme; those who maintain a belief in 'objectivity', for example?

Social constructionism, like the moment of theory more generally, emerges from a work of philosophical problematization and transformation performed on a variety of positive knowledges. As Foucault (1971) indicated in *The Order of Things*, linguistics, sociology and the 'psy' disciplines can be seen to emerge from a certain kind of interrogative work performed on the positive knowledges of classificatory language studies, political economy and biology. According to Foucault, the space in which this interrogation took place, and in which the human sciences emerged, is a field formed by three poles: mathematical formalization, the positive knowledges themselves, and a specific use of Kantian critical philosophy. As Hunter (2006) indicates, the latter in particular performs a special role in enabling theory to approach the positive knowledges not in terms of their objects, but in terms of the a-positive structures or relations that make knowledge possible for a subject. This then begs the question: what drives this philosophical problematization of positive knowledges? As we have already seen, Ian Hunter's answer (2006) concerns the forms of self-problematization that inform the activity of theory. He points in particular to the influence of Kantian and Husserlian techniques of self-problematization – means of acting on oneself with a view to suspending one's commitments to one's thoughts, perceptions, desires etc. – through which the theorist learns to problematize an object by interrogating his or her commitment to the positive knowledge in which the object resides. As Hunter argues:

> This applies to all the founding moments of theory; for example, when it is said that meaning is never present and is only accessible in a deferred way through a chain of signifiers; or when it is said that historical time is only an appearance generated by a-temporal concepts unfolding themselves in the human sensorium; or when it is said that speech is the manifestation of deep structure, or a generative grammar. Each of these moments of doubt is contingent on an act of suspension of commitment performed on oneself with a view to becoming another kind of person. (2006: 5)

According to Hunter (2006), the philosophical or metaphysical problematization of positive knowledges is precisely designed to rob them of their self-evidence and to effect a shift in the theorist's existential relation to those knowledges as a mode of inner intellectual conduct.

If such problematizations are not part and parcel of a detached investigation into a particular discipline or form of positive knowledge, but rather function as vehicles for the formation of a distinctive persona, what exactly are we to make of the critical claims made on behalf of this persona? For instance, the thesis that meanings are not free-standing and natural but are socially constructed, takes many forms. In its Lacanian psychoanalytic or deconstructive guise, we learn that meanings are produced by a system of articulation from which we, as speakers or hearers, cannot distance ourselves, because we are situated within it. Since that system (the unconscious or *différance*) is the unarticulated ground within which specification occurs, 'it' cannot be specified and always exceeds – remains after, escapes – the specification it enables. What this means, of course, is that any knowledge cannot be in possession of itself. As knowledge it cannot grasp, or name the grounds of, its possibility, and whenever it thinks it has done so, those grounds actually appear elsewhere than they seem to be (they are occluded) (Fish, 1994: 235, 1999). Ignorance, the forgetting of the enabling conditions of knowledge (conditions that cannot themselves be known), is thus deemed to be constitutive of knowledge itself. It follows from this, then, that if ignorance is the necessary content of knowledge, knowledge is not something that should be allowed to settle, since in whatever form it appears it will always be excluding more than it reveals; and indeed it is only by virtue of the exclusions it cannot acknowledge that it acquires its 'identity' (Fish, 1994: 235–6). As Fish (1994: 235–6) suggests, the deportment demanded by this insight is one of anti-knowledge: the refusal of knowledge in favour of that which it occludes. But does the practice of anti-knowledge – as a way of life – hold out the hope of anything beyond its continuous unsettling of whatever claims us in the name of positive knowledge? Clearly, as we have seen, it offers a prestigious persona, and the allure of being 'always in process' should not be underestimated. But can it, for instance, really be a criticism of an object or form of knowledge that represses its other (which one, exactly?), if everything does?

So why, then, does deployment of the term 'socially constructed' give someone any sort of advantage in the practice of revising something, compared with those who do not believe in the social constructionist hypothesis? After all, the impulse to revise – markets, curricula, accounting standards – has been experienced and acted upon many times before the advent of a constructionist programme in the intellectual field. As Fish (1999: ix) has remarked, 'the work of revision isn't furthered a whit by declaring it possible'. Neither the critic nor those who the critic manages to persuade of the analytic power of the social constructionist perspective will find themselves in a better position to revise anything than those who do not buy into the creed, or those who have never heard of it. In other words, the practical work of revision cannot be undertaken by simply announcing the thesis of social constructionism. More banally, what exactly can we learn about practices of personnel (or human resource) management, the order and rule of law, or the works of Jane Austen, by making this move; by deploying the metaphor of social constructionism? If the social constructionist thesis simply prefigures a philosophical attitude to phenomena that simultaneously robs those phenomena of their positive (non-relational) content (Hunter, 2006), we might usefully ask: what's the value added?

This book argues that such a move hampers understanding of the ways in which particular objects, persons, things are put together, assembled, or constructed in the plain, literal sense of the term (i.e. how their identity is organized). It does so because the theory deployed doesn't suit such a purpose. 'Social' constructionism, or 'theoretical' identity work, dictates its conclusions in advance, and also dictates the reaching of the same conclusion in all cases. It substitutes philosophical, preponderantly metaphysical, argument for empirical description. Let's take an example. It is one that was for a time very popular in social constructionist circles but which has, recently, like the hypothesis it represents, simply got tired. The example concerns authorship.

During the 1980s, for example, it became fashionable in certain circles to talk of the 'death of the author'. This claim was often referenced in relation to the work of Roland Barthes (1977) and Michel Foucault (1984). It did not usually appear as part of a descriptive empirical investigation – an historical argument concerning the construction of particular authorial statuses – in legal argument, say (Saunders, 1991). Rather, the claim functioned to call into question – as a philosophical truth – the very notion of an author or of a singular voice that owned its utterances. As such, its paradigmatic status within social constructionist discourse is self-evident. However, its utility for empirical debates about authorship (and copyright, one of its favourite preoccupations) appears somewhat limited, and for the reasons outlined above. If what you believe is that 'the attribution of a work to a single author will always be a mistake – not an empirical mistake, but a metaphysical mistake – because the idea of an individual voice is a myth and/or an artefact of bourgeois culture' (Fish, 2003: 396), or because authorship must always and necessarily be seen as multiple, that belief can have no significance or weight in relation to empirical questions it renders meaningless (Fish, 2003: 396).

Such 'metaphysical' preformatting does not of course begin and end with the question of authorship. It is to be found applied to a diverse range of objects and propounded by a wide range of theorists within the social sciences and humanities. Jurgen Habermas, for instance, would not be everyone's idea of a prototypical participant in 'the moment of theory', especially given his famous attacks on post-structuralism and deconstruction in *The Philosophical Discourse of Modernity* (1986). However, seen historically, Habermas's social theory appears as a central and influential example of a theoretical world view, involving as it does a philosophical (basically phenomenological) problematization and transformation of a particular disciplinary field, in this instance sociology (Hunter, 1994b, 2006). Hunter goes on to say that by representing society as an entity that evolves with its theorization, Habermas (1981) is able to present his theory of social communication in the form of a chain of hermeneutic problematizations of the work of the great sociologists (Marx, Weber, Durkheim and others):

> [T]his hermeneutic chain is envisaged as a progressive refinement of man's capacity for rational self-determination … In keeping with the Husserlian model, each stage in the process takes place in the form of a brief but fundamental breakthrough to the intuitions of the life-world – Marx's grasp of the importance of productive relations, Durkheim's conception of society as the social form of religious and philosophical categories, Weber's understanding of the rationalisation of society – which is then occluded through the elaboration of formal theorisations finally themselves complicit with society as 'system'. (Hunter, 2006)

The comparative strengths and weaknesses of these sociologists and sociologies, indeed their very purposes, are benchmarked against this goal; the possibility of a final breakthrough to the domain of the life-world, evidenced in Habermas's notion of the 'ideal speech situation'. In effect, it is this possibility that provides the entire hermeneutic chain with its *telos*.

The normative conditions furnishing this ideal speech situation are clear enough: 'Entrance into moral discourse demands that one steps back from all contingently existing normative contexts. Such discourse takes place under communicative presuppositions that require a break with everyday taken for granted assumptions; in particular it requires a hypothetical attitude toward the relevant norms of action and their validity claims' (Habermas, 1997: 164).

Because there is somewhere that has to be got to, there has to be a route, and ultimately Habermas holds the key. Here it is: the universal perspective we must rise to if the ideal speech situation is to be realized is already implicit (but occluded) in the activities we perform in the contexts that are ultimately to be transcended. Thus, without knowing it, by making the simplest of statements, we effectively buy into the strongly idealizing, context-transcendent claims of reason.

How this move works requires some attention. It begins like this: 'anyone acting communicatively must, in performing any speech action, raise universal validity claims and suppose they can be vindicated [or redeemed: *enlösen*]' (Habermas, 1997: 2). As Fish (2003: 399) argues, this is a 'must' independent of anyone's conscious intention. The intention belongs to the communicative context in general. By entering that context, one is, as it were, committing oneself to everything that communication as a universal form of action implies, including the goal of bringing about 'an agreement (*Einverständnis*) that terminates in the intersubjective mutuality of reciprocal understanding, shared knowledge, mutual trust, and accord with one another' (Habermas, 1997: 3).

> Whoever makes use of a natural language in order to come to an understanding with an addressee about something in the world is required to take a performative attitude and commit herself to certain presuppositions; ... natural language users must assume, among other things, that the participants pursue their illocutionary goals without reservations, that they tie [the possibility of] their agreement to the intersubjective recognition of criticizable validity claims, and that they are ready to take on the obligations resulting from consensus and relevant for further interaction ... That is, they must undertake certain idealizations – for example ascribe identical meanings to expressions, connect utterances with context-transcending validity, and claims, and assume that addressees are accountable, that is autonomous and sincere with both themselves and others. (Habermas, 1997: 4)

For Habermas, then, as Fish (2003: 403) indicates, a claim to universal validity is presupposed by every mundane act of communication. The programme of making good on this claim produces the project of discourse ethics that, if followed correctly, will instantiate the ideal speech situation participated in by discourse partners 'wholly committed to the universal norms now filling their consciousnesses'. From Habermas's perspective, this claim to universal validity is unavoidable. For Fish (2003: 404), though, it appears entirely avoidable by everyone except the few, but prestigious, philosophical practitioners of discourse ethics, for whom it is a baseline assumption from which to launch their project. Habermas's 'must' of communicative action, reported above, therefore belongs entirely to one particular practice – that of critical philosophy; it is not a necessary component of every particular act of assertion, communication or debate in every conceivable context. It may provide the discourse ethics philosopher with a certain metaphysical persona, but it is not a universal form of life to which all categories of person need or could aspire, or even seek 'to comport themselves according to its requirements (by giving reasons for everything, by regarding their interlocutors as free and equal, by self-consciously seeking a shared intersubjective form of understanding)' (Fish, 2003: 405).

In *Between Facts and Norms* (1997), Habermas draws a moral distinction between two communicative orientations. One, to understanding within the values, norms and practices given to you by a particular 'context' (without your assent or deliberation), the other to understanding within norms and values so general as to be applicable and appropriate no matter what the context might be. The former orientation, he argues, is preponderantly that of the 'self-interested' actor, for whom situational features are 'transformed into facts that they evaluate in the light of their own preferences'. Actors oriented to 'understanding, in general', however, 'rely on a jointly negotiated understanding of the situation and interpret the relevant facts in the light of intersubjectively recognised validity claims' (1997: 27).

The possibility of different categories and practices of personhood requiring and expressing distinctive ethical comportments irreducible to common underlying principles appears quite foreign to Habermas's mode of moral reflection, whereby a common or universal form of ethical judgement is seen to reside in the capacities of the self-reflective person. His assumption that 'self-interested' conduct is unitary and continuous, that 'self-interest' can only be one thing – selfish adherence to one's own preferences – and that thing is always and already the enemy of the common good or ideal speech situation, is a telling instance of such a world view.[2] As I indicate at some length in Chapter 3, a brief historical genealogy of 'self-interested' conduct – like that undertaken by Albert Hirschman (1977), for instance – suggests something rather more complex. The 'self' of 'self-interest' is a multiple not a singular. It does different things in different contexts, not the same thing in each and every context. Indeed, it's put together differently – normatively and technically – in relation to particular 'local' purposes. In contrast to Habermas's ahistoric uni-dimensionalism, Hirschman points to the ways in which early modern conceptions of 'self-interested' conduct were viewed in context as far from selfish and egotistical. Rather than presaging society's ruin, as Habermas would have it, early modern conceptions of 'self-interest', for instance, were aimed precisely as society's salvation, by seeking to offer a mechanism that might help to bring about an end to the ruinous religious civil wars besetting Europe at the time. Rather than interpreting 'self-interest' as intrinsically involving a mean-spirited repudiation of the public interest or common good – as the bad other to the good, reflective, deliberative, full human being – it is better to look to the particularity of the circumstances and to the business of descriptions. Then we might be able to trace how different forms of self-interested conduct are put together and thus what they enable the agents they bring into being to 'do' in particular circumstances.

If we do so, we quickly see that Habermas's distinction/struggle between self-interested understanding and a general orientation to understanding is a wrestle between two phantoms. As I have just suggested, human capacities are too positive and too various to be tied to a general 'communicative' form. It might therefore appear difficult to avoid Fish's conclusion that '[I]f an orientation to understanding as such is not built into every communicative act and thus cannot function as a bridge to itself, if intersubjective norms name a desire but not a possible human achievement, then there is no Habermasian project, nowhere to start, nowhere to go, and no possible payoff except the employment of a few rationalist philosophers' (Fish, 2003: 405). Such a conclusion has certain attractions and yet, as Hunter (1994b: 117) suggests, such outright condemnation might be less interesting, sociologically and ethically, than seeking to describe the comportment of the would-be universalist critical philosopher in its own terms. Seen in this light, the most suggestive part of Fish's critique concerns the institutional status of the critical philosopher: how a certain prestige – academically, spiritually – gets attached to this persona. More prosaically, how, in the plain literal sense of the term, is the identity of this persona organized?

Through what intellectual–technical devices does this personage achieve the spiritual problematization of other intellectual domains – of law, government, the empirical sciences – by positioning them as deficient in moral ends and theoretical reflexivity? And, if this problematization forms part of an ethic of 'world flight', then from what intellectual and institutional sources does this flight from mundanity gain its not inconsiderable authority, reverence and prestige ...? (Hunter, 1994b: 117)

This sociological–anthropological approach to the organization of identity, or the material–cultural making up of 'persons', provides this book with its key organizing logic. Such an approach involves a shift away from general social and cultural theoretical accounts concerning the formation of 'subjectivity' and 'identity' towards an understanding of the specific forms of 'personhood' that individuals acquire as a result of their immersion in, or subjection to, particular normative and technical regimes of conduct.[3] In other words, instituted norms and techniques of conduct are regarded as instruments for the cultivation of particular 'personal' deportments, whose historical circumstances, purposes and distribution are matters of sociological and historical investigation and description (Saunders, 1997). Alongside this emphasis comes recognition of the contingency and plurality of 'personhood' and the importance of not routinely or carelessly abstracting or divorcing the properties of particular 'persons' from the specific regime or milieu in which they are formed and make sense, particularly when such an exercise is undertaken under the auspices of mining 'the' concept of a person. As Amélie Rorty has argued:

[T]here is no such thing as 'the' concept of a person. This is so not only for the obvious historical reason that there have been dramatically discontinuous changes in the characterization of persons, though that is true. Nor for the equally anthropological–cultural reason that the moral and legal practices heuristically treated as analogous across cultures differ so dramatically that they capture 'the concept' of personhood only vaguely and incompletely, though this is also true. [T]he various functions performed by our contemporary concept of persons don't hang together: there is some overlap, but also some tension. Indeed, the functions that 'the' notion plays are so related that attempts to structure them in taxonomic order express quite different norms and ideals. Disagreements about primary values and goods reappear as disagreements about the priorities and relations among the various functions the concept plays, disagreements about what is essential to persons. Not only does each of the functions bear a different relation to the class of persons and human beings, but each also has a different contrast class. (1988: 31)

Why then does there appear to be such a strong – one might say permanent – metaphysical desire for one concept? Perhaps it has something to do with the unifying functions that the concept plays: 'the subject of right', 'the locus of liability', 'the autonomous, reflexive self'. Since these various functions appear to be unifying functions there is often a strong temptation to look for their unifying source. This, Rorty argues, is an elementary error. 'A desire for unity', she writes, 'cannot by itself perform the conjuring trick of pulling one rabbit out of several hats: a transcendental unity the concept of person, unifying the variety of distinct, independently unifying functions that each regional concept plays' (1988: 45).

Rorty's preference is for a strongly contextualist approach, with its privileging of description rather than theoretical colonization or (social) reconstruction; an approach that refuses to provide a general answer to the question: how are entities identified across contexts? Instead it accepts that since questions and contexts are particular 'all the way up and all the way down' (Rorty, 1988: 8), questions about identifying entities across contexts are themselves given their sense and direction by the context within which they arise. 'The question, "How are contexts identified and individuated?" is answered by the counter-question, Which contexts?' (p. 8).

Latour (2004: 231–2) appears to concur (though without using the terms 'context' and 'contextualist', which he abhors – see Latour (2005: 215)), suggesting that such a descriptive enterprise gets us closer to the objects, in this instance, persons, we seek to understand, treating them with a degree of care and concern that more elevated theories simply cannot, because they set out their coordinates too far in advance and leave no way out from their terms of reference. This latter tendency has the effect of rendering certain extremely important but often (seen from the heights of grand theory) rather banal details insignificant or even invisible.[4] Only by under-describing persons is it possible to make them conform to 'the' – illicitly decontextualized – concept of a person. To get closer requires description, and through such proximity concern for the qualities of particular personae can be registered. If nothing else, overhasty attempts to reconstruct, modernize or otherwise transform persons under the auspices of universalist or epochalist theories can then be seen for what they are, and the costs of such an exercise can be better appreciated. After all, if persons – human or non–human (states, corporations) – perform certain purposes, we should not carelessly discard or hastily 'reconstruct' or 're-imagine' them if the purposes they fulfil are ones we value and wish to see continued.

**structure and organization**     What does a sociology of persons look like? What might the relationship be between such an endeavour and contemporary social and cultural theoretical preoccupations with 'identity' and 'subjectivity'? These are the basic questions animating this book and framing the individual essays contained within it. The book is divided into two parts. Part I (Chapters 1–4) seeks to outline an approach to the study of persons focusing, in particular, upon the relations, techniques and forms of training and practice through which individuals in particular organizational settings have acquired definite capacities and attributes for existence as particular sorts of person. This approach involves a shift away from general social and cultural theoretical accounts of identity and subjectivity towards a historical and sociological understanding of the specific forms of personhood that individuals come to acquire in distinctive settings. With this emphasis comes recognition of the plural and regional character of 'personae' and the importance of not leaving them 'underdescribed'. If they are, the danger is that we will fail to see how and why each has its own history and distribution, has fashioned its own distinctive ethos, and is directed by its own techniques to its own ends (Saunders, 1997). Conversely, it is only through 'under-description' that 'social constructionist' theoretical explanation, or the normative generalizations about 'the' person seen as an autonomous self-governing whole person, gain their plausibility and effectivity. In Part II (Chapters 5–7) an attempt is made to put to work some of the intellectual resources introduced in the first part. Here, attention is focused upon a particular organizational domain – that of state service or public management – and upon a particular persona – that of the state bureaucrat or career civil servant. The aim is to show how such a persona was fashioned and for what purposes, and to chart some of the ethico-political consequences of contemporary theoretical and practical attempts to 'epochally' 're-imagine' and 're-invent' this category of person.

Chapters 1 and 2 attempt to offer an outline of a 'sociology of persons'. They do so through introducing a set of theoretical and methodological resources and by treating these as practical instruments for describing and analysing the formation of personae. These theoretical and methodological resources are associated with a small and rather disparate group of authors: Norbert Elias, Pierre Bourdieu, Marcel Mauss, Max Weber, Michel Foucault and Amélie Rorty. Without wishing to downplay the obvious problems inherent in stitching together any sort of unity from such diversity, I nonetheless want to suggest that these authors can offer useful guidance to anyone seeking to provide a suitably descriptive sociological account of the ways in which individuals have acquired definite capacities and attributes for distinctive forms of existence as certain sorts of person.

Chapters 3 and 4 seek to put this 'sociology of persons' to work by exploring the formation of two distinctive personae. Chapter 3 focuses upon the issue of 'self-interest'. In seeking to sidestep the old chestnut of whether individual human beings are 'radically socially embedded' creatures or essentially rational maximizers of their own self-interest, the chapter seeks to show how historically and in relation to particular purposes, a version of self-interested personhood was made up. The chapter begins by exploring the historical context in which this version of 'self-interest' emerged as a normative doctrine whose dissemination, far from engendering society's ruin as much post-romantic sociology would have it, was represented as a viable means to its salvation. In so doing, the chapter seeks to highlight the distinctive understanding and practice of 'self' that this doctrine promoted and its performative role as a device for securing social pacification in the context of enduring religious civil war. In historicizing self-interest in this manner, a more sympathetic understanding of the historical plurality of self-interested conducts can perhaps be developed.

Chapter 4 focuses upon the relationship between commercial devices and personal dispositions in a rather different setting: that of modern retailing. It does so through a brief historical sociology of the development of 'self-service' shopping techniques in British retailing in the years after the Second World War. Here, we concentrate upon the disparate material–cultural techniques that retailers deployed to put together a particular 'self-servicing' persona in the field of shopping and consumption. Like the 'self' of 'self-interest', the self in retail self-service does not form the trans-historical object of techniques for being human but represents only one way in which humans have been enjoined to understand and relate to themselves as certain sorts of person. This self is therefore both limited in distribution – you don't have it all the time, it is not your essence – and technically constituted – it exists in relation to a particular technological regime: the self-service shop.

In Part II some of the main themes introduced in Part I are developed in relation to a different object of analysis: recent and ongoing politico-organizational attempts to transform the conduct of a particular category of person – the state bureaucrat, public administrator or career civil servant. The essays in this section offer both a defence of the persona whose status-conduct enthusiasts for change find so difficult to appreciate, and a plea to the impatient to consider, in detail, what their own dreams and schemes presuppose and express in terms of the daily consequences of the practices and conducts they advocate. Thus, Chapter 5 seeks to make a case for the continuing indispensability of office-specific conceptions of moral agency in the realm of governmental and political action. Its main focus of concern is with the office of the state bureaucrat. This category of person has been the object of significant practical reform over the last two to three decades, and serious debate continues concerning whether such incessant reform has undermined key aspects of the role and function of the office to which this persona is attached. Indeed, rhetorics of office have played and continue to play an important part in framing debates about the status of these reforms of the state administration as an institution of government. In seeking to show the continued relevance of office-based conceptions of moral agency to the practice of state administration and to the status conduct of the public administrator, I have cause to question some of the 'enthusiastic' assumptions underpinning contemporary reforms of state bureaux and the norms of conduct they advocate. I suggest that many of the audacious experiments in public management that have been foisted upon state bureaux have had deleterious effects upon the increasingly forgotten 'core business' of public administration: running a state and operating a constitution.

In Chapter 6, attention is focused upon the 'epochalist' character of many of the contemporary critiques directed at public bureaucratic conduct and how these rely for their rhetorical power and effectivity upon the 'under-description' of that which they seek to have 're-invented' or 'modernized'. The chapter describes certain ethical and constitutional dilemmas that have arisen from enthusiastic attempts to drive through 'change' in organs of the state based upon epochally framed (and illicitly decontextualized) conceptions of organizational best practice. I argue that when it comes to 'change management' the differences between organizational personae – their distinctive purposes and typical ways of specifying and addressing ethical concerns, for instance – are as important as their similarities.

Chapter 7, the final chapter of the book, considers that fashionable term 'governance', and explores the techniques and practices advocated by its proponents and the personae they wish to see fostered. In particular, the chapter explores some of the issues of political ordering, especially those relating to sovereignty and authority, that 'expressivist' advocates of 'governance' tend to challenge, sideline or seek to transcend. It does so primarily through a brief examination of the way in which anti-statist norms of 'governance' have been deployed to explain, justify and endorse certain reforms in the organization and role of the persona of the public administrator. I argue that despite proclaiming themselves as the protectors of individual rights and community freedoms, anti-statist advocates of governance cannot be consistent defenders of these rights and freedoms, because rights and freedoms are an enforced uniformity, enforced that is by sovereign states. Not only this, they are rarely if ever guaranteed without the presence of effective, centralized state bureaucracies capable of creating and regulating them. This is a tough lesson for anti-statists to learn, but a vital one. The contemporary love-affair with decentralized and/or privatized forms of 'governance' in public administration raises serious and far reaching questions of political authority. The chapter is unconvinced of the redundancy of either Hobbesian conceptions of 'state', 'sovereignty' and 'authority' or of the vices of centralized, bureaucratic forms of public administrative conduct, and the personae they institute. It is, however, far from confident about the alternatives offered by expressivist 'governance'.

Once again the focus is on the 'lively tunes' (see n. 3) of contemporary theory and their constitutional failure to describe before moralizing. Of course, if you do not describe personae it is easy to disrespect them. Devoid of context, they can be made a critical dog's dinner of with impunity. Bizarre as it may seem to some, bureaucratic personae are highly contingent creations, dependent upon a quite limited range of material–cultural techniques and on a quite fragile ethical environment. These historically quite rare, reliable and fragile personae do not deserve to be denigrated for their failure to express a certain morality or to achieve objectives set for them by various social critics that they were not designed to meet and are incapable of so doing without ceasing to fulfil their particular purposes. Instead, perhaps it would be useful to learn to respect the limited but nonetheless important achievements of these instituted personae – such as the capacity to divorce the administration of public life from private moral absolutisms – that those of us lucky enough to live in pacified societies should not take so readily for granted.

## notes

1   This introductory essay is indebted to the work of Ian Hunter on the history of theory (2006) and Bruno Latour on the problems of contemporary critique (2004). As they both, in their rather different ways, suggest, 'Identity' work may continue to flourish but the theoretical spirit animating it is terribly tired.
2   Critical philosophy of the sort practised by Habermas seems constitutionally incapable of distinguishing two quite different senses in which 'values' might be 'personal'. Values might be personal, for instance, in the sense of deriving – comme Habermas – from processes of moral reflection that individuals (rightly or wrongly) identify with their own inner conscience. But values might also be

personal in the sense of simply providing a focus for individual moral commitment and ethical action. Clearly these two senses of 'personal' are not the same.
Individuals can and do find a (personal) focus for moral life in ethoses that
derive from impersonal ethical institutions, rather than their own individual
moral reflections. It is in this sense, as Minson (1993) and Latour (2002), for
instance, indicate that bureaucrats and judges can and should be personally
committed to the ethos of their distinctive office even though that ethos lies outside of their 'personal' moral predilections or principles.

3   This is very much Max Weber's programme as argued by Wilhelm Hennis
    (1988, 2000). Weber's contemporary, Paul Honigsheim (quoted in Hennis,
    1988: 108), recalls how Weber 'presented himself to the world as fragmented,
    and at each opportunity declared himself to belong to a particular sphere rather
    than presenting himself as a totality'. He concluded, rather dismissively, that
    '[Y]ou can't make a lively tune out of that.' Quite so. How refreshing. We have
    far too many lively tunes as it is.

4   As Latour (2005: 136) puts it, echoing Rorty's argument, '[N]o scholar should
    find humiliating the task of sticking to description. This is, on the contrary, the
    highest and rarest achievement'.

In *La Fabrique du Droit* Latour(2002) finds the jettisoning of deep philosophical and moral justifications for the work of law personally quite difficult
to achieve. Only by rigorously focusing on description of the law, and making
it compatible with the practice of the judges does the 'philosophically minded'
ethnographer begin to answer his own despairing question: 'sera-t-il jamais
*assez superficiel* pour saisir la force du droit?' (2002: 286).

It may seem churlish, but one could wish that Latour (2004) had exhibited
the same stoical self-restraint in his essay on theory and critique. After offering
a brilliant dissection of the philosophically inclined 'critical persona', Latour
(2004: 239) is unable to resist the pull of this persona himself. When he writes
'Although I wish to keep this paper short...' and then continues, the alarm bells
should be ringing. One more sentence, and it's all over: 'The solution lies, it
seems to me, in this promising word "gathering" that Heidegger had introduced
to account for the "thinginess of the thing" '.

part

1

# the identity of persons I

**introduction**    As I indicated in the Introduction to this book, 'identity' and its 'construction' has been the subject of an extraordinary amount of debate in the social and human sciences over the last two decades. Much of this remarkable upsurge of interest is inspired by and associated with the analyses of a disparate group of theorists – Althusser, Barthes, Derrida, Foucault, Kristeva and Lacan, to name but the most obvious. One consistent theme in this otherwise rather eclectic corpus is the challenge it poses to the ontological foundations of the person as the author of their own acts and centred in a unitary, reflective and directive consciousness. Disregarding for the moment the very significant conceptual and methodological differences between these authors, it is nonetheless possible to suggest that they are united in their opposition to the notion that individual human beings are essentially 'free agents', directed by a sovereign and integral consciousness. From the viewpoint of each, this idea appears little more than a metaphysical fiction.

The argument of this chapter is somewhat different. While agreeing that the idea of the 'person' as a 'free agent' may be a fiction, I want to argue that it cannot be seen as an illusion. This is because this idea of the person as a 'free agent' is implicated to a greater or lesser degree in our legal system and in many of our assumptions about education, for example. It cannot be written out of social organization just because it does not happen to comply with certain conditions of philosophical argument. Thus, as Hirst and Woolley put it some time ago, to challenge the metaphysical notion that human beings are essentially 'free agents' in the interests of a 'more complete account of the determinants of their various conducts and capacities does not necessitate rejecting social categories which organize practices, categories such as "contract", "responsibility", "obligation", "fault" and "guilt"' (1982: 132). For these categories do not depend on individuals being in some essential, ontological sense responsible or guilty, but they do require that conduct is attributable to individuals, not as its origin but as its locus (p. 132). Individual human beings may be held responsible for their acts, except in certain specified cases of incapacity, without us having to believe those acts arise from purely consciously determined purpose. The distribution of specific kinds of legal attributes – rights, standing, liability – to individuals by legal systems is a case in point. In other words, individual human beings may be constructed as 'free agents' in various practical circumstances and to varying ends without us having to assume that this means that all individuals in all circumstances are essentially equipped with 'free agency'. What it does suggest is that in some contexts and circumstances individual human beings will be held to be 'free agents' and in others they are not and cannot be. This in turn leads us to focus on both the contexts within which and the practical means through which individuals are equipped with the capacities to conduct themselves as particular sorts of person.

In this chapter and the next, then, I seek to focus on the relations, techniques and forms of training and practice through which individuals have acquired definite capacities and attributes for social existence as certain sorts of person. This involves a shift of focus away from certain theoretical accounts of the formation of 'subjectivity' and processes of 'identification' towards a more historical, sociological and anthropological understanding of the limited and specific forms of 'personhood' that individuals acquire in their passage through particular institutions. Alongside this emphasis comes recognition of the historical contingency and plurality of 'persona' and the necessity of not abstracting the properties of particular forms of personhood from the specific milieux or institutional settings in which they are formed and make sense.

The first two chapters therefore seek a certain balance of concreteness and theoretical argumentation. The theoretical resources are associated with a small group of authors whose work provides this chapter with its conceptual and methodological guidelines: Norbert Elias, Pierre Bourdieu, Marcel Mauss, Max Weber, Michel Foucault and Amélie Rorty. In their different ways and through the deployment of rather different conceptual vocabulary these authors can all be seen to provide useful tools and guidance to anyone seeking to provide a suitably descriptive account of the ways in which individuals have acquired definite capacities and attributes for distinctive forms of existence as particular sorts of person.

I begin, in Section 1.1, with a short exploration of the tendency within certain sociological discussions of 'identity' to operate with a particular conception of the 'individual' as the author of its own acts and centred in a unitary, reflective and directive consciousness. I then proceed to chart some of the ways in which this notion of the individual as a separate reality has been established in sociological thought and how and why this disposition needs to be undone if a sociologically satisfactory understanding of 'persons' is to be achieved. In particular, I explore the ways in which humans' capacities, including the capacity for self-consciousness and self-reflection, depend upon definite forms of discourse and definite sets of activities and techniques in which individuals are trained and implicated as agents. Concepts of persons, we discover, are therefore only intelligible with reference to a definite substratum of categories and practices that together give a particular agent its (complex and differentiated) form.

In Section 1.2, the limited and definite nature of instituted forms of personhood is explored in more detail through a brief case study of legal personality. Here we learn that forms of personhood, both legal and civic, depend upon definite arrays of instituted statuses and attributes, rights and duties that organize the practical deportment of individuals and groups. However, these statuses and attributes cannot be made to follow an individual's sense of 'self' or 'subjectivity'; indeed in some cases they are not attached to individual human beings at all. The task for the sociologist of 'personhood', it is argued, is to describe these instituted statuses and attributes, rights and duties, and thus the different forms of person they constitute, case by case, each in their own specific terms.

## 1.1 'individual' and 'society'
'Dualism', the understanding of reality as a dichotomy – for instance, of subject and object, meaning and structure, consciousness and being, individual and society – has been an extremely powerful tool of thought. The ability to conceive of human beings as 'individuals' standing outside of society and nature, autonomous thinking agents acting on them 'from without' was an invaluable resource in the emergence of those forms of calculative rationality, for example, that Max Weber (1978) associated with the development of 'the capitalist spirit'. Similarly, the development of 'liberalism' as a set of political and legal doctrines in Europe and North America from the seventeenth to the nineteenth centuries is frequently associated with the establishment of conducts whereby governments are encouraged to treat persons as 'individuals' (i.e. apart from social status and ascription). What is important to note here is the limited and specific nature of the dualisms constructed. These dualisms of 'individual' and 'society' are not reflective of an established reality – they do not mirror the essence of things in themselves – rather they serve specific purposes in particular contexts. So, for example, the liberal doctrine of 'equality before the law' is individualistic in a very limited sense. It means that legal systems in some societies have built into them filtering mechanisms that work to make such factors as political persuasion, religious belief, economic status and other social attributes irrelevant to the position of human beings as legal persons. In the legal sphere, then, human beings may be 'individualized' in a quite specific sense. They are not to be seen as constitutively identified with any group or role. Within that sphere there are of course still 'leakages' (racism and sexism immediately come to mind). The point, though, is that discriminatory justice tends to be defined in that domain in terms of failures in the judicial filter and not by appealing to some human 'essence' that is the same in all citizens before the law (Luhmann, 1980).

Thus it is important not to equate this form of 'individualism' with a general theory of human nature or with a general description of the 'reality' of human conduct. It needs to be understood within the limits of a specific institutional setting. This returns us to the point made earlier. Individuals are not 'free agents' in and of themselves but only in certain circumstances and for certain purposes. Not only this, that very sense of 'individuality' is something that human beings are equipped with by particular institutions, in this example, by a legal apparatus.

Regrettably, though, much philosophical and sociological work on 'identity' and 'personhood' has taken the idea of an 'individual' standing outside of 'society' as a general starting point for reflection and analysis. In other words, specific instances of conduct being attributable to individuals, not as their origin but as their locus, as in the legal domain, have been interpreted as expressions of the essential 'individuality' of human beings, of the individual as an autonomous entity, in contradistinction to society. It is this 'category error' that has led to the endless proliferation of debates within sociology (and other social sciences) concerning 'individual' and 'society' (normally both in the singular) as a problem of identifying a relationship between two distinct, pre-formed realities. How this error came about and proliferated with sociological discourse, was a key concern identified by Norbert Elias. In *The Civilizing Process*, Elias (1968b) attempted to explain some of the ways in which this idea of the 'individual' as a separate reality has been established in sociological thought and to indicate how it needed to be strenuously undone if a sociologically satisfactory understanding of 'persons' was to be achieved.

According to Elias (1968b: 247), the image of the person as 'an entirely free, independent being, a "closed personality" inwardly quite self-sufficient and separate from all other people, appears in many different academic contexts under many different guises – *homo philosophicus*, *homo economicus* and not least *homo sociologicus*'. All these expressions of what he terms the *homo clausus* presuppose the existence of individual agents with perfectly stabilized competencies. In other words, the *homo clausus* is always already competent to act; there is no hint of the context within which such a class of person might have been formed or of the social training and practice through which this category of person was equipped with the capacity to act.

But how and why exactly does Elias pin the blame on *homo clausus* for both highly objectivist (i.e. Durkheimian) and highly subjectivist (i.e. phenomenological) sociologies? According to Elias, it is because both sides set up a rigid barrier between, on the one hand, the human being as a biological and psychological individual in the 'black box' and, on the other, the 'social' world 'outside'. Both the thesis of 'over-socialization' and that of 'under-socialization' therefore rest upon a common hypothesis: that of a human being as a 'little world in himself' (Elias, 1968b: 249). Time and time again, Elias argues, the dependence on *homo clausus* leads social scientists to engage in futile debates about the relationship between individual and society as if they were two static and isolated objects, two separate and distinct realities (p. 250). Such debates, he continues, are effectively circular: they have the same endless possibilities as debating which came first, the chicken or the egg. And this misconception – in the very literal sense of the term – is re-enforced by a widespread tendency to speak not of persons but of 'the person' or 'the individual' in the singular, as if all forms of socially instituted personhood were effectively identical.

This 'conceptual trap' can only be prized open, Elias (1968b: 250) suggests, if these static notions are made to refer to ongoing processes. In saying this, Elias is keen to indicate that he does not view the 'self-perception that finds expression in the image of man as *homo clausus* and its many variations' (p. 252) as an outright illusion. It exists but it does so in specific ways in relation to specific purposes and activities. It is not a universal mode of being human, and thus it cannot act as 'a self-evident assumption incapable of further explanation'. To understand its development it is necessary to see how it has been given shape over time. Once again, the issue is clear. We need to see how particular categories of person have been formed or 'made up' in specific contexts, at a particular time and through certain practical means. In order to do this Elias introduces the notion of 'figuration'.

Elias uses the term 'figuration' to refer to 'networks of interdependent human beings' (1968b: 261). It is deployed as a more dynamic term in contrast to expressions like social structure and social system, which he regards as somewhat static, and as referring to something separate from, beyond and outside the activity of human beings. The figuration or network in this sense does not link human beings with already established identities (i.e. individuals endowed – in the manner of *homo clausus* – with a set of fixed attributes and stabilized competencies) to form what would be a static social structure constituting the framework within which individual actions are situated. In the figuration, the individuals' identities, interests and objectives – everything that might stabilize their description and their being – are variable, contingent outcomes that fluctuate with the form and dynamics of the relationship between those individuals. Both figuration and person are therefore, in a sense, two sides of the same coin. One can enter the figuration through the persons it constitutes, whereby one is immediately tempted to characterize them by the shape of their relationships. Alternatively, one can focus on the figuration itself, in which case one uses the associations of the persons it constitutes to describe it. The figuration, in other words, does not connect persons with already established identities but, rather, it provides those persons with their very dimensions or characteristics. The persons, their characteristics, what they are and do, are all dependent upon the relations in which they are involved.

What Elias enables us to see is that social relations and human attributes are necessarily interdependent. Nothing is to be gained analytically from viewing them as separate and distinct realities. In other words, as I suggested earlier, it is important not to divorce forms of personhood from the empirical settings within which they are formed. If we do so we are left only with a highly abstract, even transcendental, concept of 'the person' that literally has no location. Not only this, Elias also suggests that to understand the ways in which figuration and persons generate one another requires an historical focus.

Now, Elias was certainly not alone amongst sociologists in seeking to overcome the stasis of the individual/society dualism as a general philosophical problem and to do so through the medium of historical enquiry. The idea that time is the common medium in which social relations and individual identities generate one another is a core assumption informing the work of many different forms of sociology, from the work of symbolic interactionists such as Anselm Strauss (1977) to the 'structuration' theory of Anthony Giddens (1979). Strauss (1977: 164), for example, famously argued that 'Identities imply not merely personal histories but social histories ... individuals hold memberships in groups that are themselves products of the past. If you wish to understand persons – their development and their relations with significant others – you must be prepared to view them as embedded in historical context.' This is not simply a matter of recognising the historical background to the present. Rather, as the historical sociologist Philip Abrams (1982: 16) put it, 'it is an attempt to understand the relationship of personal activity and experience on the one hand and social organization on the other as something that is continuously constructed in time. It makes the continuous process of construction the focal concern of social analysis.' At an intuitive level this makes good sense. After all, it suggests a way of understanding what Giddens (1979) describes as a central problem in sociological theory: how the actions of human subjects constitute a social world that in turn constitutes the conditions of possibility of the actions of those subjects. And yet it often gives rise to a misconception every bit as powerful and ultimately as disabling as the generalized philosophical distinction between 'the individual' and 'society'.

The misconception at issue arises as a result of a presumption that a reading of Elias already puts into question: that human beings whether conceived of as 'subjects', 'selves' or 'free agents' have a continuous history. As I have argued, Elias's work suggests that categories such as the 'self' are dependent upon particular socio-cultural practices. These categories cannot therefore be deployed as universal data of human existence and experience. They should not be 'taken for granted' in some foundational sense. In other words, the forms of personhood ascribed to human beings in their passage through social institutions do not have a grounding in some essence within those beings – whether that essence is described in terms of self-consciousness or the capacity for agency. In a brilliant, but rarely cited, article, 'The biographical illusion', Pierre Bourdieu (1987) takes issue with certain sociological under-standings of personhood that seek to do precisely that. His target is the 'life-history' approach currently popular within certain forms of social and human scientific enquiry.

One of Bourdieu's first tasks is to unpack the presuppositions underpinning the 'life-history' approach to analysing and describing an individual's 'identity'. Among the most important of these he includes the 'fact that a "life" constitutes a whole, a coherent and directed ensemble, which can and must be grasped as unitary expression of a subjective and objective "intention" of a project' (1987: 298). This life organized like a story 'unfolds according to a chronological order which is also a logical order'; it has not only direction but also a purpose. In this way, the 'life-history' appears to be an account of the unfolding of the individual self, from its beginning to its end. Life is a story and the individual subject is its author. Again, the contexts within which and practical means through which this 'self' comes into being are left undescribed. The 'self' is seen to be the core of what it means to be a person and is therefore not in need of further elaboration. We only need to map its journey through life and unpack its very special 'story'.

Having indicated the key philosophical presuppositions underpin-ning the 'life-history' approach, Bourdieu proceeds to indicate some of their more pressing problems. First, he argues that the 'life-history' cannot be regarded as a transparent reflection of life in itself but rather must be seen as a specific technique for constructing experience. Memory of one's life-history, for example, cannot be assumed to be an essential psychological capacity but rather to be socially organized through rituals of storytelling. The mode of storytelling that the 'life-history' exemplifies is that of the linear novel. Through his brief discussion of the very different philosophy of life underpinning modern novelistic conventions (citing Proust and Robbe-Grillet, in particular ) – the real as discontinuous, events as unfore-seen and often random – Bourdieu highlights the contingency of the novel-istic discourse on which the life-history is based, and thus questions the claims of the life-history to reflect the unity and totality of the self (1987: 298–9). In other words, rather than giving voice to the unfolding of a pre-established self, Bourdieu argues that the life-history must be seen as a mechanism for producing the experience of self as unity and as totality.

Like Elias, Bourdieu is keen to emphasize that the unified self is not in and of itself an illusion. The point is, rather, that it is not a natural or essential element of being human, but historically variable and contingent upon particular socio-cultural practices. Bourdieu goes on to indicate that modern societies contain 'all sorts of institutions to totalise and unify the self' (1987: 300). He chooses the example of the 'proper name' to make his point. The proper name – the name on your passport or driving licence, for example – is a particular way of establishing a constant and enduring social identity that guarantees the identity of the 'biological individual' (or 'raw' human being) in all the possible fields in which that biological individual is constituted as an agent. As an institution the proper name assures nominal consistency, identity in the sense of identity with oneself, that constancy which social order requires of a responsible being. As Bourdieu puts it, 'the proper name is the visible affirmation of the identity of its bearer across social times and spaces, the foundation of the unity of its successive manifestations and of the socially recognised possibility of totalising these manifestations in official records, curricula vitae, cursus honorum, criminal records, obituaries and biographies which constitute the life as a totality completed by the verdict pronounced on a provisional or definitive report' (p. 300). The proper name is not expressive or affirmative of a pre-established personality or identity. It is not therefore an abbreviated definite description of the 'true me'; it does not refer to a cluster of descriptive features that stay the same across time and social space. Rather, as Bourdieu indicates, 'any description is only valid within the limits of a given time and place' (p. 301). Therefore the 'proper name' cannot affirm 'the identity of the personality, as socially instituted individuality except at the cost of considerable abstraction'.

The life-history 'illusion' consists precisely in the opposite belief: that it is possible for a proper name to refer to a cluster of features, of positive properties, no matter how minimal, that defines the permanent essence of an individual 'self' across time and space. For the life-history approach it is the existence of a prior core self and a founding consciousness – which the proper name expresses and affirms – that provides the common ground for all forms of socially instituted personhood, whether legal, governmental, aesthetic or economic. As Bourdieu (1987: 301) makes clear, though, no such common ground exists. Legal, governmental and aesthetic personalities stand in no general relationship to one another. No claim can be made that one of them is, as it were, the person itself. Each institutes its own definite but limited form of personhood. And these separate and distinct forms are not capable of being summed up into a fully recognized 'person'. In the legal sphere, for example, it's not just that non-humans (i.e. corporations) may be legal persons, though this is in fact the case; it is, rather, that elements of legal personality do not exactly attach themselves to persons in the conventional sense at all, but to certain statuses that are 'supported by' persons (I will examine the instance of legal personality in more detail in Section 1.2). Status may be defined as a condition signifying an individual's membership of a particular category or class of persons to which special legal rules apply. For example, the law classifies persons on the basis of their sex, age, nationality, race, marital status, occupation or income. It then confers legal rights, duties, privileges and immunities on the various forms of person – for example, in the form of landlord and tenant legislation or health and safety legislation. A person may fall into one or several categories at the same time, such as landlord and tenant or employer and employee. The legal consequences of being in a particular category are often completely unrelated to other aspects of a person's status. A person has rights and duties as an employer that are unassociated with the same individual's rights and duties as a spouse. As Bourdieu (1987: 300) suggests, 'the proper name is thus the support (we might be tempted to say the substance) of what we call our <u>legal status</u>, i.e. of that bundle of personal attributes (nationality, gender, age etc.) which in civil law have juridical effects and which are instituted, rather than simply recorded as it might seem, in the terms defining our legal status'.

Having established the difference between the unity of the 'subject' of the 'life-history' approach and the very different 'impersonal' unity designated by the proper name, Bourdieu goes on to show what a more sociologically informed examination of an individual biography might look like. As Bourdieu indicates:

> To try and understand a life as a unique and autonomous series of successive events without any link other than association with a 'subject' whose constancy is doubtless only that of a proper name, is almost as absurd as trying to account for a journey in the Metro without taking into consideration the structure of the railway network, i.e. the matrix of objective relations between the different stations. (1987: 302)

This is a crucial point. To track the 'trajectory' of a specific category of person requires a detailed description of the field in which that trajectory is to be accomplished (and which provides that category of person with its constitutive characteristics). Without such a clear idea of the structure of the field in question, and thus of the possibilities it offers to the agents it constitutes, it would be impossible to chart the direction of movements leading from one position to another (from one secretarial post to another or from one managing directorship to another). Without this detailed description and mapping exercise we would not be able to understand the trajectory a particular category of person undertakes in a given social space (Bourdieu, 1987: 301–2). As Bourdieu suggests, it is only possible to understand a trajectory like social ageing – which he stresses is linked to but independent of biological ageing – in a given field (why is 30 considered 'old' for traders on the floor of the London International Financial Futures Exchange and yet frequently a reasonable age for 'new blood' appointments in academia?) on condition of having 'previously constructed the successive states of the field in which the trajectory was accomplished, thus in the set of objective relations which united the agent in question – at least in a certain number of pertinent states – with the set of other agents engaged in the same field and facing the same space of possibilities' (p. 302). Only by engaging in this form of detailed description and mapping is it then possible, Bourdieu insists, for the sociologist to understand what he describes as the 'personality' designated by the 'proper name' – 'the set of positions simultaneously occupied at a given moment by a socially instituted biological individuality acting as the bearer of a set of attributes and attributions capable of permitting it to intervene as an effective agent in different fields' (p. 302).

As Bourdieu (1987) suggests, how could we understand what it means to be a certain sort of person if we do not describe the context in which forms of personhood are located and which provide them with their content – 'who would dream of describing a journey without an idea of the landscape in which it was made?' Too frequently, he says, we seem to think we can because we believe that all the forms of personhood ascribed to individuals in their passage through social institutions have an ultimate grounding in the self. This is the 'illusion' that the 'life-history' approach labours under.

To sum up. Elias's work invited us to face up to – and discard – the assumption that all the forms of personhood ascribed to biological and psychological individuals ('raw' human beings) in their passage through social institutions have an essential (moral or theoretical) ground in what he describes as the *homo clausus*. This was an invitation that Pierre Bourdieu responded to in 'The biographical illusion'. As I argued, Bourdieu's critique of the 'life-history' indicates that the 'self' cannot be considered as a given, the unchanging centre of a 'life'. Human capacities, including the capacity for self-consciousness and self-reflection depend upon definite forms of discourse and definite activities. These capacities vary. Concepts of persons are therefore only intelligible with reference to a definite substratum of categories, practices and activities which together give the agent its complex and differentiated form. The task, as Bourdieu's work suggests, then becomes one of describing the different categories, practices and activities, and thus the different forms of person, case by case, each in their own terms. In seeking to live up to Bourdieu's injunctions I attempt in Section 1.2 to describe one very specific form of personhood, that of 'legal personality'.

## 1.2 the distinctiveness of persons: the case of legal personality

As Bourdieu (1987: 300) argues, any given biological and psychological individual in modern societies is likely to support a number of personae. He goes on to indicate, however, that these several personae cannot be usefully summed up into a whole. In this section I will explore why this might be the case through a brief examination of one particular form of socially instituted personhood – legal personality. I have chosen 'legal personality' for two main reasons. First, it is an example that has already, albeit very briefly, been introduced in the discussion of Bourdieu and 'the biographical illusion'. Secondly, and more importantly, the very specificity and technicality of legal personality provides a useful concrete example of the approach to persons being developed more generally in this chapter.

In order to begin to get to grips with the specificity of this idea of 'legal personality', we need first to step inside the legal sphere and familiarize ourselves with our surroundings. We will do so using a legal scholar, Ernest Weinrib, as our guide. In an essay entitled 'Legal Formalism: on the immanent rationality of law', Weinrib (1988) sets out to answer the question 'What is the Law of Torts?' ('tort' refers to a wrongful act, other than a breach of contract, for which a civil action for damages can be brought). What he has to say about tort law has some important consequences for our understanding of the (relative) autonomy and grounded rationality of the legal system more generally.

Weinrib begins his endeavour by stating that:

> When we seek the intelligibility of something, we want to know what that something is. The search for 'whatness' presupposes that something is a this and not a that, that it has, in other words, a determinate content. That content is determinate because it sets the matter apart from other matters, and prevents it falling back into the chaos of unintelligible indeterminacy that its identification as a something denies. (1988: 958)

It follows from this, Weinrib continues, that 'nothing is more senseless than to attempt to understand the law from a vantage point extrinsic to it', on the reasoning that any such attempt is more likely to give rise to an understanding of that 'extrinsic vantage point' (whatever it may be) and not of law (p. 958). For Weinrib, legal understanding is an immanent (internal) affair, and 'legal phenomena' will come into view only under the pressure of a legal analysis; otherwise they would not be legal phenomena but something else entirely (p. 958).

'Immanent understanding' as Weinrib describes it, is not to be apprehended by itemizing features of the internal landscape, but by grasping the coherent set of purposes that confer value and significance and even shape on those features. It is that set of purposes, when they inform an insider's perception, that is responsible for her sense of what is and what is not 'intuitively plausible' in the consideration of any legal problem. As Fish (1995: 21), for instance, has argued, when a legal practitioner listens to a client's story she listens with legal ears and what she hears is quite different in its emphases from what the client hears when he offloads his story on to her. The client may stress a moment or an action that appears to him to be defining of his cause only to hear the legal practitioner say that it is not something that can be brought under categories with which and within which the law thinks.

What this means is that justification – the process by which a move in a game is declared valid – is always internal and is never a matter of looking for confirmation to something outside of the law's immanent intelligibility. The client who complains that their experience of an event has not been accommodated by the law's understanding or interpretation of it will remain unhappy because 'the crucial consideration is not what happened, but how one is to understand the justificatory structure that is latent in the legal arrangements that might deal with what happened' (Weinrib, 1988: 985). Weinrib indicates that this account of justification renders it somewhat circular, since it 'does not strive for any standpoint beyond the law, the most it can do is plough over the same ground in ever deeper furrows' (p. 985). However, he regards this inherent circularity as a source of law's considerable strengths rather than as a weakness because 'if the matter at hand were to be non-circularly described by some point outside it, the matter's intelligibility would hang on something that is not itself intelligible until it was in its turn integrated into a wider unity' (p. 975).

If we are to avoid such an infinite regress, Weinrib (1988: 956) argues, we have to see the law not so much as an 'instrument in the service of foreign ideals but as an end in itself, constituting as it were, its own ideal'. He elaborates his argument by reference to the example of tort law, which he describes as a continuing mediation (by tort law itself) on 'the relationship between tortfeasor and victim' (p. 969) – that is between someone who wrongfully inflicts an injury and someone who suffers it; the unfolding of that meditation will necessarily induce considerations of fault, causation, duty, foreseeability and proximity. It is of course always possible to view a tort case through the lens of a different complex of concerns – a desire to redistribute wealth as evenly as possible regardless of any finding of fault or demonstration of loss, for example; but if a case were decided in the name of such a foreign ideal, it would be a tort decision in name only, for a 'conception of tort liability in which the plaintiff can recover from the defendant for injury in the absence of wrongdoing, or in which the defendant is liable to the plaintiff for a wrong that does not materialize in injury, would be a "conceptual monstrosity"' (p. 969). It would be employing the language of tort law while bypassing and destroying the very rationale (internal and immanent) for there being a tort law in the first place. In this regard, as Fish (1995: 21) has argued, it would be something like 'if a goalkeeper in a football match, aware that the opposing striker is in danger of losing his job and unhappy at the prospect of contributing to his loss of livelihood, allowed a goal past him rather than saving it; the criticism would not be that he was playing badly but that he was not playing the game at all'.

Now all this talk of 'immanent intelligibility' and 'foreign ideals' may seem a little strange when my avowed aim is the investigation of 'legal personality'. Yet, it is crucial to understanding the forms that legal personality takes. For if, as Weinrib argues, the source of the law's validity lies within the legal system itself – i.e. it is 'immanent' – in the legal norms regulating legislative and judicial decision-making, then the source of legal personality or standing will lie firmly within the legal system, too. In other words, the statuses and attributes of legal personality will be seen to be inseparable from the definite yet limited parameters of particular legal systems. Legal personality, then, cannot usefully be viewed as an expression of human subjectivity in some general sense. It is an artefact too particular and specialized to be counted as 'the subject' (or 'the person'). A couple of further examples should help clarify this point.

In modern western societies judicial decision-making is typically guided by what Niklas Luhmann (1980) termed 'conditional programmes'. Such programmes specify that if a certain situation occurs, then a particular legal decision is to be made (judicial discretion may of course come into it). Such an approach serves to differentiate the legal system from other social institutions in two distinct ways. First, only specific kinds of information about a situation are considered relevant for the case in question. Secondly, the foreseeable consequences of a judicial decision do not constitute a factor in the deliberation leading to the decision. For instance, a judge doesn't have to take into account how the verdict may affect any of the defendant's other social roles – for example, how it might affect her marriage or her career. Of relevance is only whether the given situation is of the sort specified in the conditional programme. In effect, both this general indifference to the consequences of particular decisions as well as the systematic tendency to disregard the (general) social standing of the individuals involved in the case serve to make those individuals 'equal before the law' (remember the discussion at the beginning of Section 1.1 of the limited and technical form of individualism embedded in the liberal doctrine of 'equality before the law'?). These individuals are not 'equal' in some ontological sense, because they have something within themselves that the law is forced to recognize as essential to every human being qua human being – a 'self' or 'subjectivity', for example – but, rather, because the legal system requires, on occasion, that conduct be attributable to individuals, not as its origin but as its locus. In this legally specific sense, and only in this sense, can individuals be said to be 'equal before the law'.

The specificity of legal forms of personality and their non-reducibility to an individual's 'inner self' or subjectivity is further evidenced by the simply legal truism that not all individuals are legal persons and not all legal persons – corporate bodies or states, for instance – are human beings. As this extract from *Black's Law Dictionary* makes clear, a legal person is such, not because he [*sic*] is human, but because rights and duties are ascribed to him. The person is the legal subject or substance of which the rights and duties are attributes … Every full citizen is a person; other human beings, namely subjects who are not citizens, may be persons. But not every human being is necessarily a person, for a person is capable of rights and duties, and there may well be human beings having no legal rights, as was the case with slaves in English law. (1968: 61–2)

For legal purposes, then, any entity, whether human or not, whom the law regards as capable of rights and duties is a person. An entity that is not so capable in the law's eyes, again, whether human or not, is not a person for legal purposes. In legal terms persons, as we have seen, are nothing but the substances of which rights and duties are the attributes. Only in this respect do persons possess juridical significance. Thus legal personality 'refers to the particular device by which the law creates or recognizes units to which it ascribes certain powers and capacities' (*Blacks Law Dictionary*, 1999: 1162–3). Considered in this light it becomes clear that the statuses and attributes of legal personality are inseparable from the norms, techniques and practices of the legal system. They are not universal modes of 'being human'.

In a discussion of the idea of 'legal personality', Helena McFarquhar (1987) points out that the law adopts a wide definition of what constitutes a 'person'. This includes not only human beings seen individually or placed in groups, but also artificial persons such as companies and corporations. Specific legal systems, she indicates, prescribe the manner and circumstances in which they will attribute legal personality. The person is the legal subject and substance of which rights and duties are attributes. This has two further consequences. First, the forms of legal personality that the law recognizes do not predate the act of legal recognition itself. Rather, they are constituted through the very act of recognition. Secondly, legal personality is not all of a piece. It's not simply a matter of recognizing that legal personality can be attributed to non-humans but that the very elements that make up legal personality are not attached to persons per se but to certain statuses that are 'supported by' persons. As McFarquhar (1987: 128) puts it 'persons have different legal capacities depending upon their status. Status may be defined as a condition signifying an individual's membership of a particular category of persons to which legal rules apply'. She goes on to indicate that the law classifies persons along a range of dimensions – age, sex, nationality and so forth – and then proceeds to confer legal rights, duties, capacities and incapacities on the different categories of person in the forms of various types of legislation. As she points out, individuals may fall into one or several categories at the same time but the legal consequences of being in 'a particular class are often unrelated to other aspects of a person's status. As a parent, for example, a person has rights and duties which are not associated with the same person's rights and duties as an employer or trade unionist' (McFarquhar, 1987: 129).

Moreover, as we have seen, not all persons are individuals, for legal personality can be possessed by non-humans. McFarquhar indicates that the law can treat some groups or associations as legal persons in their own right, separate from their individual memberships at any given time. She distinguishes two types of artificial legal persons – unincorporated and incorporated bodies. The former are not treated as full legal persons in their own right; their powers and duties are those of their individual members. The members 'bear individual responsibility for their association's actions and property cannot be held in the association's name; it is usually held in trust for the association' (McFarquhar, 1987: 130). Unincorporated bodies can be set up for certain clearly defined purposes including the mutual benefit of members (e.g. social and sports clubs), employment (e.g. trade unions) or profit-making (e.g. partnerships such as the John Lewis Retail Partnership). Incorporated bodies are the most usual method for creating an artificial legal person. According to McFarquhar (1987: 130), 'incorporation' is the device whereby a group or association is treated in law as if it were an independent legal person, a corporation. The point to focus on here is not simply that non-humans as well as humans may be legal persons; rather it is that legal personality is nothing more than a heterogeneous set of statuses and capacities that attach themselves to different classes of object for different purposes in the legal sphere. Human beings may be the most obvious example of persons bearing rights and duties but we must remember that a person is such in the legal sphere not because it is human, but because and only because rights and duties are ascribed to it.

In his classic article, '*Mens Rea*: a note on sexual difference, criminology and the law', Mark Cousins (1980) elaborates this point. Cousins questions the ways in which the terms 'men' and 'women' are used as definite, stable, trans-discursive categories within certain forms of sociological argument. Taking the law as an example, Cousins seeks to indicate the ways in which the heterogeneous collection of statuses and capacities in law that bear upon the organization of sexual difference cannot be made commensurate with such definite categories of 'men' and 'women'. Cousins's article has at its core an attempt to explore what it would mean for the law to recognize women as women. The article begins with a brief examination of the concept of 'sexual division' as it has been deployed within certain forms of sociology; however, Cousins notes a paradox at the heart of the concept. On the one hand, the content of sexual division is viewed as an effect of social forces. He points to ways in which differential crime rates and pay levels are explained sociologically as the effects of definite social practices. Yet, on the other hand, the category of sexual division itself appears to rely upon the idea of a natural division underpinning these social practices. How so? By way of explanation, Cousins points to the ways in which much sociological writing on 'sexual division' has proceeded as if what it referred to – men and women – was itself quite unproblematic. The categories 'men' and 'women' are assumed for the purposes of social analysis to be stable. This has the consequence of according them a discursive privilege as 'definite categories' within theoretical argument. As Cousins argues, 'it is thought that the entities "men" and "women" are possible objects of investigation for two reasons: they are human subjects in general, and in particular they share the characteristics of the entity to which they belong as a group. Things and persons can act upon them, and thus it appears plausible to speak of the action of men or law upon women' (1980: 117). Cousins seeks to problematize this approach by indicating that 'men' and 'women' as 'persons' cannot provide stable referents for the categories 'male' and 'female', 'masculine' and 'feminine'. Instead, they will be produced 'as definite forms of difference by the particular discourse and practices in which they appear' (p. 117). In order to make his point, Cousins turns to the law for support.

He begins his excursion into the law and its bearing upon the organization of sexual difference by indicating the way in which the sociological representation of 'men' and 'women' as stabilized 'persons' is deployed to criticize the law as exclusionary and unjust. One problem with such an approach, he suggests, concerns its assumption that men and women, as persons, have their personalities recognized or denied by the law; that what law does is recognize or fail to recognize what already exists. This in turn is held to support two related assumptions: first, that the personality that is recognized predates the act of recognition; secondly, that legal recognition is unitary and continuous – you are either recognized or you are excluded. On each of these counts, for Cousins, sociological analysis is found wanting.

First, legal personality is not unitary and continuous but, rather, technical and limited. As Cousins points out, women who have been excluded from one category of legal personality have not ceased to be persons for other legal purposes. Nor has there been a general exclusion of women from the term 'person' in the legal sphere that 'would require, or could be repaired by, a singular reform'. Secondly, these technical and limited elements of legal personality are not capable of being summed up into a fully recognized person. This is not simply because the term person within the legal sphere refers to non-humans as well as humans but also because, as we saw earlier, elements of legal personality do not attach themselves to persons in the conventional sense at all but, rather, to certain statuses that are supported by persons. Status is the condition of belonging to a particular class of persons to which the law assigns particular legal capacities or incapacities or both. Such might be 'husband' or 'wife', 'father' or 'mother'. These statuses are not specialized functions of the basic or foundational categories of 'men' and 'women' because, as Cousins (1980: 117) points out, they include categories such as 'parent' and 'spouse'. In other words, these statuses refer to a collection of rights and duties, capacities and incapacities, in respect of the legal status of marriage and parenthood. These heterogeneous collections of statuses and capacities simply cannot be made commensurate with the sociological categories of 'men' and 'women' as full persons thought to underpin them. This in turn means that 'women' and 'men' as whole persons do not simply take on legal subjectivity by dint of their recognition as such from the law. Is it possible to make a general 'legal personality' out of the range of statuses and capacities that individuals might carry at various times in different forms of legal encounter? Cousins says 'No' and argues clearly why he thinks this is the case:

> If legal personality is not of a piece, and moreover if it is comprised of differentiated elements in respect to the type of legal action, then it is not a ticket that permits the holder to walk in to and out of legal actions as a member of humanity at law. Rather, it is that law designates in particular actions what forms of legal personality are appropriate for joining or being joined in particular actions. What is important is what form of agency the law recognises/constitutes as the appropriate subject. Sometimes, this can be a person, a man or a woman as defendant, sometimes it might be a man as father or a woman as mother, sometimes it might be a man or a woman as representative, agent or servant of a corporate body … [T]he point is that the materiality of these legal categories, of the distribution of types of agent that appear within the law, cannot be made reducible to men and women and their identities. (1980: 119)

It is for these reasons that the law cannot recognize 'men' as 'men' or 'women' as 'women'. Cousins (1980: 119) argues that this has important consequences for the ways in which law sets the terms both for analysis and for political evaluation of legal transformation. As there cannot be any simple calculation of interests and the legal instruments for realizing them, it is instead important to analyse the effects the law and the agents that appear within it have upon the organization of sexual difference, and thus to attempt to evaluate what legal reforms are necessary conditions for its transformation. These reforms will, of necessity, be technical and limited (in coverage, duration and distribution), contingent upon certain jurisdictions and their instruments. Being legal reforms they will be products of, what Weinrib (1988) described as, law's 'immanent rationality'.

In examining 'legal personality' I have proceeded to unpack or disaggregate the almost reflex tendency within a range of social scientific discourses to identify 'person' with 'individual' and 'individual' with 'self'. As we have seen, 'legal personality' cannot be made commensurate neither with the 'individual' as a (raw) biological and psychological being, nor with the particular mode of being human we associate with having a unique 'self'. In this sense, our brief engagement with 'legal personality' not only enables us to see how the peculiar statuses and attributes of legal personality are inseparable from the definite yet limited parameters of the legal system but also provides us with a vocabulary and method for exploring other forms of socially instituted personhood. If forms of personhood, and not just forms of legal personality, depend on the definite arrays of instituted statuses and attributes, rights and duties that organize the practical deportment of individuals and groups, then focusing on those statuses and attributes will enable us to differentiate between types of person, and help us to understand the specific circumstances of their functioning. This is a point that was forcefully argued some time ago by T.H. Marshall in 'A note on status'. In this classic piece Marshall (1977) indicated how a sociological extension of the legal concept of status (a move that he insisted should not cause sociologists to abandon the older usage nor to lose sight of the differences between sociological and legal usage of the term) provides us with a useful tool for describing different forms of civil personhood.

As we have already seen, legal status refers to the condition of belonging to a particular category or class of persons to whom the law assigns certain legal capacities or incapacities or both. Marshall suggested that in both its legal and sociological conceptions 'status' referred to membership of a particular class of persons. The sociological conception differed from the legal one, though, in concerning itself with 'socially recognized rights and duties and so to socially expected behaviour within the frame of specified relationships' and not solely with legally established capacities and incapacities. Both conceptions are necessary for an effective sociological analysis, Marshall argued, for without them it would be impossible to satisfactorily describe certain forms of socially instituted personhood. As he indicated, 'it is impossible to make comparative studies of the family', for instance, 'if one does not pay attention to the shifting borderline between the legal rights and the socially approved and expected conduct of the husband–father or wife–mother' (1977: 226).

Having first critiqued the slide of 'status' into the territory of personality studies and then delineated the similarities and differences between sociological and legal usage of the term, Marshall went on to clarify the confusion between these conceptions of 'status' on the one hand and those of 'social status' and 'ranking' on the other. Marshall was particularly worried about the popular usage of 'social status' to denote position in a hierarchy of social prestige. He argued that this rather general notion of 'social status' as a position on a prestige scale has nothing whatsoever to do with the sociological conception of 'status'. However, it had, in Marshall's view, had a number of negative effects on the ways in which sociologists approached questions of status. By focusing so closely on hierarchical position within various groups and institutions, Marshall believed some social scientists have effectively marginalized the 'primary concept of status as the fact of membership itself' (1977: 226). 'Status' in its sociological sense, he suggested, should include a range of relationships, not only those of superiority and inferiority. 'Social status', however, was exclusively concerned with the latter and assumed, in effect, that it was possible to somehow add up into a 'general' status all the distinct statuses that any one individual occupied in her or his passage through different associations and institutions. As Marshall rather wistfully put it, it was 'impossible to do the required sum. How do you add together, for instance, doctor, father, councillor, wicket-keeper, church warden and husband to get a unitary result?' (pp. 226–7).

Having established some clear distinctions between legal and sociological conceptions of status and between the latter and 'social status', Marshall went on to distinguish between status and other terms with which it was often elided, namely 'rank', 'standing' and 'rating'. He did so through a fleeting – and now somewhat dated – case study of a particular category of person; however, the precision with which he uses the conceptual tools at his disposal to describe persons is worth noting:

> Let us take, as a summary example, a University Librarian or senior administrative officer such as a Registrar or Bursar. His [sic] status differs from that of a Professor, because his role and the functions of his post differ from those of a Professor. But his university rank may be the same. He may, however, have a lower social status in the community at large than most Professors (perhaps because of family origins), and a rather lower rating for intelligence or general culture or social graces. In consequence of all of these factors his standing in the university is not quite what he would like it to be. (Marshall, 1977: 229)

Like Elias, Bourdieu and Cousins, Marshall's work makes clear that forms of personhood depend upon definite arrays of instituted statuses and attributes, rights and duties that organize the practical deportment of individuals and groups. The task he set himself and other social scientists was one of describing these instituted statuses and attributes, rights and duties, and thus the different forms of person they constitute, case by case, each in their own specific terms. It is to this task that we turn in Chapter 2.

# the identity of persons II

**introduction**  Engagement with the work of Elias and Bourdieu, and the investigation of 'legal personality' in Chapter 1 suggests that what is understood by the term 'self' cannot be seen to furnish the ground for all forms of personhood. However, despite this conclusion a problem remains that needs addressing: how is it that this notion of 'self' – individualized, interiorized, psychologized – has come to be thought of as the sine qua non of what it means to be a person in the present? How did one way of being a person come to be seen as the 'true' or essential form of human subjectivity? Chapter 2 is concerned with sketching possible answers to this problem.

Through an engagement with recent work in the sociology of 'identity' I seek to explore in Section 2.1 some of the main theoretical and methodological tools for conducting what Foucault (1985) termed a 'genealogy of subjectification'. If we use this term 'subjectification' to refer to the multifarious processes and practices through which human beings come to relate to themselves as persons of a certain sort, then we can begin to see that this 'subjectification' has its own history, one that is more practical, technical and less unified than many general philosophical accounts perhaps allow for or appreciate.

The variable relations of person, individual and self that we began to uncover in Chapter 1 are then explored in further detail in Section 2.2 through an engagement with the classic work on the history of 'persona' undertaken by the anthropologist and sociologist, Marcel Mauss. In his canonical published lecture, 'A category of the human mind: the notion of "person", the notion of "self"', he draws important distinctions between person, individual and subject (Mauss, 1985), ones that are quite different from those that we instinctively deploy today. Whereas Mauss views 'individuals' as relatively unstructured biological and psychological beings ('raw, human material'), 'persons' represent the definite complexes of instituted statuses and attributes that have provided the means of actually conducting oneself and one's relations with others. Mauss's distinction, as Hunter and Saunders (1995: 72) have pointed out, rests upon evidence drawn from societies in which not all individuals are or have persons. Moreover, those individuals who are or who have persons do not necessarily bear this personhood in what we would regard as an individual manner – that is within themselves. The forms of having or being a person have varied considerably across time and space; sometimes they have been invested in trans-individual institutions, such as name systems or mask-wearing rituals. Finally, 'subjects' differ from persons and individuals in that they represent a historically contingent and specific manner in which individuals come to possess the attributes of personhood allocated to them (Hunter and Saunders, 1995: 72). This manner is one in which the public attributes of the person are internalized and identified with an inner entity (conscience, consciousness, 'the self') rather than with a public institution, such as the totem or religious ritual. According to Mauss this 'internaliza-tion' of personhood does not represent the 'true' or essential form of human subjectivity; rather, it is simply one amongst many potential and actual ways of being a 'person'. As he famously argued, 'it was formed only for us, among us' (1985: 22); it is the result of the distribution of specific cultural techniques for constructing and monitoring a 'self' – those 'techniques of conscience' first inculcated on a wide scale by the Puritan sects and churches that were to form the subject of Max Weber's *The Protestant Ethic and the Spirit of Capitalism* (1930).

Mauss's historical and anthropological approach to studying the formation of persons in distinct instituted cultural settings shares much with Max Weber's interests, as we discover in Section 2.3. Of Weber's historical sociologies of 'personae', perhaps the most famous is that of the Puritan he described in some detail (1930). This was the persona housed in the distinctive order of living associated with the Protestant sects in the seventeenth century, where life was methodically conducted by daily Bible-reading, constant keeping of spiritual account-books, intense monitoring of one's spiritual progress through each day and throughout life. However, Weber explored many other personae and their cultural settings: the modern bureaucrat in the administrative office and the peasant in the agrarian life order of eastern Germany, for example (Hennis, 1988). The historical particularity of personae fitted to existence in particular cultural settings also figured large in Weber's famous address on 'the profession and vocation of politics'. Here he drew this lesson for his audience: 'We are placed in different orders of life, each of which is governed by different laws' (1994b: 362–3). For Weber it was crucial to grasp the historical particularity of these different 'life-orders' in order to see that they do not constitute a ranking or continuum of human cultural development.

In the light of Mauss's concern with techniques and practices of the person and Weber's emphasis on the relationship between specific 'conducts of life' and 'departments of existence', we move on to engage more closely with Michel Foucault's analysis of the 'self' as a historically and culturally specific comportment of the individual, one dependent on special techniques or procedures of 'subjectification'. In Section 2.4 we discover

Foucault whose analysis of 'the subject' approaches this creature not as some trans-historical object of techniques for being human but as a specific way in which individuals have been enjoined to understand and relate to themselves as 'persons' of a certain sort. As Christian Jambet (1992: 238–9) put it, 'there is a subject, for Foucault, because a certain type of "relationship with the self" comes into being in a culture'. In his final work on 'techniques of the self' in late antiquity, Foucault analyses the distinction between the code of a morality and the ethic or way of life of those attempting to live by the code. Taking as an example the injunction towards conjugal fidelity as a core element of the Christian moral code, Foucault comments that knowledge of this code tells us nothing of the practical means through which Christians have learned to relate to themselves and conduct themselves as faithful persons. The modes of conjugal living are as diverse as the code is seemingly monolithic. Only by focusing attention on these practical means or techniques can we learn to appreciate how Christians were equipped with the capacity to live as faithful persons. Foucault describes these means as ethical techniques and argues that they belong to the domain of spiritual discipline. In Section 2.4, then, we view Foucault's work as an investigation into the specific spiritual practices through which individuals come to concern themselves with themselves and seek to compose themselves as 'subjects' of their own conduct.

The chapter concludes by focusing attention on some lessons for the sociological study of 'identity' that might be drawn from the work discussed in both Chapters 1 and 2.


## 2.1 subjectivity and social relations: genealogies of 'subjectification'

What do we mean by this unwieldy term 'genealogy of subjectification'? The term is most frequently associated with the work of Michel Foucault (1986a) who deployed the term 'subjectification' to refer to the multifarious processes and practices through which human beings come to relate to themselves as persons of a certain sort. Seen in this light, 'subjectification' clearly has a history and, as the sociologist Nikolas Rose (1996: 128) has argued, it is one that is more practical, technical and less unified than many social theoretical accounts perhaps allow for or appreciate.

For one thing, as Rose (1996: 128) makes clear, a genealogy of subjectification is not another attempt to write an historical account of changing ideas about the person as these have figured in social theory, philosophy or literature, for example. While such an endeavour is interesting Rose does not believe it is possible to derive 'from an account of notions of the human being in cosmology, philosophy, aesthetics or literature, evidence about the organization of the mundane everyday practices and presuppositions that shape the conduct of human beings in particular sites' (p. 128). A genealogy is therefore not a history of ideas; rather, it focuses on changing practices and techniques of conduct. It is interested in exploring the practical and technical means through which human beings have learnt to conduct themselves as particular sorts of 'person'. Secondly, genealogy is not concerned with delineating a narrative history of the person as a psychological entity, in order to see how different ages produce humans with different psychological characteristics – beliefs, emotions, pathologies. This would involve privileging a particular conception of what it means to be a person – an interiorized, psychologized, individualized one that only emerged in the relatively recent past – by making it the pre-established grounds or foundation of historical investigation, rather than the site of an historical problem that needs investigating.

Having established what a genealogy is not, it is perhaps easier to provide a more positive description of what genealogical analysis involves. Given that 'subjectification' refers to 'all those heterogeneous processes and practices by means of which human beings come to relate to themselves and others as subjects of a certain type'(Rose, 1996: 130–1), a genealogy of subjectification would focus on the changing – i.e. historically contingent – practices through which human beings have been located in particular 'regimes of the person'. In other words, it would examine historically the relations that human beings have been enjoined to establish with themselves as certain sorts of person. A genealogy of subjectification, then, would involve tracing the ways in which a particular conception of what it means to be a person – 'the self' – that functions as a regulatory ideal in so many aspects of contemporary life has been put together or 'made up', contingently and haphazardly 'at the intersection of a range of distinct histories – of forms of thought, techniques of regulation, problems of organization and so forth' (p. 129). For genealogists, then, 'the self' does not form 'the transhistorical object of techniques for being human but only one way in which humans have been enjoined to understand and relate to themselves' (p. 136). Once again, we see the importance of the context, the practices and techniques through which human beings become persons of a certain sort, in this instance how they come to live as persons with a distinctive 'self'.

Following Foucault, Nikolas Rose provides a detailed, but by no means exhaustive, set of interlinking criteria framing a 'genealogy of subjectification'. These function as a sort of theoretical and methodological grid. He frames them under five headings:

*Problematizations*
Where, how and by whom are aspects of being human rendered problematic and according to what systems of judgement and in relation to what concerns?

*Technologies*
What means have been invented to govern human conduct, to shape and fashion in certain desired directions, and how have these been given a technical form?

*Authorities*
Who is accorded or claims the capacity to speak truthfully about humans, their nature and their problems, and what characterizes the truth about persons that are accorded such authority?

*Teleologies*
What aims, attitudes and ideals function as exemplars for these different practices for working upon the conduct of persons? What codes of knowledge support these ideals and to what ethical valorization are they tied?

*Strategies*
How are these processes and practices for regulating the conduct of persons linked to wider moral, political and social objectives concerning the desirable and undesirable features of populations, workforce, family etc.?

(Rose, 1996: 131–4)

As indicated earlier, each of these 'directions for investigation' is inspired by or derived from the writings of Michel Foucault, in particular his work on the arts of government – those more or less rationalized strategies and programmes for regulating the conduct of persons. The term indicates a perspective from which one can attempt to make intelligible the diversity of attempts by authorities of different kinds 'to act upon the actions of others in relation to objectives of national prosperity, harmony, virtue, productivity, social order, discipline, emancipation, self-realization and so forth' (Rose, 1996: 135).

Rose regards this perspective as significant precisely because it directs our attention to the ways in which these strategies and programmes so often operate through trying to shape what Foucault termed 'technologies of the self' (see Section 2.4). These are techniques for conducting one's self, for example, through requiring one to relate to oneself epistemologically (know yourself), despotically (master yourself) or in other ways (care for yourself). They are embodied in particular practices (confession, diary-keeping and group discussion) and they are always conducted under the actual or imagined authority of some system of truth or some authoritative individual, whether theological and priestly or psychological and therapeutic (Rose, 1996: 135). Rose is keen to indicate that this idea of 'technologies of the self' does not represent 'the self' as the essential characteristic of being human but, rather, as only one way in which human beings have been encouraged to understand and relate to themselves as persons. 'In different practices, these relations are cast in terms of individuality, character, constitution, reputation, personality and the like, which are neither merely *different versions* of a self, nor do they *sum* into a self' (p. 136).

While Rose regards Foucault's work on the relations between government and technologies of the self as furnishing some crucial pointers for conducting a genealogy of subjectification, he also believes that it is imperative to move beyond what he sees as Foucault's sometimes singular focus on 'ethical styles of life' – those ways of relating to oneself that are structured by divisions of truth and falsity, the permitted and the forbidden. Instead he delineates a number of other lines of enquiry that he regards as important to the genealogical project.

First among these is a concern with 'corporealities or body techniques' (Rose, 1996: 136–7). Referring in passing to the work of Marcel Mauss (see Section 2.2) on the differential manner in which the body is used as a technical tool in various cultural settings, Rose suggests that genealogists of subjectification should be concerned with the 'ways in which different corporeal regimes have been devised and implanted in rationalized attempts to enjoin a particular relation to the self and others' (p. 137). Rose points to the work of Norbert Elias (see Section 1.1), and in particular to his historical sociological investigation of *The Court Society* (1983) as an exemplar of genealogy in this regard. In this work Elias demonstrates how the warrior aristocracy in early modern France moderated their warlike propensities and mutated into a social group stressing a particular economy of manners associated with etiquette and the self-monitoring of conduct.

Secondly, Rose (1996: 137) stresses the heterogeneity of the relations between 'the government of others and the government of the self'. He points to the diversity of modes in which a certain relation to oneself is enjoined. The injunction to 'master oneself', for example, takes on a variety of forms depending upon the context within which it occurs. As Rose (1996: 137) indicates, the mastery of the will in the service of 'character' or 'virtue' by the inculcation of habits and rituals of self-denial, prudence and foresight, for instance, is very different from the psychotherapeutic project of mastering one's desire. Here one seeks to free oneself from the destructive consequences of repression, projection and/or identification by bringing its root to conscious awareness.

Rose (1996) distinguishes these characteristic elements of a 'genealogy of subjectification' from the preoccupations of conventional sociological and psychoanalytic approaches to identity and the subject. Focusing briefly on the work of such sociologists as Anthony Giddens (1991) and Zygmunt Bauman (1993, 2004), Rose shows how these authors read off changes in forms of subjectivity and identity from wider social and cultural transformations – whether characterized through the term 'modernity' or 'postmodernity'. This kind of analysis, he argues, regards changes in the ways in which human beings understand and act upon themselves as the effects of epochal shifts located in somewhat abstract overarching designations – production regimes, technology, the family and so on and so forth. By contrast, Rose (1996: 130) insists that no matter how ostensibly significant such changes might appear to be, it is nonetheless important to stress that they 'do not transform ways of being human by virtue of some "experience" they produce. Changing relations of subjectification ... cannot be established by derivation or interpretation of other cultural or social forms' (p. 130). To assume that they can, he argues, is to presume that human beings stand outside of history and are naturally or essentially equipped with the capacity of endowing events with meaning. This would be a mistake for, as we have seen, the ways in which humans give meaning to experience is multifarious and historically contingent. 'Devices of meaning production', Rose argues, 'vocabularies, norms and systems of judgement, produce experience; they are not themselves produced by experience' (p. 130). These techniques do not come ready-made. They have to be invented, stabilized and disseminated in different ways in diverse settings. Instead of assuming changes in identity from grand theoretical accounts of social and cultural transformations, Rose suggests that we should instead examine the intellectual and practical instruments and devices enjoined upon human beings to shape and guide their ways of 'being human'. Rose is advocating a change of focus for the analysis of 'identity', one that pays greater attention to the context within which actual human capacities and attributes are formed and distributed, and to the practices and techniques through which human beings learn to become persons of a certain sort. If we maintain too grand a perspective, he suggests, we will render crucial contextual details insignificant, unremarkable and ultimately invisible. With 'identity', he suggests, the devil is often in the details. If our analytical gaze is too lofty or too generalized we risk overlooking the specificity and particularity of the different forms of personhood.

Rose (1996: 140–1) also has a few words to say about the differences between the genealogical project and psychoanalytic approaches to the 'subject' and 'identity'. He focuses on the work of some contemporary feminists – most notably Judith Butler – who have deployed Lacanian psychoanalytic insights to offer a general account of the ways in which certain practices of the self become inscribed in the bodily comportments of 'the gendered subject'. He suggests that their project is somewhat paradoxical. By arguing that norms and techniques of conduct only reach human beings via the detour of the unconscious, these authors reuniversalize and dehistoricize the concept of the subject and its 'formation'. This detour through the unconscious transmutes 'technologies' into 'representations', by transforming them into that which the individual subject 'fails to know'; that is, into representations which bring the individual into being as the subject of (failed) consciousness. The cost of bringing the unconscious 'into play' is therefore adherence to a single general model of subject-formation, grounded in the play of conscious and unconscious representations.

According to Mark Cousins and Athar Hussain (1984: 254–6), psychoanalytic and genealogical approaches operate with rather different

**46**

assumptions concerning what they describe as the relative depth and thickness of human material. Psychoanalytically informed observers tend to operate with a relatively 'thick' view of this 'human material'. They elaborate a psychical apparatus whose primary process entails an unconscious whose effects have to be inferred from interpretation. From a psychoanalytic viewpoint, there is necessarily, not contingently, a complex layering and interpenetration of conflicting elements derived both from the inner history of the individual and from its 'external' environment.

By contrast, genealogists of subjectification require or presuppose only a weak, minimal or 'thin' conception of the human material on which history operates. As Rose (1996: 142) argues, genealogists are primarily interested in the 'diversity of strategies and tactics of subjectification that have taken place and been deployed in diverse practices at different moments and in relation to different classifications and differentiations of persons'. They are, in other words, primarily interested in describing and analysing the practices and techniques through which human beings are equipped with the capacities to conduct themselves as certain sorts of person. In order to indicate in more detail what such a genealogical focus entails, I turn first to the work of the sociologist and social anthropologist Marcel Mauss and in particular to his detailed work exploring the ways in which an individual's bodily capacities are not naturally given but are in large measure the outcome of (and vary with) social beliefs, norms, practices and techniques. If, as Foucault (1986a: 76) claimed, 'genealogy' is 'grey, meticulous and patiently documentary', then Marcel Mauss surely qualifies as a genealogist par excellence.

## 2.2  marcel mauss: techniques of the body and categories of the person  
Marcel Mauss once observed that '[T]he physical training of all ages and both sexes is made up of masses of details which pass unobserved, we must undertake to observe them' (quoted in Lévi-Strauss, 1987: 4). In his classic essay 'Techniques of the body', Mauss (1973) provided a catalogue of the ways in which social conventions, physical techniques and their forms of training and practice organize activities and abilities we tend to regard as 'natural', such as walking, spitting, sleeping and so forth. The latter, he argued, are acquired attributes and abilities that vary across time and space between different cultural milieux. This is a standard anthropological observation and it functions only as the starting point of Mauss's venture, for he is predominantly concerned with investigating what bodily attributes are actually attributes of.

Mauss begins by describing a number of examples of differential 'body techniques'. He cites the amusing instance of working with British and French troops in the First World War. The English troops he was attached to didn't know how to use French spades, which forced them to

two • the identity of persons II

change 8,000 spades a day whenever they relieved a French division and vice versa. English and French soldiers' techniques of digging were very different. They couldn't easily adapt to each others' techniques. Mauss (1973: 71) observes that 'this plainly shows that a manual knack can only be learnt slowly. Every technique properly has its own form.'

Having observed the fact and variety of different uses of the body, Mauss admits to being somewhat uncertain as to how to classify them. He begins by attempting to place them within a traditional anthropological division of actions into either rites or techniques, the latter being the actions necessary to attain some definite goal. However, the role of tools in this notion of 'technique' proved to be something of a dead end until Mauss began to conceive of the body itself as both the instrument and the object of its own making:

> In this case all that need be said is quite simply that we are dealing with techniques of the body. The body is man's first and most natural instrument. Or more accurately, not to speak of instruments, man's first and most natural object, and at the same time, technical means, is his body. (Mauss, 1973: 71)

If this comment appears at first sight to be somewhat trivial, that may well be due to our extensive reliance on external apparatuses and mechanical and electronic aids to do the work or perform the tasks previous civilizations and other cultural groups used their own bodies to do. Nonetheless, Mauss's point still holds. Hearing, seeing, smelling, resistance to extremes of heat and cold all bear out this radical divergence of bodily attributes and the role of socially transmitted techniques in producing them (Hirst and Woolley, 1982).

In linking the attributes of the body to 'body techniques' Mauss is able to overcome the problems posed by competing biological, psychological and sociological explanations. To describe 'body techniques', Mauss suggests, requires the development of what he calls 'the triple viewpoint' because each 'body technique' – whether it be swimming, spitting or resting – is a particular, indissoluble, 'assemblage' of biological, psychological and sociological elements. Techniques of swimming and diving, for instance, have an evident biological and anatomical component; even so, not all peoples have been swimmers. At the same time, such techniques involve taking into account and overcoming specific psycho-physical reflexes, such as the reflex of shutting one's eyes when underwater. If reflexes are to be overcome and the body put to a new purpose, techniques will have to be transmitted, a specific training undergone – such as being shown how to keep your eyes open underwater. This transmission of techniques is the sociological element, as techniques are only developed, stabilized and transmitted through particular organizational forms and certain sorts of relationship (Hunter and Saunders, 1995: 71).

For Mauss, chief amongst the sociological elements 'of the art of using the body' were 'the facts of education' (1973: 73). Education, here, was classified so as to include imitation and apprenticeship in informal settings as well as the more formal elements of instruction within institutional settings. In all cases, though, authority is involved. In learning a technique, Mauss argues, 'what takes place is prestigious imitation. The child, the adult, imitates actions which have succeeded and which he has seen successfully performed by people in whom he has confidence and who have authority over him' (p. 73). For Mauss, then, the adaptation of the body towards specific goals through the mastery of particular techniques is inseparable from the social order and relationships embodied in training. 'The ensemble', he stresses, 'is conditioned by the ... elements indissolubly mixed together' (p. 74).

As a result of following this line of thought, Mauss feels able to offer a more 'precise classification' of the techniques of the body:

> The constant adaptation to a physical, mechanical or chemical aim (e.g. when we drink) is pursued in a series of assembled actions, and assembled for the individual not by himself alone but by all his education, by the whole society to which he belongs, in the place he occupies in it. (1973: 76)

Bodily attributes, for Mauss, are 'the material, cultural and historical artefacts of particular "gymnic" arts and technologies' (Hunter and Saunders, 1995: 71). Moreover, as we have seen, a diverse range of these attributes are acquired through the direct inculcation and imitation of 'body techniques', techniques that are neither solely controlled by the mind nor presented to it in the form of unconscious representations (Hunter and Saunders, 1995: 71). Such attributes may be 'unconscious' in the sense that their inculcation does not require prior hypothesizing, testing or rational verification. As Hunter and Saunders have argued in this respect,

> this does not mean that such techniques lie beyond the reach of conscious knowledge, in an unconscious domain. It simply means that these sorts of technique happen not to be governed by those special disciplines – of hypothesis, conditional acceptance, testing, confirmation – that we call 'knowledge'. They fall neither within or beyond the reach of knowledge, because they belong to another department of existence. (1995: 75)

This is the domain that Mauss calls 'prestigious imitation'. It is characterized not by rational, conscious circumspection but by what Hunter and

Saunders (1995: 75) term 'habitual virtuosity' (or what Bourdieu (1987) terms 'habitus').

What Mauss's work indicates is that it is possible to treat a diverse range of human attributes as the contingent outcomes of an array of 'body techniques'. Individuals and groups acquire these various attributes – dancing, swimming, riding a bike, reading – not as a condition of consciously representing the world but as a basic outcome of a practical involvement in a given activity or way of life.

Having established this possibility, Mauss attempts to extend its remit. In his famous 1938 lecture 'A category of the human mind: the notion of person, the notion of self', Mauss (1985) sets out to explore whether the capacity to conduct oneself as a 'subject' or 'self' is directly comparable with these other techniques (for swimming, spitting, dancing, etc.). In other words, he asks whether the capacity to problematize one's actions and abilities by relating them to an inner principle of self-scrutiny and control might itself be the product of special techniques and practices and not, as was often argued in his and is argued still in our own time, the foundation of all human abilities and modes of human existence (Hunter and Saunders, 1995: 73).

In this essay, Mauss challenges the idea that the conception of person as self is a natural concomitant of human experience, a given feature of being human. Forms of specification of individuals exist in all societies he argues, but they are not necessarily specified as individual subjects, as unique entities with inherent capacities for self-representation and self-reflection. Individuals may be 'named', specified as places within the systems of persons and ritual entities of the clan or tribe. Names and statuses specify, but do not 'individualize' in the modern sense of the term. Rather, they may repeat ancestors – successive generations occupying a specific named social place; or identity might change with status – with social maturity and so on (Hirst and Woolley, 1982: 118). Particular culturally embedded conceptions of social agency may neither individualize nor identify agency with consciousness. Mauss comments on what he describes as certain traditional Chinese forms of specification of individuals:

> His individuality is his *ming*, his name … yet at the same time [it] has removed from individuality every trace of its being eternal and indissoluble. The name, the *ming*, represents a collective noun, something springing from elsewhere: one's corresponding ancestor bore it, just as it will fall to the descendant of its present bearer. Whenever they have philosophized about it, whenever in certain metaphysical schools they have attempted to explain what it is, they have said that he is a composite, made up of *shen* and *kwei* – two other collective nouns – in this life. (1985: 14)

Mauss (1985: 14) concludes that 'those who have made of the human person a complete entity, independent of all others save God, are rare'.

If the modern western conception of the person as an individualized, interiorized entity is a historical and cultural rarity, what is its specific genealogy? Now Mauss, it is true, represents the emergence of a modern western conception of the person as the history of an 'idea'; however, this is due to compression of argument rather than any specific methodological proclivity on his part. As the nephew and a chief disciple of Emile Durkheim, Mauss appears to assume that conceptions of persons are only intelligible with reference to a definite substratum of categories, practices and activities which together give their agent its complex and differentiated form (Hirst and Woolley, 1982: 120).

Mauss's historical anthropology – or genealogy – of the modern western conception of the person as 'subject' really begins with 'the Romans, or perhaps rather the Latins' (1985: 14). The first relatively even distribution of persons to individuals, he argues, comes about with the establishment of rights ascribed to all those individuals who were citizens under the laws of Rome. While the Romans developed the concept of persona from that of a particular legally based status or role, to which were attached certain obligations, into that of a person as an independent moral entity, a being whose conduct is self-governed,[6] it was Christianity that invested this legal and moral persona with additional metaphysical attributes (p. 19). As Hirst and Woolley (1982: 119) have argued, 'it became both an agent and an immortal soul', the well-being of the soul being dependent in part upon the conduct of the agent. According to Mauss, it is Christianity in particular that produces a conception of the individual as a unity in its conduct, as a unique entity independent of particular social statuses, and of a transcendental value irreducible to considerations of social utility (pp. 19–20). It is not until after the Reformation that identity and consciousness are linked in the individual subject, with self-consciousness emerging as the ground of individual moral existence (Hirst and Woolley, 1982: 119). For Mauss (p. 21) this development is premised upon specific forms of Christian belief and practice, in particular an unmediated relationship between the individual Christian and God, a relationship based on prayer as a dialogue, on introspection and an inner regulation based upon the continual examination of 'conscience'. For Mauss (as for Max Weber; see Section 2.3), the Christian sects in early modern Europe played a crucial role in the formation of this particular conception of the person and its more generalized dissemination to other cultural practices:

We cannot exaggerate the importance of sectarian movements throughout the seventeenth and eighteenth centuries ... [T]here it was that were posed the questions regarding individual liberty, regarding the individual conscience and the right to communicate directly with God, to be one's own priest, to have an inner God. The ideas of the Moravian Brothers, the Puritans, the Wesleyans and the Pietists are those which form the basis on which is established the notion: the 'person' (*personne*) equals the 'self' (*moi*); the 'self' (*moi*) equals consciousness, and is its primordial category. (1985: 21)

The fact that a large number of individuals come to acquire the ability to locate a moral personality within their 'self' is, for Mauss, a matter of historical-anthropological contingency. Mauss is thus quite clear that the identification of the individual with an internalized moral persona is not the essential form of human subjectivity. The modern concept of the person is no less a construction placed upon certain specific human capacities and attributes than any of the other conceptions that Mauss discusses in his essay. Following in the anti-evolutionary tradition of his uncle, Emile Durkheim, Mauss rejects any teleological or evolutionary reading of his historical anthropology of the person as an individual subject, a self:

> Who knows even whether this 'category', which all of us here believe to be well founded will always be recognised as such? It is formulated only for us, among us. Even its moral strength – the sacred character of the human 'person' is questioned ... in the countries where this principle was discovered. We have great possessions to defend. With us the idea could disappear. But let us refrain from moralising. (1985: 22)

Commenting on the importance of Mauss's work for a 'genelaogy of subjectification', Hunter and Saunders (1995: 71) stress the important distinctions that Mauss draws between person, individual and subject – distinctions quite different from those that we instinctively deploy today. Whereas 'individuals' are seen by Mauss as relatively unstructured biological and psychological beings ('raw, human material'), 'persons' represent the definite complexes of instituted statuses and attributes that have provided the means of actually conducting oneself and one's relations with others. Mauss's distinction, as Hunter and Saunders (1995: 72) point out, rests upon evidence drawn from societies in which not all individuals are or have persons. Moreover, those individuals who are or who have persons do not necessarily bear this personhood in an individual manner – that is within themselves. As we saw earlier, the forms of having or being a person have varied considerably across time and space; sometimes they have been invested in trans-individual institutions, such as name systems or mask-wearing rituals. Finally, 'subjects' differ from persons and individuals in that they represent a historically contingent and specific manner in which individuals come to possess the attributes of personhood allocated to them. This manner is one in which the attributes of personhood are internalized and identified with an inner entity (conscience, consciousness) rather than with a public institution, such as the totem or religious ritual. According to Mauss this 'internalization' of personhood does not represent the 'true' or essential form of human subjectivity; rather it is simply one among many potential and actual ways of being a 'person'. As he famously argued, 'it was formed only for us, among us'

(1985: 22); it is the result of the distribution of specific cultural techniques for constructing and monitoring a 'self'.

As Hunter and Saunders (1995: 73) make clear, the sort of historical-anthropological approach to studying the formation of persons, and their bodily and mental attributes and capacities, in distinct instituted cultural settings suggested by Mauss is also the 'central theme' of Max Weber's work and, indeed, of Michel Foucault's later work on what we have already referred to as 'technologies of the self'. It is to the work of these two scholars that we now turn.

## 2.3 max weber: persons and 'life orders'

In recent years, a somewhat axiomatic sociological image of Max Weber as a 'grand' theorist of the 'instrumental rationalization' of modern life has been challenged by a range of work emerging from the social sciences and the humanities (Hennis, 1988, 2000; Turner, 1992; Saunders, 1997). In the 'traditional image' – influenced in particular by the reading of Weber's oeuvre associated with the work of Talcott Parsons – western history is represented as a process involving the rationalization of all social relations and of increasing disenchantment, in which all world-views become progressively devalued. Although diverse and far from constituting a mutually agreed 'line', recent interpretations have sought to undo this image of Weber as a sociologist of 'rationalization' and have instead begun to paint a picture of a historical anthropologist whose concerns centred on the problem of *Kulturmensch*, on 'man' as a cultural being.

For this Weber we are cultural beings because 'we are not natural, living, social, religious or political beings' (Turner, 1992: 44). We have no 'essence' waiting to unfold itself but are instead remarkably malleable creatures whose capacities and dispositions are formed and reformed in the various spheres of life in which we are placed and place ourselves. In other words, because we are not 'natural' but 'cultural' beings, our becoming a certain sort of person – a politician, a bureaucrat, a priest – is dependent upon historically contingent socio-cultural conditions of training and practice. Thus, in his famous essay on the relationship between Puritan ethics and the development of a capitalistic way of life, Weber stresses the sets of ethical techniques and practices through which members of the Protestant sects learned to conduct their lives in the absence of collective guarantees of religious salvation. The Puritan ethics that Weber describes can be viewed as a set of practices and techniques in which the status and attributes of a particular form of Christian personhood are attached to an inner – conscious and conscientious – principle of monitoring and self-control. Weber's Puritan internalizes in the form of an ever watchful inner conscience the public norm embodied in the predestinarian doctrine or code, rather than externalizing that norm in religious ceremonies and images or, for that matter, in a legal system. The manner of bearing one's person, he argues, depends on a diversity of factors and has no general or necessary form.

For Weber, the question is not how well a particular persona equates with the truth of human experience or subjectivity in general, but how one gets individuals willing and competent to bear that form of personhood which fits the circumstances of a given sphere of life (Saunders, 1997). Like Mauss, Weber is concerned with constructing a practical account of the ways in which individuals learn to conduct themselves as certain sorts of person, an account that shows the actual 'conducts of life' involved and the technical conditions for producing and deploying them.

According to one of the most powerful advocates of the recent interpretation of Weber as a historical anthropologist of *Kulturmenschen*, Wilhelm Hennis (1988, 2000), this relationship between form of personhood and sphere of life or 'life-order' (*Lebensordnung*) is in fact the 'central theme' of Weber's work. Hennis (1988, 2000) is in no doubt that the attempt to find 'a theme running through Max Weber's work – and this in the singular!' would strike most sociologists as absurd. Yet, his patient, detailed surveys of Weber's oeuvre lead him to the conclusion that just such a 'theme' can be detected. For Hennis (1988: 104), Weber's theme concerns the relationship between individuals as 'cultural beings' – as endlessly malleable creatures – on the one hand and 'the "orders of life"' – the orders of social life and its powers – on the other. It is this relation that provides what Weber's wife Marianne (quoted in Hennis, 1988: 62) refers to as the 'universal point of view' of his work. By this phrase, she does not mean to suggest that Weber was somehow able to take a God's eye view of the world that was transcendentally 'objective' or 'impartial', but rather that an abiding concern with the ways in which humans as 'cultural' beings are differentially 'made up' as certain sorts of person, through their insertion in distinct socio-cultural settings or 'life-orders', characterized his oeuvre. It is this problematic that she and, following her lead, Hennis (1988) regard as the 'universal point of view directing his questions'.

Weber's lesson therefore concerns the work that has gone into fashioning novel personae to meet the exigencies of particular socio-cultural settings. For Hennis, it is not so much the complexity but the relative simplicity of Weber's theme that has proved to be such an obstacle to its comprehension. For what Hennis (1988: 104) considers to be an often high-theory obsessed social science, one which sought, as Weber himself put it, 'to shift its location and change its conceptual apparatus so that it might regard the stream of events from the heights of reflective thought', the relationship between 'personae and the life-orders' would 'have little interest'. If one can come down from those heights, Hennis argues, then the relations of 'personality and life-orders' might become rather more important (p. 104). More specifically, for Weber, Hennis continues, it was a matter of investigating the formation of 'personalities' appropriate to particular 'life-orders' (p. 104).

'Conduct of life' (*Lebensführung*) specifies the ethical techniques and practical means through which a particular 'persona' is methodically organized. As we have seen, perhaps the most famous of these Weberian 'personalities' is the Puritan, the typical product of that ethos which emerged in the life-order associated with the radical Protestant sects. However, Weber explored many other personae and their cultural settings: the bureaucrat in the administrative office and the peasant in the agrarian life order of eastern Germany, for example. In each case, though, Hennis argues, Weber's exploration of a specific persona consists of three main elements. The point of departure is that of the external given conditions of any life-order, the 'conditions of existence', in a material–cultural sense, of the life-order in question. Secondly, Weber analyses the organized form of rationality possessed by a given life-order and the demands on individual conduct that it makes. This also involves an assessment of the conditions making for the possibility of 'personality' within any given life-order. Finally, Weber is concerned with the tensions and antagonisms, actual and potential, between the regularities of these orders, 'spheres' or 'values'. As Weber (1994b: 362) put it, 'we are placed in various orders of life, each of which is subject to different laws'. No transcendental moral or philosophical justification for a given life-order is possible precisely because 'the different value systems of the world stand in conflict with one another'. Between these value spheres there is a battle between gods of different religions '[a]nd destiny, certainly not "science", prevails over these gods and their struggles. One can only understand what the divine is for one system or another, or in one system or another' (Weber, 1989: 23). For Weber it was vital to grasp the inherent plurality of 'life-orders' and the personae they give rise to in order to see that they do not constitute a ranking or continuum of human cultural development.

As I have already argued, recent interpretations of Weber have disputed traditional assumptions about the central themes of his oeuvre. In particular, authors such as Hennis (1988, 2000) and Turner (1992) have argued that the development of western 'rationalism' as a process of increasing disenchantment or, rather, as an increasingly purely rational and functional order of all social relationships is certainly not the main theme of Weber's work. Instead, as we have seen, Hennis (1988, 2000) and others have argued that the development of individuals as 'cultural beings' lies at the heart of Weber's concerns. According to Hennis (1988: 28), Weber's primary concern is to analyse the relationship between the various 'life-orders' and the forms of person they give rise to. As support for this thesis, Hennis (1988: 29) refers to an illuminating remark of Weber's concerning the intentions that guided him when writing *The Protestant Ethic and the Spirit of Capitalism*: 'it was not the furtherance of capitalism in its expansion which formed the centre of my interest, but the development of the type of mankind that was brought about by the conjunction of religiously and economically conditioned factors'. In particular, Weber indicates that he was concerned with 'the clarification of the "characterlogical" effects of specific forms of piety' (quoted in Hennis, 1988: 29). Chief among the latter, as we shall shortly see, was the development of a comportment of the person we have come to know as 'the subject' or 'self'.

Having introduced the basic tenets of Calvinist doctrine and contrasted these with those of other Protestant sects, such as Lutheranism, Weber indicates that the source of the 'utilitarian character of Calvinist ethics' and 'the important peculiarities of the Calvinist idea of the calling' lies with the Calvinists' 'special consideration of the doctrine of pre-destination' (1930: 109). As Weber says: 'For us the decisive problem is how was this doctrine borne' (p. 111). In Calvinism, Weber stresses, 'two principal, mutually connected, types of pastoral advice appear for those seeking a sign that they are after all members of the elect' (p. 111). On the one hand, it is held to be an absolute duty to consider oneself chosen and to combat all doubts as temptations of the devil. And on the other hand, in order to attain that self-confidence, 'intense worldly activity is recommended as the most suitable means. It and it alone disperses religious doubts and gives the certainty of grace' (p. 112).

Worldly activity is asserted as the very means of salvation when previously the worthiest individuals in the religious sense had been seen as those who withdrew from the world. This results from changes in the types of Christian conduct that the Calvinists viewed as serving to increase the glory of God. Weber writes:

> Just what does so serve is to be seen in his own will as revealed either directly through the Bible or indirectly through the purposeful order of the world which he has created ... It was through the consciousness that his conduct, at least in its fundamental character and constant ideal ... rested on a power within himself working for the glory of God; that it is not only willed of God but rather done by God that he attained the highest good towards which this religion strove, the certainty of salvation. (1930: 114–15)

One is instructed to use one's life as a calculated means of at once fulfilling God's plan, and assuaging one's own inner need for certainty. A conscientious and conscious, self-driven and driving existence is proposed:

> In practice this means that God helps those who help themselves. Thus the Calvinist, as it is sometimes put, himself creates his own salvation, or as would be more correct, the conviction of it. But this creation cannot, as in Catholicism, consist in a gradual accumulation of individual good works to one's credit, but rather in a systematic self-control which at every moment stands before the inexorable alternative, chosen or damned. (Weber, 1930: 115)

**56**

The techniques and practices of Calvinism – the methodical conduct of daily Bible reading, the constant keeping of spiritual account-books, the intense monitoring of one's spiritual progress through each day and through-out life – are aimed at enabling its adherent 'to maintain and act upon ... his constant motives'. In other words, 'it tried to make him into a personality' (Weber, 1930: 119). Thus individuals located in the life-orders of the Protestant sects came to acquire the attributes of personhood in a particular way. This manner of comporting the person we have termed 'the subject'. It involved the public attributes of personhood being internalized and identified with an inner entity (consciousness, conscience) rather than with a public insti-tution, such as a religious ceremony or, for that matter, a legal system. As we have seen, the fact that a large number of individuals come to acquire the abil-ity of locating public attributes of personhood within themselves is, for Weber (as for Mauss), a matter of historical contingency. It does not represent the truth or essence of what it means to be human. It is simply one amongst many ways of conducting oneself as a person.

In *The Protestant Ethic and the Spirit of Capitalism* (as in 'The pro-fession and vocation of politics' (1994b) and 'Science as a vocation' (1989)) Weber's 'central theme' comes through clearly. Here, his key question con-cerns the practical means through which one cultivates individuals willing and competent to bear that 'personality' which the circumstances of a given sphere of existence or life-order requires. His point is therefore to construct a historical and practical account of the cultural attributes required to sus-tain a given way of life, an account that indicates the actual 'conducts of life' involved and the conditions necessary for producing and deploying them. In this respect, as I indicated earlier, Weber's work has much in com-mon with that of Mauss and with the later studies of Michel Foucault into the manner by which 'individuals' come to see and act upon themselves as 'subjects' of a certain sort. It is to the work of Michel Foucault that we now turn.

## 2.4   michel foucault: 'techniques of the self'

As I have sug-gested in relation to the work of Mauss and Weber, the self-reflective and self-responsible person – the 'subject' – is not the source of its own capaci-ties and dispositions but is the product of particular practices and disci-plines. What both Mauss and Weber's work indicates is that ideas are not by themselves actionable. General philosophies or social and cultural theo-ries of 'the subject' tell us nothing about how – practically – individuals have learned to comport and conduct themselves as 'self-responsible' and 'self-reflective' persons. It is therefore necessary to pull apart accounts of the 'subject' to be found in various philosophies and social theories from the practical disciplines through which individuals become 'subjects' in given contexts. In their different ways, the work of Mauss and Weber does precisely this and their more practical and technical concerns find interesting parallels in the work of Michel Foucault.

In his last works on ethical 'practices of the self' in late-antiquity, Foucault (1986b) indicates that the presence of a moral code tells us little about how practically those attempting to live by the code conducted themselves on a day-to-day basis. Taking as an example the injunction to conjugal fidelity as a core element of the Christian moral code, Foucault (1986b) indicates that knowledge of this injunction signally fails to tell us anything about the means by which Christians have attempted to practically conduct themselves as faithful persons. The means of conjugal living, he argues, are as diverse as the code is seemingly monolithic. Fidelity has been practised – at different times and in different ethics – as a lesson in self-restraint to oneself and one's social or political subordinates; as a way of managing the sexual energies and achieving an optimal economy of the body and mind; and so on and so forth. These means can be called ethical techniques and they belong to the domain of spiritual discipline. And it is this domain, Foucault argues, that holds the key to the development of that which we have come to call 'the subject' – the self-reflective person.

As we have seen, ethical practices for Foucault were to be distinguished from codes of morality in that the latter tended towards relatively formal systems of interdiction and injunction – thou shalt or shalt not do this or that. Ethics, on the other hand, refers to the practical means through which individuals come to conduct themselves as persons of a certain sort in relation to a given 'code'. In order to understand how modern individuals could experience themselves as subjects of a 'sexuality', for example, it was, Foucault argued, essential first to analyse the practical ethical means through which 'Western man' [sic] had been 'brought to recognize himself as a subject of desire' (1986b: 329). This necessitated a 'genealogy of ethics', understood as 'a history of the forms of moral subjectivation and of practices of the self that are meant to ensure it'.

Such a genealogy would explore the ways in which the various forms of spiritual practice found in Greek and Greco-Roman culture were assimilated into 'the exercise of priestly power in early Christianity, and, later, into educative, medical, and psychological types of practices'. It would do so along four interrelated axes. The first of these Foucault terms 'the determination of the ethical substance'. By this he means 'the way in which the individual has to constitute this or that part of himself as the prime material of his moral conduct'. Greek and Greco-Roman ethics, for example, Foucault argues, is primarily concerned with 'the use of pleasures' (*aphrodisia*), observing their dangers and seeking their moderation, whereas Christianity works on the flesh as the locus of impurity and sinful desires, 'a characterization of the ethical substance based on finitude, the Fall, and evil' (Foucault, 1986b: 239). Secondly, each form of ethical relation can be examined according to its distinctive 'mode of subjectification' (*mode d'assujettissement*). Here Foucault is referring to the different ways in which individuals establish a relationship to the moral code and recognize their responsibility for putting it into practice. Using the example of conjugal fidelity once again, Foucault (1986b: 239–40) points out that one puts this into practice and complies with the precept that imposes it in many different ways, for instance, 'because one acknowledges oneself to be a member of the group that accepts it, declares adherence to it out loud, and silently preserves it as a custom' or because 'one regards oneself as a an heir to a spiritual tradition that one has the responsibility of maintaining or reviving'. Thirdly, one must explore the means of transformation, the actual ethical work (*travail éthique*) that 'one performs on oneself, not only in order to bring one's conduct into compliance with a given rule, but to attempt to transform oneself into the ethical subject of one's behaviour' (pp. 240–2). This transformative activity is achieved through the medium of a variety of 'techniques' or 'technologies' of the self: dialogue, listening, meditation, training of memory, examination of conscience and self-examination, diary and note-book keeping, letter writing and so on and so forth. Thus in relation to the problem of 'sexual austerity', Foucault indicates that this precept can be practised 'through a long effort of learning, memorization, and assimilation of a systematic ensemble of precepts, and through a regular checking of conduct aimed at measuring the exactness with which one is applying the rules'. However, it can also be practised 'through a decipherment as painstaking, continuous and detailed as possible, of the movements of desire in all its hidden forms, including the most obscure'. Finally, Foucault indicates that a 'genealogy of ethics' must concern itself with the *telos* of the individual's relationship to him/herself, the mode of being in which the ethical practice is embedded and which forms its goal or end. The *telos* is as varied as the practices themselves. Returning once again to 'conjugal fidelity', Foucault indicates that this precept 'can be associated with a moral conduct that aspires to an ever more complete mastery of the self; it can be a moral conduct that manifests a sudden and radical detachment vis-à-vis the world; it may strain toward a perfect tranquillity of soul, a total insensitivity to the agitations of the passions, or toward a purification that will ensure salvation after death and blissful immortality' (pp. 240–2).

For Foucault, like Mauss and Weber before him, it is neither the capacities for consciousness nor the structures of language that qualify the individual as a subject. Instead the individual is seen as 'raw material' for a certain kind of ethical labour, one using ethical techniques that result in that comportment of the person we have come to call 'the subject'. Two features of this material–cultural labour through which individuals are 'subjectified' are worth emphasizing here. First, as Foucault makes clear, before individuals can begin to reflect upon themselves as the subjects of their own conduct – before they begin to take an ethical interest in themselves – they must undergo a certain form of problematization. They must first cross what Ian Hunter (1994a: 53) has called a 'threshold of interrogation', and this is only done through initiation into specific practices of self-problematization. As the 'Introduction' to *The Use of Pleasure* (Foucault, 1984) makes clear, Greek, Greco-Roman and Christian cultures contain a multiplicity of such practices. Whether in the form of Stoic self-testing or in the Christian interrogation of the flesh – Protestant self-examination or Catholic confession – a whole series of inventions exist for taking an interest in oneself as the subject of one's own conduct. Secondly, the specific ways in which individuals conduct themselves as persons with a 'self' are the product of certain forms of ethical work that Foucault terms 'technologies of the self'. Once again, classical and Christian spiritual practice is the source of a plethora of such forms: self-examination, sexual austerity and fasting, for example. These provide the 'ascetic' means through which individuals can learn to comport themselves as the responsible agents of their own (sexual, visionary, dietary) personhood, in pursuit of 'self-imposed' spiritual goals.

In keeping with Mauss and Weber, then, Foucault treats the persona of 'the subject' as a particular comportment of the individual made available to certain populations by specific spiritual practices. If something like this sort of genealogy has any explanatory reach, then it has a number of implications for the idea that the subject is the source of its own capacities. Not only this, though, it also has some important consequences for the idea, propounded in the 'subject of language approach', for example, that one can infer forms of 'subjectivity' from the operations of a linguistic system. In the first instance, it should now be clear that 'the subject' is not the source of its own capacities because those capacities – whether for self-consciousness or swimming – are the products of socially instituted forms of training and practice. Secondly, it should also be clear that it is simply not possible to infer from the operation of linguistic systems the same capacities for cultural development or individuation in all human social organizations. Thus there can be no general 'subject of language'. Indeed, as Ian Hunter (1993: 128) has pointed out, 'there is no general subject of swimming or of algebra or of brick-laying, as individuals can acquire these and a host of other positive attributes without subjecting them to the techniques of ethical problematization. By the same argument, there is indeed a subject of (Western) sexuality but this special inner comportment is not the ground of our other capacities, and it is an historical contingency that our inner selves are not organized around diet.'

In other words, it is possible to treat human attributes, including the capacity for language use, as the outcome of an array of techniques of living and forms of social practice and training. Individuals and groups acquire these attributes – talking, reading, spitting, digging, dancing – in many different ways and certainly not solely or even primarily on the basis of conscious self-reflection or rational verification. The arguments put forward by Mauss, Weber and Foucault suggest that the capacity to conduct oneself as the 'subject' of one's thoughts and actions – and indeed to problematize oneself by treating the latter as 'unconscious', hence in need of reflective ethical work – is directly comparable with these other attributes. It is the product of particular socially instituted forms of training and practice, the result of exposure to certain 'techniques' of conduct. Although, as Mauss, Weber and Foucault have all pointed out, we now take this capacity for granted and see it as a natural concomitant of modern life, it is nonetheless important to understand that being a 'subject' is rooted in particular conducts of life; it is not something that all individuals pursue at all times with equal vigour.

**concluding comments**    The work of Mauss, Weber and Foucault and the gloss on these by Rose provided some important theoretical and methodological guidelines for historicizing the emergence of the 'subject' as a particular comportment of the person. I termed this historicizing and contextualizing approach 'genealogical'. A genealogy of 'the subject' or 'self' I argued, is concerned with exploring the ways in which a particular conception and comportment of the person has been put together or practically 'made up' in different places, spaces and times. Where the separate lines of enquiry undertaken by these three authors converged was in their rejection of the self-reflective person as the author of its own capacities and dispositions. Rather, they focused our attention on the domain of spiritual practices and ethical labour through which individuals came to concern themselves with themselves and sought to compose themselves as the 'subjects' of their own conduct. Their object was to investigate the 'subject' or 'self' as a particular practice or comportment of the person, deriving ultimately from western spiritual disciplines. Seen in this light, Weber's account of the rise of the Protestant ethic in the sixteenth and seventeenth centuries, for example, is a description of a massive exercise in spiritual training (Hunter, 1994a). Protestantism appears in this sense as an attempt to spiritualize church and society through the systematic transfer of 'ethical disciplines' from the priesthood to the lay population. As we saw earlier, this transfer involved the systematic use of devices for mass spiritual problematization which, as Weber argues, destroyed the certitude of salvation that had come from collective participation in the sacraments of the church. And it involved the systematic transmission of particular forms of ethical labour: practices of self-watchfulness and self-control, special forms of devotional reading and writing, through which the faithful monitored and reassured themselves of their ethical standing. The result, as we saw, was a profound individualization of Christian spirituality, as ordinary members of the flock were introduced to a practice of ethical life that made them 'personally' responsible for their own salvation (Hunter, 1993; 1994a).

The arguments put forward by Mauss, Weber and Foucault suggest that the capacity to conduct oneself as the 'subject' of one's thoughts and actions is the product of particular socially instituted forms of training and practice, the result of exposure to certain 'techniques' of conduct. Although, as Mauss, Weber and Foucault all pointed out, we now take this capacity for granted it is nonetheless important to understand that being a 'subject' is the product of training in specific techniques rooted in particular conducts of life; it is not something that all individuals pursue at all times in all domains. Rather it is, as Mauss put it, an arrangement forged 'only for us, among us', distinguished by its rarity and delicacy, not by its universal truth and necessity. For all three authors, being sensitive to the specificities of context is crucial to understanding the formation of persons and their uneven and limited distribution.

In this chapter, then, I have focused attention on the relations, techniques and forms of training and practice through which individuals have acquired definite capacities and attributes for social existence as certain sorts of person. This involved a move away from more philosophical accounts of the formation of subjectivity towards a more sociological, historical and technical understanding of the limited forms of personhood that individuals acquire in their passage through various social institutions and other cultural milieux. Alongside this emphasis came recognition of the historical contingency and plurality of 'personhood' and the necessity of not divorcing or carelessly abstracting the properties of particular forms of personhood from the specific cultural milieu in which they are formed and within whose boundaries they make sense.

My main argument is that the emergence of plural spheres of life (or 'life-orders' to use Weber's term) gives rise to many different and non-transferable conceptions and comportments of the person. Many of the intractable debates about persons and 'identity' that arise today do so when the concerns of one context are imported into another, different context. The appearance of 'forced options' – such as whether post-structuralism or psychoanalysis gets 'the subject' right – often arises from attempts to derive decisions from 'the' (illicitly decontextualized) concept of a person. As Hirst and Woolley suggested (1982: 132), this temptation to unity is 'an elementary error', the 'error' in question being a failure to recognize that specific concepts and comportments of the person perform quite different functions in different cultural contexts or social institutions. Given their contextual specificity, forms of personhood and their definite but limited settings must not be underdescribed. If they are, we will fail to see the job that each is doing, that each has its own history and distribution, has fashioned its own ethos, and is directed by its own techniques to its own ends. The ends of clinical psychoanalysis, for instance, are very different from those of 'subject of language' philosophy. It is not so much that one is right and one is wrong when it comes to understanding the 'subject' or the 'person' but that each is a different practice, doing a different job of work in its own particular context. As such, they are not really working with the same conception of persons. The 'subject' of language is simply not the same entity as the 'subject' of clinical psychoanalysis. Attempting to integrate them in pursuit of a more rounded understanding of 'the' (decontextualized) subject may end up generating more heat than light. As Amélie Rorty would have us ask: how can we actually identify what we might term as this 'trans-contextual subject' if conceptions of persons and the practices that bring them into being are context specific 'all the way up and all the down' (Rorty, 1988: 8)? The approach outlined in this chapter has suggested that persons only come into view within the vocabularies and practices of specific enterprises (law, finance, psychoanalysis, medicine) and in relation to the purposes of which that enterprise is the vehicle. The set of purposes and practices that constitute the persona of the 'cultural theorist' and the set of purposes and practices that constitute the persona of the 'financial adviser', for example, are quite different and there is no reason to assume that the purposes and practices of one can or should have any practical value in the other's 'life-order'. If you wanted professional advice on your taxes would you go to a cultural theorist? If you wanted to learn how to undertake a semiotic analysis of Hithcock's *Vertigo* would you go to see a financial adviser? As we have seen, the vocabularies, practices and techniques of a given 'life-order' are not extrinsic to the persons they constitute. Discard them in favour of other vocabularies, practices and techniques and you risk losing, for good or ill, the person they call into being.

# which is the 'self' in 'self-interest'?

**introduction**  I argued in Chapters 1 and 2 that specific concepts and comportments of the person can be seen to perform quite different functions in different contexts. Given this sort of specificity, I suggested, it is important not to underdescribe forms of personhood and their definite but limited settings. If we fail to heed this advice, it is more than probable that we won't be able to see the job that each is doing, how each has its own history and distribution, has fashioned its own ethos, and is directed by its own techniques to its own ends.

In this Chapter, I seek to live up to this injunction by unpacking the concept of 'self-interest'. This concept has frequently functioned as a unifying device. 'Self-interest' is regularly viewed, by its friends as well as its foes, as one of those concepts that, in Rorty's (1988: 45) words seeks 'to pull one rabbit out of several hats', by providing a transcendental unity of the concept of the person. All the better then to show how historically there have been quite discontinuous changes in the characterization of the 'self' deemed to be 'self-interested'. 'Self-interest', I will argue, refers to a number of historically distinct conceptions and behaviours. There is, in other words, no such thing as *the* concept of 'self-interest', just as there is no such thing as *the* concept of a person 'whose various components form a harmonious structure that could provide adjudication among competing normative claims about what does or does not fall within the domain of the rights and obligations of persons' (Rorty, 1988: 31).

Above all, perhaps, it is neo-classical economics that has accustomed us to the image of human beings as 'rational maximizers' of their own 'self-interest'. As many economists would hasten to point out, though, this idea of rational self-interest is not intended to function as a complete description of human conduct. Rather, it is a theory. A deliberate, reductive move designed to construct mathematically tractable models of human behaviour that, in turn, yield testable predictions. This is an important point. Yet, under the sway of such economic modelling, a not insignificant number of social scientists have come to see such maximizing behaviour everywhere, and to install self-interest as the central generating mechanism of all social relations; in effect, to establish 'self-interest' as the hard rock on which all of social life is founded (Niskanen, 1971; Buchanan, 1978; Becker, 1981, 1986; Schotter, 1981).[1]

As Callon (1998), for instance, has argued, such reductionism has been regularly denounced by sociological commentators who, in pointing to the poverty, atomism and basic fictiveness of this conception of humanity, seek instead to reassert the primacy of 'the social' in 'man's' complex constitution: 'the sociologist denounces this *(economic)* reductionism in order to disqualify economic theory and propose replacing it by another theory, a sociology of real man, one taken in a bundle of links which constitute his sociality and hence his humanity' (p. 51).

In what follows, I seek to sidestep the issue of whether individual human beings are radically 'socially' embedded creatures, or essentially rational maximizers of their own interests, and focus instead on how, historically, particular 'self-interested' conducts were programmed. I argue that 'self-interested' conduct does indeed exist, but is not an unchanging human essence. I then attempt to show how, at a certain historical period and in relation to specific purposes, a particular version of self-interested personhood was made up.

I begin by exploring the historical context in which this version of 'self-interest' emerged as a normative doctrine whose dissemination, far from engendering society's ruin, as much post-romantic sociology would have it, was represented as a viable means to its salvation. In so doing, I seek to highlight the distinctive understanding of 'self' that this doctrine promoted and its performative role as a device designed to secure social pacification. In historicizing self-interest in this manner and treating its theorization as culturally performative, rather than as simply empirically descriptive, a more sympathetic understanding of the historical plurality of self-interested conducts can, perhaps, be developed.


**persons and contexts**    For as long as sociology has been practised, capitalism, or markets, or rational self-interested conducts, have been the target of considerable critical opprobrium/denunciation. The mode of critique has varied with the theoretical position favoured, from Marx's theory of alienation, Durkheim's *anomie* or Freud's thesis of libidinal repression up to, and including, more recent visions of contemporary economic conducts as destructive of morality (Sayer, 1997). In these, and other, implicit or explicit critiques of capitalism the stress, more often than not, is on the repressive, alienating, or otherwise inhibiting aspects of economic conducts on the development of, what we might term, 'the full human personality'. Without wishing to dispute, or indeed interrogate, the veracity of these critiques, it is nonetheless worth pointing out that rather than being an unforeseen side-effect of commercially 'self-interested' conduct, one to be denounced and eradicated at the earliest opportunity, the one-sided, predictable, rational and in some senses 'repressed' personality it produced, was exactly what its advocates trusted that it would accomplish. And this for good reasons, as Albert Hirschman has indicated:

> This position, which seems so strange today, arose from extreme anguish over the clear and present dangers of a certain historical period, from concern over the destructive forces unleashed by the human passions with the only exception, so it seemed at the time, of 'innocuous' avarice. *In sum, capitalism was supposed to accomplish exactly what was soon to be denounced as its worst feature.* (1977: 132)

In other words, commercially directed forms of 'rational' self-interest were viewed, in context, as possible solutions to the disastrous conflicts besetting early modern Europe, particularly those associated with religious war and aristocratic adventurism. From this perspective, the focus on interest-governed conduct, commercial or otherwise, was a product of an urgent quest 'for a new way of *avoiding society's ruin*, permanently threatening at the time because of precarious arrangements for internal and external order' (Hirschman, 1977: 130). For its early modern advocates, 'self-interested' conduct appeared as a potential cultural counterweight to the menace posed by the world of the 'full human personality', replete with its destructive passions. From the perspective of the present, such a belief in the efficacy of 'self-interest' can appear remarkably naive or just plain monstrous. The ravages of contemporary economic globalization, for instance, are regularly held up as exemplars of the full horrors of unbridled self-interest. And yet, if we exercise our historical imaginations just a little, we might also wonder at contemporary critics' forgetfulness of the dire consequences of a time when social and political existence was dominated by rival religious zealotries and the search for 'glory'.

**passions, interests and persons**   In *The Passions and the Interests*, subtitled 'arguments for capitalism before its triumph', Albert Hirschman (1977) explored why and how certain, frequently commercial, ideas of self-interest were popularized, and particular self-interested conducts endorsed by a wide variety of seventeenth- and eighteenth-century thinkers. The latter, many of whom were personally antithetical to money-making and commerce, came to look favourably upon commercial self-interest, he argues, because they saw it as a relatively peaceful and harmless alternative to the violent passions that had fuelled the European wars of religion and inspired military and aristocratic adventurism. Weary of the destruction caused by the unbridled passions, and bent on reform, a number of these thinkers were hopeful that the 'mild' passion for money-making and calculation, 'although admittedly ignoble and uncouth, could defeat and bury the violent passions that so ruinously stoked the endless cycles of civil butchery' (Holmes, 1995: 54). These attempts to harness the moderating effects of enlightened self-interest were therefore driven by a need to counteract and neutralize what were seen as the destructive consequences of mobilizing passion in the service of a religious cause and aristocratic ideals.

The idea that self-interest was a relatively harmless and even beneficial form of human conduct was, according to Hirschman, a novel idea, contradicting the old association of avarice with sin. Its relative novelty and contrariety with prevailing cultural norms suggested that its advocates would have their work cut out in establishing its standing as a prestigious doctrine (Johnston, 1986). And yet, as Hirschman (1977: 31–48) argues, such was the desperation to find a way out of 'perpetual war', and such was the impotence of the two established categories that had 'dominated the analysis of human motivation since Plato', namely 'passions' on the one hand and 'reason' on the other, in promoting that endeavour, that the emergence of a 'third way', the category of 'interest', that could potentially counteract the weaknesses of the first two, was received with remarkable enthusiasm, given its established (negative) connotations:

> Once passion was deemed destructive and reason ineffectual, the view that human action could be exhaustively described by attribution to either one or the other meant an exceedingly sober outlook for humanity. A message of hope was therefore conveyed by the wedging of interest in between the two traditional categories of human motivation. Interest was seen to partake in effect of the better nature of each, as the passion of self-love upgraded and contained by reason, and as reason given direction and force by that passion. The resulting hybrid form of human action was considered exempt from both the destructiveness of passion and the ineffectuality of reason. No wonder that the doctrine of interest was received at the time as a veritable message of salvation! (Hirschman, 1977: 43–4)

Given this context, it seems unsurprising that 'interest' could come to assume a 'curative' connotation that its prehistory and established meanings would otherwise have rendered unthinkable. And that, in turn, the association of 'interest' with a more enlightened idea of governing human affairs and attenuating some of the latter's more destructive propensities, helped to bestow upon certain practices of 'interest'-governed conduct, a similarly positive and 'curative' set of meanings. Commerce, for instance, might be low, but in contrast to the bloody and destructive consequences of the pursuit of glory or religious fanaticism, it might be a more civilized and less unpredictable form of life. Interests might be base, but they could also be seen to 'raise the comfort level of social interaction' (Holmes, 1995: 54).

Self-interested agents, whether commercially motivated or not, were regarded as acting with a certain coolness and deliberation, cultivating a particular approach to human affairs which appeared to be the very antithesis of that expected from a 'full human personality'. Interest thus assumed a certain standing because it seemed to offer a counterweight to pre-eminent – dangerous and unpredictable – human motivations. Here lies the heart of Hirschman's argument. By failing to discern the implicit contrast with the violent passions, and continuing, therefore, to conceive of interest as fundamentally inhumane, we may be at a loss to explain the positive and curative attitude towards 'interest' and 'interests' displayed by a wide range of thinkers in seventeenth- and eighteenth-century Europe (Holmes, 1995: 55). Moreover, by ignoring the irrational and destructive antonyms of self-interest, we might fall into the sort of error popularized by R.H. Tawney (1926) and C.B. Macpherson (1964), for instance, and continuing today in the work of critical intellectuals such as Jürgen Habermas (1997), where affirmations of calculating self-interest end up being represented as a mea-spirited repudiation of the common good.[2]

**the 'self' in 'self-interest'**    If, then, we continue to either view self-interest as a hard-wired, and unvarying, human capacity, the 'rock' upon which all of social life is built, or, alternatively, consider it as always and already the enemy of the common good, we may fail to appreciate the ways in which 'self-interested' conduct varies conceptually and materially over time, and the distinctive purposes particular forms of 'self-interest' are designed to meet. This becomes evident when attention is focused on the kind of person deemed capable of acting in a 'self-interested' fashion.

It has become a commonplace in contemporary sociological debates about personal identity to argue that individual human beings are not essentially 'free' or 'self-interested' agents, directed by a sovereign and integral consciousness. What is, or should be, at issue here, though, is not the *status* of 'free agent', or 'subject of right' but, rather, the claimed or assumed ontological foundations of that status (Hirst and Woolley, 1982: 132). In other words, the idea that individuals are 'free agents' is not an illusion. As Hirst and Woolley (1982: 132) argued some time ago, while categories of person such as 'the free agent' are correctly described as fictional, in the sense that they are artificial and not natural kinds, they are not illusions in the sense of having no practical basis in cultural life. The idea of the 'free agent', for instance, could not be understood as 'imaginary' in this sense precisely because it is implicated, to a greater or lesser extent, in our legal systems, in our conceptions of contract and the employment relationship and many of our assumptions about education (p. 132). It exists, not in a natural or, indeed, singular state, but in many conceptual and material forms. It is differentially 'formatted, framed and equipped', to use Callon's phrase (1998: 51).

With regard to 'self-interested' personae, then, we can say that for individuals to take an interest in their own conduct as its ethical subject requires the elaboration and transmission of specific ethical disciplines and practices. In other words, before an individual can act on the basis of their own 'interests' they must first become the sort of person disposed to and capable of relating to themselves as the responsible agents of their own conduct. In seventeenth- and eighteenth-century Europe, as we shall shortly see, an enormous amount of work went into supplying the cultural 'equipment', the norms and mechanisms necessary for cultivating such capacities among elite populations culturally habituated to other, frequently antithetical, ideals and forms of conduct (Hirschman, 1977; Pocock, 1985; Tully, 1988).

In contrast to those who would seek to explain all forms of behaviour through the prism of rational self-interest (in the singular) and, equally, to those who would only view self-interest (again, in the singular) as the harbinger of the destruction of social relations, thinkers such as Hobbes and Hume, for example, had a very different agenda. First, their respective works are characterized by an acute awareness of human irrationality and the diversity of destructive human motivations, rather than the monochrome psychological reductionism levelled at them by critics (and a number of supporters) alike. In other words, they do not assume that 'human beings' are essentially, or even frequently, self-interested creatures. Quite the contrary, they continually point to the massive historical impor-tance of self-destructive human irrationality and impulsiveness and the socially ruinous consequences of the uncontrollable passions (Holmes, 1995). By focusing upon the passions and their deleterious social conse-quences, their respective anthropologies set up 'the full human personality' as a dangerous creature in need of civil restraint. They also position 'inter-est', albeit in non-reducible terms, as a beneficial mechanism by which such restraint was to be engendered.

It is precisely such an ethico-cultural intent that underlies the prescriptive and performative aims of Hobbes's so-called 'egoistic' model in *Leviathan*, for instance, as I seek to indicate at greater length later in the chapter. Rather than assuming that human beings are by nature self-inter-ested, rational maximizers of their own utility, the purpose of Hobbes's philosophical anthropology was rather to promote a 'cultural transforma-tion' in their ethical make up. Only when the lives of human beings were invested less in religious passions and more in 'caring for necessary things' would they begin to possess those characteristics required of political sub-jects in the sovereign state, which Hobbes represented as necessary condi-tions for the securing of civil peace (Johnston, 1986: 215–16; Minson, 1993: 167; Tuck, 1993: Ch. 7). Self-interest here functions as an element in a philosophical anthropology designed to counteract destructive human passions, not as an imperialistic attempt to explain all forms of behaviour through the prism of one human capacity.

For Hobbes, Hume and, indeed, Adam Smith, 'interest' – while differentially formatted to suit their respective purposes – would be a useless category if it were not reserved for one motive vying with others. Representing it as the primary, or natural, human motivation robs 'calculating self-interest' of the specificity it acquires when seen against the backdrop of selfless urges and thoughtless acts. For these thinkers, as Holmes (1995: 57) has put it, 'the rational pursuit of utility, far from being universal, is a rare moral achievement, possible only for those who undergo an arduous dispositional training'.

So what exactly is this 'self' that is deemed to be 'self-interested', if it approximates neither to the always already rational maximizer of much economically influenced social science, nor to the unbridled egoist invoked in much critical sociology? An answer to this question begins to present itself when we focus on the philosophical anthropologies through which particular seventeenth- and eighteenth-century versions of 'self-interest' were constituted. In seeking to redescribe 'self-interest' as a comportment of the person derived from a distinctive philosophical anthropology, I will have recourse to a particular approach that investigates philosophies in terms of the 'ascetic' relation to self that they impose, and the 'spiritual exercises' they require (Oestreich, 1982; Foucault, 1984, 1986b; Gaukroger, 1995; Hadot, 1995a; Hunter, 2001).[3] Characteristically, histories of philosophy conducted in this manner

> focus on the anthropologies, psychologies and cosmologies through which members of specific intellectual elites acquire the capacity to take up a particular relation to themselves and their world. This is typically a relation that imbues such individuals with a conviction of their deviation from an ideal way of thought or life – a relation of self-problematisation. In this way, they are inducted into a particular intellectual regimen or practice of self-cultivation, through which they may reshape themselves in the image of this ideal. (Hunter, 2001: 23)

Despite some significant differences in method and emphasis, studies framed by this historiographic and anthropological approach treat their respective philosophical objects as reflexive ethical instruments – that is, as means by which 'individuals are inducted into new existential relations to themselves' (Hunter, 2001: 23). As such, they approach the 'self' not as a subjectivity transcendentally presupposed by experience, but in terms of 'one historically cultivated to meet the purposes of a particular way of life' (pp. 23–4).

We have already seen that certain seventeenth- and eighteenth-century conceptions of 'self-interest' were promulgated with specific purposes in mind – to act as an ethical and cultural counterweight to religious ideals of conscience and aristocratic ideals of glory. Hume (1998: 38–43), for instance, viewed Christianity as an almost intolerable moral provocation. He certainly conceived of commercially directed, self-interested conduct as a relatively peaceful alternative to sectarian zealotry. He also viewed enthusiasm as socially undesirable, and just as alien to a calculating mindset as the nobility's addiction to glorious adventurism. As Holmes (1995: 4) has put it, the principal aim of those who wrote favourably of self-interest at this time was

to bridle destructive and self-destructive passions, to reduce the social prestige of mindless male violence, to induce people, so far as possible, to act rationally, instead of hot bloodedly or deferentially, and to focus on material goals such as economic wealth, instead of spiritual goals such as avenging a perceived slight or compelling neighbours to attend church.

In so doing, as a number of commentators have pointed out, they had recourse to the certain tenets of Hellenistic philosophy, most notably Stoicism and Epicureanism (Oakeshott, 1975: 154–8; Hirschman, 1977; Oestreich, 1982; Tuck, 1993; Brown, 1994; Hunter, 2001).

Brown (1994) and Force (2003), for instance, are simply among the latest scholars to point to neo-stoicism as a primary influence on Adam Smith's ethical thought. As is well known, the Stoics were centrally concerned with perturbations and disorders of the soul. A passionate person, they believed, was unable to pursue their own best interests in a coherent fashion being ungoverned by reason. Thus, rational choice was impossible until the individual had achieved a state of 'apathy'[4] or emotional serenity. Equanimity or tranquillity of mind, in turn, presupposed a strenuous process of self-discipline, a mental therapy in which the unruly passions were not simply moderated but extirpated (Nussbaum, 1994).

According to Brown (1994: 217) it is extremely difficult to code 'the overall structure of Smith's discourse' through the tropes of unbridled egoism, the embrace of crass materialism and the repudiation of the common good, for instance, precisely because the stoic moral hierarchy underpinning his oeuvre suggests a rather different interpretation of key concepts such as 'self', 'interest' and 'liberty'. She argues that the self-love praised by Smith in *The Theory of Moral Sentiments*, for instance, is the very antithesis of the celebration of unbridled egoism frequently ascribed to him by his critics. Such assumptions about the status of 'self-love' and other related concepts overlooks their Stoic pedigree (Brown, 1994: 94). As she makes clear, here 'self-love is akin to *amour de soi*, a caring for the self that is entirely consistent with moral behaviour' (p. 94). Stoic self-love cannot be seen as a synonym for selfishness in the modern sense of the term. Rather, it refers to the command of one's faculties and the control of one's impulses. By being in control of oneself – an unrelaxing vigilance for the stoics – one is fundamentally being attentive to oneself, caring for oneself in that one is seeking to ensure progress towards an ideal of wisdom (Hadot, 1995a:  87). The wise person will take an interest in their own health and choose to live a healthy life not because a healthy life is an end in itself, but because it is reasonable for a person to do this; such a person, however, will be indifferent to the outcome in a moral sense in that they will accept ill health or good health with equanimity (Brown, 1994: 77; Long, 2001).

Similar issues arise when the 'concept' of liberty is invoked. Once again the neo-stoic underpinning of Smith's conception of 'liberty' entirely disappears in much modern interpretation of Smith's oeuvre. As Brown (1994:  219–20) argues, with regard to the current paradigmatic status accorded the *Wealth Of Nations* as the founding text of free market economics, 'freedom came to be seen as negative freedom and an end in itself, an ultimate moral and political good against which other claims would appear subordinate, whereas the Stoic concept of freedom was bounded by an insistence on the ultimate moral indifference of worldly outcomes'. Liberty of action, then, is not about freedom to do whatever the individual desires so to do, precisely because freedom for the Stoics 'is not acquired by satisfying yourself with what you desire but by destroying your desire' (Epictetus, quoted in Brown, 1994: 218). This state of freedom, then, is not a natural state of being as it has to be fastidiously worked at (Nussbaum, 1994). Nor is it a state of self-indulgence or self-obsession – a celebration of unbridled egoism. Quite the contrary. It offers up a view of freedom as a kind of ethical *askesis* – the work one performs to turn oneself into an ethical subject capable of shaping one's own nature.

Given this, it seems implausible to assume that seventeenth- and eighteenth-century advocates of self-interest were simple motivational reductionists. There is little here to support the view of rational self-interest either as an inherent element of human personality or as the harbinger of a corrupted humanity. For neo-stoics, self-interest was a rare moral ideal. It could only be achieved after a strenuous process of moral (self) disciplining (Oestreich, 1982; Tuck, 1993).[5]

## 'caring for necessary things': hobbes and the politics of cultural transformation

As I argued above, early modern formulations of self-interest may be better understood as normative projects, framed by particular neo-hellenistic philosophical anthropologies, rather than as descriptive claims about human motivation. We can see this most clearly, perhaps, by focusing in more detail on the works of Thomas Hobbes.

Hobbes is frequently represented as the first important political theorist to conceptualize human beings as essentially rational animals devoted solely or primarily to self-preservation and, in effect, as the great proto-theorist of bourgeois society (Macpherson, 1964). However, Hobbes held no such reductionist view and, as a consequence, could not have bequeathed it to his contemporary social scientific successors (Holmes, 1995: Ch. 3). Indeed, he held directly the opposite view. He emphatically denied that human beings are essentially rational animals who, by nature, are driven to pursue their own self-interest. Instead, according to Hobbes, mankind appears throughout history to have been driven by self-destructive passions and urges. Put bluntly, 'human beings dread dishonour and damnation more acutely than they fear death' (Holmes, 1995: 3). The arguments in *Leviathan* and *Behemoth*, for instance, reinforce this insight. Both explicitly reject the rational-actor model as an accurate description of actually existing humanity even if, at the same time, they partly seek to reconstruct human conduct in its image.

According to David Johnston (1986: 215), for example, 'Hobbes's new view of man' as a rational agent driven by self-interest was not a representation of reality as he saw it. 'On the contrary, it was a carefully constructed model of man as Hobbes believed it would have to be in order to live in a peaceful and lasting political community.' In this reading, Hobbes's work is viewed as a political act of 'cultural transformation', an attempt to bring a world into being rather than simply reporting on the world as it is. After all, if most human beings, most of the time, were rational pursuers of their own self-interest, Hobbes suggests, history might not be a perpetual chronicle of slaughter and destruction. Civil wars are so frequent, instead, precisely because at least some people are prepared to risk death for the sake of 'higher' ideals such as 'glory' or 'salvation' (Holmes, 1995: 72).

To help put a stop to the destructive violence of civil war, it was therefore crucial for Hobbes to discredit those ideals that tempt human beings to defy death. According to Johnston (1986) this is the main aim of Hobbes's project of 'cultural transformation'. In a reformed polity – a commonwealth – people will, for the most part, rationally pursue their self-preservation, oblivious to the siren songs of aristocratic glory and religious redemption. As I suggested earlier, only when people's lives were invested less in religious imaginings and more in 'caring for necessary things' would they possess 'those characteristics required of political subjects in a Commonwealth or Sovereign State (especially constancy and a fear of death and insecurity) which Hobbes regarded as essential to the securing of civil peace' (Minson, 1993: 167–8).

In order to discredit his chosen targets Hobbes had recourse to a particular philosophical anthropology, in this instance Epicureanism (Oakeshott, 1975: 154–8). In attacking his rivals – both religious and civic republican – Hobbes relied upon an Epicurean anthropology in which man was represented as a dangerous creature, a passion-driven and self-destructive being, in desperate need of civil re-education and political and legal restraint (Johnston, 1986; Hunter, 2001; Skinner, 2002). *The Elements of Law National and Politic* and *Leviathan*, for instance, both begin with a lengthy treatise on human nature in which this Epicurean anthropology looms large. In both texts, human beings are represented, by nature, as remarkably self-destructive entities. Left to their own devices they will inevitably come into conflict with one another. Hobbes cites a number of causes of the 'offensiveness of man's nature one to another'. In *Elements of Law* he highlights, on the one hand, the insatiability of people's appetites and, on the other, their desire for glory, which is 'that passion which proceedth from the imagination or conception of our own power, above the power of him that contendenth with us' (1969: I.9.1). Taken together, these explain why men are always in conflict with one another. For 'some are vainly glorious, and hope for precedency and superiority above their fellows, not only when they are equal in power, but also when they are inferior' (1969: I.14.3). His hope for superiority makes even those who are moderate and ask for nothing more than recognition of their equal standing with other people 'obnoxious to the force of others, that will attempt to subdue them' (1969: I.14.3). Even if people's appetites were not insatiable, their vanity would lead them into conflict with one another, and it would do so even if there were some men who were neither vain nor immoderate of appetite.

A similar coding of human motivation is to be found in the first part of *Leviathan*. Here, '[N]ature hath made men so equall' in both 'ability' and 'right' (Hobbes, 1991: I.XIII.60) that 'from this ... there ariseth equality of hope in the attaining of our Ends. And therefore if any two men desire the same thing, which nevertheless they cannot both enjoy, they become enemies; and in the way to their End ... endeavour to destroy or subdue one an other' (1991: I.XIII.61). In the state of nature, therefore, 'they are in that condition which is called Warre; and such a warre, as is of every man, against every man' (1991: I.XIII.62). In 'such condition, there is no place for Industry; because the fruit thereof is uncertain ... and which is worst of all, continual feare, and danger of violent death' (1991: I.XIII.62). Both texts represent a view of humanity that is far from rational and prudent; instead, they paint a picture of human beings as compulsive and impulsive creatures, frequently unreflective and prone to torrid emotional outbursts.

The destructive consequences of this 'natural offensiveness' would be inevitable were it not for the existence of countervailing elements in human nature. The most important of these is fear of death. In *Elements of Law*, Hobbes argues that 'necessity of nature maketh men to will and desire *bonum sibi*, that which is good for themselves, and to avoid that which is hurtful; but most of all that terrible enemy of nature, death' (1969: I.14.6). Similarly, in *Leviathan* Hobbes states that 'Feare of Death' is a crucial feature of human nature that can help 'encline men to peace' (1991: I.XIII.63). The second is the potential of Reason. In *Elements of Law*, Hobbes argues that the capacity to reason provides human beings with the potential means required to avoid the greatest of all evils: death. It is therefore 'reason' which 'dictateth to every man for his own good, to seek after peace ... and to strengthen himself ... ' (1969: I.15.1, I.14.6, I.14.14). This contention is repeated in *Leviathan* where Hobbes states, for instance, that 'Reason suggesteth Articles of Peace, upon which men may be drawn to agreement' (1991: I.XIII.63). If the consequence of natural appetite is pride and fear, then the 'suggestion' of Reason is peace. But how can this 'suggestion' be translated into a concrete solution? The answer to this question is contained in what Oakeshott called Hobbes's 'hypothetical efficient cause of civil association' (1975: 43). It is an account that owes not a little to neo-stoicism as well as to Epicureanism (Oestreich, 1982; Tuck, 1993: Chs 2 and 7).

For Hobbes, as Oakeshott (1975: 38) has it, 'the precondition of deliverance is the recognition of the predicament. Just as for Christians, the repentance of the sinner forms a crucial first step towards salvation', so for Hobbes, humanity must first control its violent passions. So long as human beings are in the grip of these passions they will continue in a state of 'Warre'. The controlling counter-emotion is, as we have seen, fear of death. This fear illuminates prudence, and what begins in prudence is continued in reasoning. For while reasoning may well help guide individuals 'in the pursuit of their own private felicity, it is also capable of illuminating certain axioms in respect of their competitive endeavours to satisfy their wants' (Oakeshott, 1975: 38). As Oakeshott continues, 'since what threatens to defeat every attempt to procure felicity in these circumstances is the unconditionally competitive character of the pursuit (or in a word, war), these truths found out by reason for avoiding this defeat of all by all may be properly called the articles of Peace' (1975: 39). Such reasons are practically fruitless, however, unless they can be translated into maxims of human conduct and from maxims into laws; that is until they are recognized as 'valid rules of known jurisdiction, to be subscribed to by all who fall within that jurisdiction and to which penalties for nonsubscription have been annexed and power to enforce them provided' (p. 39).

At first sight, it might appear that the operation of 'right Reason' itself is capable of doing this job, and thereby of securing 'lasting peace'. This would be a mistaken conclusion, however. Inspired by the fear of death, Reason 'suggesth' the means by which 'warre' might be ended by articulating the 'convenient articles of Peace'. But reason in and of itself is incapable of securing such peace precisely because it is already part of the problem it seeks to remedy. In *Elements of Law*, Hobbes indicates why. He argues that 'right Reason' is not a singular but a multiple. 'Commonly, they that call for right reason to decide any controversie do mean their owne.' The invocation of 'Right Reason' thus returns us instantly to the dead end of natural equality and freedom and the crucial question: Who is to decide what is reasonable and what is right?[6]

The articles of Peace that 'Reason suggesth' are summed up by Hobbes in one phrase: *'Do not that to another, which thou wouldest not have done to thy selfe'* (1991: I. XV. 79). Here, rather than commanding them to honour and cherish the inherent worth of their fellow humans (who are to be treated as ends, not means), Hobbes invites people to join in a defensive compact based on mutual mistrust. Rather than calling people to the higher perfection of charity and universal love, Hobbes preaches instead the universality of self-interest. Moved by fear of death, instructed by the conclusions of reasoning about how the disasters of 'perpetual Warre' might be mitigated, and endowed with the ability to set these conclusions to work, human beings have at their disposal the means of escaping from the horror of their 'natural state'. The solution is elegant and simple. The mechanism by which a transformation from a 'natural person' to a 'civil person' is to be effected requires the establishment of a neutral arbiter: an artificial, unitary person whose judgements must be accepted in advance as beyond appeal. This is the 'Sovereign'. It is in every individual's self-interest to submit to the power and authority of the sovereign, Hobbes argues, because the consequences of refusing allegiance to the only body capable of protecting them will always be worse, individually and collectively, namely 'the miseries and horrible calamities' that accompany 'Warre' (1991: II.XVIII.128). As Hobbes puts it in *Elements of Law*, the person who occupies the place of 'Right Reason' must be 'he, or they, that hath the Soveraigne power', from which it follows that 'the civil Lawes are to all subjects the measures of their Actions, whereby to determine, whether they be right or wronge, profittable or unprofitable, vertuous or vitious; and by them the use, and definition of all names not agreed upon, and tending to Controversie, shall be established' (1969: II.10.8: 188–9).

A 'constant and lasting Peace' is therefore dependent upon settled and known rules of conduct, embodied in Laws, and a power sufficient to coerce those who fall within their jurisdiction to observe them. The nature of mankind being such that 'during the time that men live without a Common Power to keep them all in awe', they will be 'in that condition which is called Warre; and such a warre , as is every man against every man', it is in every individual's self-interest, their very hope of pursuing their own 'felicity', that they surrender their 'natural rights' to such a common power. By giving up their 'Right to self-government' to a sovereign authority endowed with 'the use of so much power and strength' they thereby ensure that peace is enforced equally on everyone (Hobbes, 1991: II.XVII.120). Human beings who are equal in power and desire are now equal in subjection; each surrenders their natural freedom and liberty on the condition that their fellows do the same, and in this way peace and security are established for everyone. By surrendering a potential liberty to everything – and equally the potential loss of everything – people are establishing the most viable means for securing their own self-interest.

**76**

**self-interest, liberty and necessity**   It is in this discussion of liberty and self-interest that Hobbes's debt to neo-stoicism is, perhaps, most apparent. His conception of liberty revolves around the compatibility of freedom and necessity (e.g. liberty and coercion, liberty and absolute authority), which many critics have taken to be at best inconsistent and at worst a category error (even sympathetic critics, such as Ryan, 1996: 235ff.). For the stoics, however, determinism and freedom were not merely compatible, they actually presupposed one another (Oestreich, 1982: 7; Long and Sedley, 1987: 392), and it is this stoic vision that Hobbes mines in his discussion of the relationship between 'natural liberty' and the 'liberty of subjects', the cardinal distinction framing his discussion of the topic in *Leviathan*. As I indicated earlier, nature and artifice are viewed by Hobbes as two separate 'conditions of mankind' and *Leviathan* is, in effect, a cultural and political roadmap aimed at aiding the transition from the former to the latter 'condition'.

It is in relation to this duality between 'nature' and 'artifice' that we need to assess the coherence of Hobbes's views about the capacity of laws to abrogate freedom and hence about the relationship between necessity and liberty (Skinner, 2002). For Hobbes, liberty, in the proper sense of the term, is always marked by the absence of something, most explicitly by 'the absence of externall impediments' (1991: I. XIV. 91). 'A FREE-MAN' is therefore one 'that in those things which by his strength and wit he is able to do, is not hindered to doe what he has a will to' (1991: II.XXI.146). A free man is one who in respect of his powers and capacities 'can do if he will and forbear if he will' (Hobbes, quoted in Skinner, 2002: 211).

Now, in one sense, as Hobbes makes clear, the institution of civil law does appear to limit 'naturall liberty' in that the force of the law definitely limits our freedom as subjects. For subjects are by definition human beings who have given up the condition in which everyone is naturally placed, where 'every man holdeth this Right, of doing anything he liketh' (Hobbes, 1991: I.XIV.92).

> For *Right* is *Liberty*, namely that Liberty which the Civil Law leaves us: But *Civill Law* is an *Obligation*; and takes from us the Liberty which the Law of Nature gave us. Nature gave a Right to every man to secure himselfe by his own strength, and to invade a suspected neighbour, by way of prevention: but the Civill Law takes away that Liberty, in all cases where the protection of the Law may be safely stayd for. (Hobbes, 1991: II.XXVI.200)

However, for Hobbes, such 'naturall' freedom isn't really a freedom worth having as it is so arbitrary and uncertain. While the institution of civil law means that subjects must relinquish their potential right to everything, they also gain from the fact that no individual has the potential right to take away their life or property simply because they happen to be more powerful. 'Naturall liberty' as 'exemption from laws' is, in effect, a form of servitude since it is a condition in 'which all other men may be masters' of our lives and our goods (1991: II.XX.141).[7] Hence the emphasis Hobbes places on 'that misery that accompanies the Liberty of particular men' (1991: I.XIII.90). Nonetheless, despite this, Hobbes is insistent that to speak of the liberty of a Subject is to speak first and foremost of the 'Silence of the Law' (1991: II.XXI.152). If there are 'cases where the Soveraign has prescribed no rule, there the subject hath the Liberty to do, or forebeare, according to his own discretion' (1991: II.XXI.152). Where the law demands or forbids a certain action, there the subject is required to act or forbear to act as the law and hence the sovereign command. However, as Skinner (2002: 221) correctly notes, 'the main point on which Hobbes wishes to insist is that, even in those cases where the freedom on the state of nature is undoubtedly abridged by our obligation to obey the civil laws, this does nothing to limit our liberty in the proper signification of the word'. In other words, the presence of the laws does not fundamentally affect the capacity of a human being to 'do if he will and forbear if he will' and thus to be free in Hobbes's 'proper' sense of the term.

At first sight this seems a category error of the highest order and yet, for Hobbes, it is of the utmost importance. To understand why this is the case, it is necessary first to explicate the account that Hobbes gives of the distinctive ways in which any system of civil law operates to ensure the obedience of its subjects. Hobbes delineates two routes by which this can be achieved. First, he argues, as we saw earlier, that because the basic aim of the law is to establish and maintain civil peace by protecting life and liberty, all reasonable people will agree to obey the law because they will see it is in their own interests so to do. 'So the liberty of such agents to act as their judgement and reason dictate will not in the least be infringed by their obligation to obey the law. The dictates of their reason and the requirements of the law will prove to be one and the same' (Skinner, 2002: 221–2). In submitting to the law, people therefore express rather than restrict their liberty. As Hobbes puts it, 'The use of the Lawes is not to bind the People from all Voluntary actions; but to direct and keep them in such a motion, as not to hurt themselves by their own impetuous desires, rashnesse, or indiscretion; as Hedges are set, not to stop Travellers, but to keep them in the way' (1991: III.XXX.239–40).

Secondly, however, Hobbes is aware that this is not the main reason that human beings obey the law, moved as they are, he believes, by the unruly passions. Ultimately, they can only be brought to obey because the fear of not so doing is so enormous. Only if there is a 'common power to keep them all in awe' with overwhelming force at its disposal, can human beings be made to obey the law and thus to forbear from acting as partiality, pride, revenge and so forth would otherwise dictate (Hobbes, 1991: II. XVII. 117). Hobbes's point here is that liberty and coercion are not antithetical. For the presence of such a common power does not in and of itself deprive a subject of his or her capacity to act as their will and desires dictate. As he puts it, 'generally, all actions which men doe in Common-wealths, for feare of the law, are actions, which the doers had liberty to omit' (1991: II.XXI.146).

According to Skinner (echoing Bishop Bramhall), Hobbes is here reviving a quintessentially 'Stoic vision of the compatibility between liberty and necessity' (2002: 226). Vitally, absolute sovereignty, regardless of form, 'so far from being inimical to liberty, is a necessary condition for it. Liberty of the natural state is intolerable and, in its proper signification, almost meaningless as a ubiquitous feature of existence' (Condren, 2002: 71). Rather than being a designed destruction of individual liberty, as many have argued, the sovereign state is, in fact, 'the minimum condition of any settled association among individuals' (Oakeshott, 1975: 66). It furnishes individuals with a secure basis for the exercise of their liberty and the pursuit of their interests in a way that the state of nature, where everyone is potentially free to do anything and hence free to be enslaved, simply cannot.

Hobbes thus grants nothing to 'natural sociability'. To do so would be to open the door to the very demons his work was striving to extirpate. For Hobbes, the classical republican theory of liberty espoused by so many of his contemporaries, and trading on the idea of the liberty to self-government as a 'natural birthright', was a provocation to 'warre', fuelling rather than controlling the 'licentious passions' (1991: II.XXI.149–50). Such a formulation posed a direct challenge, in his view, to the liberty of subjects properly understood as founded in the laws of the sovereign civil power. Demanding a right to opinions about justice and natural law independent of the sovereign is, for Hobbes, to invite a sort of anarchy. The appeal to 'nature' is, in effect, 'a mechanism for returning us to it' (Condren, 2002: 72).

This is why it would be 'absurd' to see Hobbes as the progenitor of an image of humanity as 'naturally equipped' with the capacity to rationally maximize its own self-interest. The capacity for 'self-interested' conduct is a product of entry into the civil state. It is not a natural faculty, but a politically and culturally superimposed mode of conducting civil life. To argue for such a natural capacity would, in Hobbes's schema, be to support the forms of passionate egoism and partiality found in the state of nature, the worst features of which the institution of the civil state was designed to allay.

That 'self-interest' is not a 'natural' faculty for Hobbes should give no succour to those who, by contrast, decry the inhumanity and reductionism of rational (civil) 'self-interest', stressing the damage it does to the 'full human personality' seen as 'the person' embedded in her or his full social context. Again, to talk of the 'full human personality' in this way is immediately to return us to the state of nature and to a problem not a solution. As Hobbes was only too aware, the world of the full human personality with its diverse passions needed to be exorcised to the greatest degree possible. It was a social menace, not a social good. True 'sociality' could only be produced in the civil state, it was not something that existed as a 'moral good' in its own right, independent of the *civitas*. If it were granted such autonomy, it would allow, by default, a respecification of 'natural law' independent of sovereignty and in effect a reintroduction of tyranny in the form of the 'warre of all against all'.

From all this we can adduce that, for Hobbes, the pursuit of one's self-interest cannot be equated with unbridled egoism, for such conduct is akin to a natural rather than an artificial condition. Similarly, true self-interested conduct, that which is caring of necessary things within the bosom of the sovereign state, is indeed antithetical to the development of the 'full human personality'. For the latter, too, in Hobbesian logic, is simply the product of a natural rather than artificial condition. Hobbes's self-interested person is therefore only produced and suited to existence in the *civitas*.

As we have already seen, Hobbes indicates that those who 'clamour for liberty and call it their birthright' always make a fundamental error. For if they demand 'liberty' in the proper signification of the term, then they already manifestly possess it. In other words, the presence of the sovereign state does nothing to undermine 'corporall liberty' or 'freedome from chains and prison'. Such liberty already exists. But if they demand 'exemption from the laws' – if they do not want to be subjects – then this really is mad. For asking for such freedom is, in effect, to call for your own servitude – that form of unrestricted liberty 'by which all other men may be masters' of your being and possessions. Far from outlining the conditions in which human individuality and self-interest is undermined, Hobbes is, in effect, seeking to delineate the only secure forms in which individuality and self-interest could be pursued peacefully and effectively. The proper liberty of subjects to pursue their self-interest thus derives from their giving up the right to govern themselves according to their own desires. It is instituted through their absolute obedience to the civil laws and commands of sovereign. Here Hobbes's neo-stoicism is evident. As Tuck (1993: 346) points out, Hobbes's human beings 'find peace and security by denying themselves individual judgement: by subordinating their own wills and desires to those of the sovereign, not because the sovereign knows better, but because the disciplining of an individual psychology is necessary for one's well being'.

**concluding comments**    What can we take away with us from this brief and rather perfunctory discussion of 'self-interest'? If nothing else, perhaps, a somewhat sceptical attitude both to the routinely ahistorical and censorious critical sociological association of the 'self' of self-interest with unbridled egoism, crass materialism and a repudiation of the common good, and to the similarly ahistorical, preponderantly economistic, conception of persons as naturally rational maximizers of their own utility. Historically, as I have sought to suggest, there have been quite discontinuous changes in the characterization of the 'self' deemed to be 'self-interested'. 'Self-interest' thus refers to a number of historically distinct conceptions and behaviours. There is, in other words, no such thing as *the* concept of 'self-interest', just as there is no such thing as *the* concept of a person 'whose various components form a harmonious structure that could provide adjudication among competing normative claims about what does or does not fall within the domain of the rights and obligations of persons' (Rorty, 1988: 31). As I indicated earlier, Hirst and Woolley (1982: 131–3) pointed out some time ago that the temptation to unity in relations to 'persona' for sociologists, as for other social and human scientists, represents an elementary error: 'a metaphysical fiction'. The error in question lies in a failure to recognize that specific conceptions and comportments of the person perform quite different functions in different socio-cultural circumstances and contexts. Given their context specificity, forms of personhood, and their definite but limited settings, must not be underdescribed. If they are, the danger is that we will fail to see the job that each is doing, that each has its own history and distribution, has fashioned its own ethos, and is directed by its own techniques to its own ends.

In this chapter I have therefore attempted to approach the 'self' of predominantly early modern conceptions of self-interest, not as a subjectivity transcendentally presupposed by experience, but as one historically cultivated to counter the exigencies of particular circumstances – the disaster of perpetual 'warre' in seventeenth-century Europe – and to meet the purposes of a particular way of life – existence in the *civitas*. It has been my contention that homogenization of the term 'self-interest' – in sociological and economic discourse – has resulted in many misconceptions about what particular doctrines of 'self-interest', and the practices with which they were associated, were instituted to achieve at certain historical periods and in specific cultural milieux. At its worst, I have suggested, this has led to a misunderstanding of the import of particular doctrines of self-interest, which are read in terms of general tradition – such as that which views self-interested conduct as a natural faculty – rather than in terms of the context-specific aims of those advocating them.

In so far as such homogenization is successful – and the standing accorded to 'rational-actor' modelling in the social sciences suggests it has been remarkably successful – it inevitably brings in its wake another abstraction, the demand for enrichment. Here, as I argued earlier, the presumed poverty and atomism of (homogenized) 'self-interest' is taken as the occasion for the 'return' of that which it is held to repress: passion, emotion, desire, culture, spontaneity, morality, virtue (the list is as long and varied as the basic premise is misguided). An obsession (particularly among critical sociologies) with the social, moral and cultural 'negativities' of 'narrowly' self-interested conduct (seen as the apogee of 'pure' calculation, whatever that might be) fuels the demand for a more complete conception of humanity; a return, in effect, to 'the full human personality'. What we are confronted with here, it would seem, are two abstractions feeding off one another in a seemingly never ending dialectical frenzy. Interest begets passion begets interest and so on and so forth ad infinitum. What is lost, though, is the contextual specificity of particular doctrines of self-interest, the problems that they were designed to address, and the conceptions of persons they gave rise to in so doing. As Hirschman (1977: 132) points out, only by forgetting the desperate conditions that had fostered the emergence of early modern doctrines of 'self-interest' could the Romantic critique, for example, represent 'self-interested conduct' as incredibly impoverished in relation to an earlier age of nobility, freedom and passion.

Hobbes also knew only too well that 'self-interested' conduct, as he envisaged it, would always be a remarkably fragile achievement. In *Leviathan*, he argues that the experience of the English Civil War provided a unique opportunity to alter the terms of debate, and the terrain, of political, cultural and ethical life. However, he thought that this window would only stay open as long as the memory of the horrors of that conflict remained vivid in people's minds:

> There be few now (in England), that do not see, that these Rights [of sovereignty] are inseparable, and will be so generally acknowledged, at the next return of Peace; and so continue, till their miseries are forgotten; and no longer, except the vulgar be better taught than they have hetherto been. (Hobbes, 1991: II.XVIII.93)

If the neo-stoical vision of 'self-interest' that Hobbes proposes seems hostile to many current sociological and political hobby horses, such as the contemporary revival of interest in popular conceptions of political community, we may do well to recognize that many of the problems to which he was attempting to respond are still real enough, and should be approached by us, today, only with great circumspection. In other words, we should remind ourselves, occasionally, of the ills which Hobbes's conception of 'self-interest' was attempting to escape or at least mitigate. Only by turning Hobbes's specific creation into a travesty of itself can the demand for enrichment make any sense at all.

As Hobbes was only too aware, though, it was a mistake to count out the ideals of the unity of personality, or of 'natural liberty', by assuming they were permanently 'driven from the field' (Pocock, 1985: 122).[8] The appeal of siren voices, religious and metaphysical, he argued, 'can never be so abolished from human nature' (Hobbes, 1991: I.XII.58).

Self-interest, as a 'singularly cool and deliberate passion' (Holmes, 1995: 67) was, for Hobbes, always one impulse vying with many others. Instead of continually homogenizing its multiple conceptions and behaviours into a simplified 'tradition', thus exaggerating the paradigmatic control of only one version of 'self-interest', we might do better to exercise our historical imaginations a little more and learn to appreciate early modern conceptions of self-interest as remarkable human achievements, especially given the incredibly fallow earth in which they were expected to grow.

## notes

1   As Becker (1986: 112), for instance, has it,

> the economic approach is a comprehensive one that is applicable to all human behavior, be it behavior involving money prices or imputed shadow prices, repeated or infrequent decisions, large or minor decisions, emotional or mechanical ends, rich or poor persons, men or women, adults or children, brilliant or stupid persons, patients or therapists, businessmen or politicians, teachers or students.

2   According to Habermas (1997: 27), for example, '[F]or self-interested actors, all situational features are transformed into facts they evaluate in the light of their own preferences, whereas actors oriented toward understanding rely on a jointly negotiated understanding of the situation and interpret the relevant facts in the light of intersubjectively recognized validity claims.'

3   *Askesis*, here, does not refer simply to the interdictions we place upon ourselves but rather to the work one does to turn oneself into a particular ethical subject.

4   Stoic 'apathy' is not complete impassivity or insensibility but rather the absence of uncontrollable and irrational impulses (Holmes, 1995: 282 n. 67).

5   As Oestreich (1982: 7) puts it,

> neo-stoics ... demanded self-discipline and the extension of the duties of the ruler and the moral education of the army, the officials, and indeed the whole people, to a life of work, frugality, dutifulness and obedience. The result was a general enhancement of social discipline in all spheres of life, and this enhancement produced, in its turn, a change in the ethos of the individual and his self-perception.

6   As Hobbes makes clear in *Leviathan*, all reasoning depends on naming; but in moral reasoning all naming depends upon individual passion and prejudice. The implication is that those who champion the settlement of moral disputes by 'reason' are in effect calling for 'every of the passions, as it comes to bear sway in them, to be taken for right Reason, and that in their own controversies: bewraying their want of right Reason, by the claym they lay to it' (Hobbes, 1991: I.V.33). As Skinner (2002: 139 n. 322) argues, Hobbes's contention is thus that moral consensus can only be created politically.

7   As Oakeshott (1975: 66–7) argues in this respect,

> Hobbes conceives the sovereign as law-maker and his rule, not arbitrary, but the rule of law ... [T]hat law as the command of the Sovereign holds within itself a freedom absent from law as custom or law as reason: it is Reason, not Authority that is destructive of individuality. And of course, the silence of the law is a further freedom; when the law does not speak the individual is sovereign over himself. What is indeed, excluded from Hobbes's *civitas* is not the freedom of the individual but the independent rights of spurious authorities and of the collections of individuals such as churches, which he saw as the source of the 'civil strife of his time'.

8   Hirschman (1977: 135) suggests that Cardinal de Retz got it right when he insisted that the passions are not to be discounted in situations where interest-motivated behaviour is assumed to be the norm. Or, as Hobbes (1991: I.XII.58) himself remarked 'Powers invisible, and supernaturall ... can never be so abolished out of humane nature.' Recent corporate scandals give credence to this view. In time, the distinctive role of 'the full human personality', 'natural liberty' and other metaphysical ideals in these developments may be more fully discerned.

# self-service: retail, shopping and personhood

BP Marketing Men saw one customer read the instructions several times, scratch his head, push a pound note up the nozzle and shout at the pump through cupped hands 'Four gallons of commercial please.'

(*The Times*, 17 August 1972, 'Self-Service Petrol', p. 23)

**introduction**   This chapter focuses upon a rather different terrain and rather different techniques of person-formation. We shift attention away from the problem of forming civic personae in the context of religious civil war in early modern Europe to a rather different issue: the difficulties facing British retailers as they set about attempting to operationalize a self-servicing persona in the years after the Second World War. In a nutshell, this is the problem. How do you get people to adopt a technology – in this case a technology of shopping – when those people have little to no previous experience of that technology and when its use goes against their understandings of the proper way to conduct a given activity? How do you get them to see something that they have conceived of as work, undertaken for them by other people for a wage, as something they should do themselves, for free? Not only this but to see themselves as enhancing their own liberty in so doing?

This chapter seeks to address these questions through a brief, attenuated 'history' of the development of 'self-service' shopping technologies in British retailing from the period directly after the Second World War (roughly, from the late 1940s to the mid-1960s). The chapter does not claim to be definitive but rather attempts to explore the relationship between retail techniques and devices (*dispositifs*), shopping practices and the constitution of persons. The focus on 'self-service' has two main objectives. First, despite the enormous significance attributed to the development of 'self-service' techniques in the growth of retail power in the second half of the twentieth century, and to the related shifts in the relations of production and consumption they engendered, little empirical research has been conducted into how these techniques achieved the dominance they are now presumed to have.[1] Certainly, much explanatory weight is placed on the slender shoulders of 'self-service', but this is not matched by appropriately detailed or convincing attention to the provision of empirical evidence to back up the claims made on its behalf. Secondly, and relatedly, the chapter argues that the rather epochalist arguments that these analyses deploy do not aid understanding of the shifts in the personae of retail shop workers and consumers that self-service effects. In particular, approaches to the study of service work and consumption that have tended towards the deployment of a standard set of dialectics of control/resistance and oppression/emancipation and so forth (even when these are not framed exclusively in terms of management/worker relations but are expanded to include worker/consumer and worker/consumer/manager relations) exhibit a distinctly ahistoric conception of the formation of persons. Indeed, they tend to work with an understanding of 'the person' (in the singular) as a subject almost preternaturally equipped with the capacity to bestow meaning on experience (see Chapters 1 and 2 for a discussion of this tendency within certain sociologies and social theories).

**retail, shopping and personhood**  Anyone undertaking a review of the sociological, and related social-science-based, literature on retailing is likely to be struck by two things. First, by how little sociological work on retailing – whether as a site of work and employment or of shopping and consumption – actually exists, despite the cultural, economic and social significance routinely attributed to this sector. And secondly, how the work that does exist often relies on what we might term an 'unexplicated historical context'. By this I mean that the same historical claims appear time after time as a backdrop to the particular study being conducted. Of especial interest is the frequency with which the development of 'self-service' shopping techniques in the period after the Second World War is accorded an elemental role in 'revolutionizing' both retail work and consumption and thus fundamentally altering the relationship between retail employee and consumer (Bamfield, 1980; Davies and Howard, 1988; Gardner and Sheppard, 1989; Ducatel and Blomley, 1990). What is so intriguing about this sort of work is not only the paucity of historical evidence deployed to back up the dramatic claims made about the effects of self-service but also the teleological quality of the arguments being advanced. Because self-service can be seen from the vantage point of the present to have contributed to a reduction in the number of sales staff required by the industry, for instance, this then becomes one of the reasons advanced for its success. In other words, the dominance of self-service is taken as a given because its innate economic logics are bound to make it the most efficient and effective system for maximizing the speed up of all retail operations and thus the turnover time of retail capital. Similarly, from the consumption side of the equation, an equally teleological set of arguments appear, linking the success of self-service and related retail technologies to their capacity to both express and reflect unconscious or emergent consumer desires – for increased autonomy and expanded choice, pleasure and self-expression, for instance (Gardner and Sheppard, 1989; Shields, 1992; Falk and Campbell, 1997; Bauman, 1998) . Either way, the question of how, practically, self-service changed the conduct of retail work and consumption remains unanswered.

In what follows, I attempt to offer a more grounded, but far from exhaustive, historical account of the growth of self-service retailing in one particular context – mid-twentieth-century Britain. This brief account sets out to question many of the teleological and epochalist assumptions on which much current analysis is based. It is my provisional contention that the growth of self-service was a more uneven and contingent affair than many of the industry accounts and critical commentaries suggest. There was nothing preordained about the growth of self-service; nothing deriving from its innate logics that guaranteed its success. Indeed, for many years it looked as if it would make little to no headway in the British context. Even as late as 1963, 16 years after the opening of the first self-service store in Britain, of the 580,000 shops operating in the country only 13,000 operated on a self-service basis (Towsey, 1964).[2] Indeed, it is difficult to overestimate the amount of work that retailers and related trades engaged in to try and convince their publics of the benefits of 'going self-service' when it came to shopping. I characterize this work as 'cultural economic' in that it was both purposefully geared towards an economic end – getting more consumers to go self-service with attendant benefits for retailers in terms of reduced overheads and increased volumes – and yet frequently represented to consumers in terms of a series of distinctly non-economic benefits – as enhancing convenience, personal autonomy and individuality, for instance (du Gay and Pryke, 2002; Slater, 2002).

I then move on to focus on the practical development of self-service; this allows us to undertake a more nuanced understanding of how, what we might somewhat unhappily term, 'consumer identities' are formed and how they relate, or not, to work-based identities. As we saw in Chapter 1, one of Foucault's great insights (1993), one he shares with Max Weber (1978), Marcel Mauss (1979) and Pierre Bourdieu (1987) among others, is that forms of personhood are not unitary and continuous but technical and limited (see also Saunders, 1991).[3] If we use the Foucauldian term subjectification (see Chapter 1) to refer to the ways in which individuals come to relate to themselves as persons of a certain sort, then subjectification can be seen to have its own history. And this history is more technical, more practical and less unified than many sociological and cultural theoretical accounts allow for or appreciate. The aim here, then, is to explore how consumers came to see themselves as persons of a certain sort – as creatures of freedom, of liberty, of personal powers of choice and of self-realization in relation to their everyday practices of shopping – through their immersion in that range of technologies we have come to know as 'self-service'. Or, to put it another way, the focus is on the ways in which 'self-service' technologies 'made up' the consumer as a particular sort of person. The self in self-service, then, does not form the trans-historical object of techniques for being human but only one way in which humans as consumers have been enjoined to understand and relate to themselves as persons. This self is therefore both limited in distribution – you don't have it all the time, it is not your essence – and technically constituted – it exists in relationship to a particular technological regime: in this instance, the self-service shop. As Foucault (1993: 222) put it: 'Maybe our problem is to discover that the self is nothing else than the historical correlation of the technology built in our history.'

Although the 'self' of 'self-service' is, I will argue, precisely technical and limited in distribution, many sociologies of service work (Hochschild, 1983; Sturdy, 2001; Taylor, 2002) and of consumption (Featherstone, 1991; Falk and Campbell, 1997; Bauman, 1998) continue, whether consciously or unconsciously, to represent this self as unitary and continuous and to use this presumed continuity and unity as the basis for critique. Thus, for some sociological critics the self in 'self-service' is not an authentic self. It not only denies 'the self' of the retail worker but offers only a superficial, commercial distortion of a real self to the consumer. The failure of self-service to meet the criteria of authentic humanism – the fully realized self – becomes the motor of that repressed self's revenge: resistance (Ogbonna and Wilkinson, 1990; Sturdy, 2001). Yet, as Foucault (1993) indicated, resistance – if by that contested term one refers to opposition to a particular regime for the conduct of conduct – requires no unitary and continuous subject or agent, one with an innate love of liberty, who automatically seeks to enhance their own powers or capacities, or compulsively strives for emancipation in opposition to the demands of any external authority. Rather, as Nikolas Rose (1996: 136) has argued, human beings live their lives in a constant movement across different practices that address them as persons of varying sorts. Within these different practices persons are presupposed to be different sorts of human being, and acted upon as if they were different sorts of human being. Techniques of relating to oneself as a subject of choice and liberty come up against practices of relating to oneself as a subject of discipline and duty. The humanist demand that one decipher one's actions in terms of their authenticity (Hochschild, 1983) – as I indicated, probably the benchmark that most sociological critics have utilized – runs up against the demand that one abides by the rules of the organization for which one works even when one is personally opposed to them. Thus the existence of conflict and contestation in practices that conduct the conduct of persons should come as no surprise nor should it be allotted extraordinary explanatory or political weight. Certainly, it does not require any appeal to the unity and continuity of human beings as agents of history (Saunders, 1991; Rose, 1996).

**technologies of 'self-service'** At its most basic, the term 'self-service' is used in the retail environment to describe any method of displaying goods in a manner that enables customers to help themselves. Its singularity is therefore multiple. There are many degrees of 'self-service' – as the trade terms 'partial self-service' and 'assisted self-service' testify. The trade journal *Shop Review* gives one broad definition; a self-service system is one in which:

> 1. Every item of stock must be pre-packaged and clearly price-marked and displayed within reach of the customer in an easily-seen, suitably-classified, quickly identified section of open shelving, bins, trays or gondolas. 2. Each customer must be handed or pick up a basket (or light trolley) as they enter, into which all their purchases must be placed. 3. Customers must leave the self-service store, shop or department via a check-out counter, where the borrowed basket is emptied, the cost of the goods added up, payment made and the goods placed in the customers own basket or a free bag provided for this purposes by the store. 4. There must be an adequate and efficient system of quick and constant replenishment of stock from an immediately adjacent store-room. 5. The lay-out must be such that freedom of movement is assured and that executives and staff have an uninterrupted view of the whole self-service area. (1955: 35–42)

Now, this definition would not hold for every instance of self-service retail one might come across in 1955 as well as today, but the basics are still thoroughly recognizable. So are the benefits assumed to flow to the retailer from its operation. These were described in the same article as:

> 1. Increased sales turnover due to increased custom and additional spend per customer. 2. Reduction in overheads through reduced staff costs. 3. Greater efficiencies due to more rational management of the store; for instance more statistical information available through the cash register thus enabling better comparison of profitability of different departments and thus ability to mix product selection. (p. 42)

One of the things that unites these industry reports about the introduction of self-service with much critical social scientific work on retail is the manner in which the assertions about the success of self-service are swallowed wholesale, as it were. Self-service, we are told, was a clear and immediate hit with the shopping public. The British retailer, Marks and Spencer, for instance, indicates in its official company history that their first self-service store, opened in 1948 at Wood Green in London, 'was a great success' (http://www2.marksandspencer.com/thecompany/whoweare/our_history/1932_1955.shtml). The same goes for the company histories provided by other large British retailers such as Sainsbury's and Waitrose, for instance. *Shop Review* (1955: 38), however, reports things somewhat differently, indicating that Marks and Spencer's first attempt at self-service (in a food department at their Wood Green store in London) was simply an experiment and one that was quickly dropped by the company when it did not take off. Similarly, the high street multiple retailer Tesco converted one of it stores to self-service in 1947, only to have to return it to counter service when customers complained of the inconvenience of having to shop for themselves (Humphrey, 1998: 73). Finally, opening day at the first Sainsbury's self-service store in Croydon found a queue of only one person – the branch manager's wife! The idea that, once unveiled and put to work, self-service just took over the retail environment should not be taken at face value. Despite much rewriting of the historical record for promotional purposes, many of the established household names in British commercial retail such as Marks and Spencer and Sainsbury's did not enthusiastically adopt self-service. Instead, they were very concerned about the impact on their customers of going self-service and took a distinctly cautious and experimental approach to the technology. Indeed, by 1953, 66 per cent of all self-service stores in Britain were still operated by Britain's true self-service pioneer, the otherwise deeply unfashionable, Co-Operative Society.[4] So why the caution if the benefits – in terms of reduced overheads and enhanced turnover – were so clear and unambiguous?

First, it is important to pay attention to the economic and political context in which self-service was introduced. For many years after the Second World War rationing continued to be the norm for many goods. Not only this, the British government continued to exercise very detailed controls on the prices of goods to ensure that they were distributed relatively fairly to all sections of the population (Towsey, 1964; Seth and Randall, 1999). Competition on price was therefore restricted and this had a negative pull on the willingness of many retailers to invest in new methods. Those that did, it would appear, tended to be at the lower end of the market where pressures on staffing (due to labour shortages) were intense and the need to cut costs was perhaps most strongly felt. In the case of the Co-Operative Society, this combined with a political sense of mission to provide a service for the working-class family. It is this, perhaps, that accounts for the dramatic conversion rate of Co-Operative Society stores to self-service in the years immediately after the Second World War (I will discuss the implications of this move for shop-floor workers, a little later).

Given the lack of positive incentives it is hardly surprising that the stores with the most to lose – those catering to the middle classes, in particular – were extremely cautious about self-service. The early failure of self-service – such as at Marks and Spencer – were frequently represented in the national press as the result of a consumer distaste for serving oneself (*The Times*, 1957). Established class-based cultural norms about 'service' and the relative responsibilities of shopper and worker did not always tally with the more individualized ethos of self-service and, in particular, the redistribution of responsibilities for serving from workers to consumers that it instigated (Glazer, 1993; Humphrey, 1998; Bowlby, 2000). Lord Sainsbury's experience at the opening of the Purley self-service branch might serve as a paradigm of what retailers to the middle classes most feared from the self-service experiment. Lord Alan Sainsbury, the managing director of the company carrying his name, stood at the entrance to this store on opening day shaking hands with customers as they entered and passing them a shopping basket. The company history reports the wife of a local judge screaming abuse at Lord Alan and throwing the basket back at him with contempt when she discovered that she was required to do the work of a shop assistant and then to carry home her own purchases (J. Sainsbury plc, http://www.j-sainsbury.co.uk/company/history.htm). This perhaps is the crux of the cultural problem facing the would be self-service retailer. How do you get a population used to being served over the counter, or even of not having to go to the shops at all, to agree to do the work previously done by shop assistants on their behalf. Not only this, but to come to see it as enhancing their economic and personal freedom?

## the material culture of self-servicing: shopping and work

The effort to persuade sceptical or uninitiated consumers to see 'self-service' in a positive, even emancipatory, light seems always to begin with the development of a large network of agents – not simply retailers, but manufacturers, packagers, marketers, advertisers, fixture makers and fitters, and psychologists, all of whom had a specific part to play in the job of getting the housewife – for the object of their attentions were nearly always this category of person – to see the activity of shopping in a different light (Cochoy, 1998, 2003; Humphrey, 1998; Bowlby, 2000).

Early in 1950 Edgar Pennell, Head of Vocational Training at the British retailer, The John Lewis Partnership, embarked on a fact-finding tour of shops in the USA. He had never before encountered self-service and it left a lasting impression upon him. He wrote:

> At a very early stage in my travels I encountered in one large store a 'Greeting Cards' department which was entirely without staff! The customers just helped themselves and paid for their purchases at the neighbouring perfumery department. My enquiries into this strange procedure put me onto a remarkable trend in American retailing – the enormous growth of Customer Self-Service. (*The Gazette of the John Lewis Partnership,* 6 May 1950, p. 158)

Despite the fact that Pennell was visiting the USA somewhat towards the end of the first self-service boom there, self-service nonetheless came as a complete revelation to him. He was an immediate convert and set about formulating his thoughts about self-service for dissemination within the senior echelons of the management of the John Lewis Partnership. In particular, he was concerned to outline 'the mechanisms and devices whereby this steadily increasing degree of "Customer Self-Service" had been made profitable and practicable' (1950: 158). He lists five main factors. (Their similarity to those listed in the *Shop Review* article mentioned earlier should be noted.)

They are (1) a greater accessibility of merchandise to the customer, brought about by (2) a re-design of Fixtures and Shop-layout and by (3) an increased and better use of signs, directional notices and informative tickets of all kinds. This is accompanied by (4) more flexible and simplified methods of payment ... I was continually aware, however, that there was some 'mysterious' factor which was eluding me, and it was not until I was a quarter way through my trip that I saw clearly what it was. The whole technique of 'Customer Self-Service' ... depends on 'No.5' – a Reclassification of the Merchandise *from the customer's point of view*, instead of from the store's point of view ... This is the *sine qua non* of Customer Self-Service, and without it the other four factors have little or no weight. (*The Gazette of the John Lewis Partnership*, 6 May 1950, p. 158; italics in original)

For Pennell, if merchandising spoke to the consumer as an individual – if it was effectively 'personalized' – then the consumer would be more willing to take on the work of serving herself. For a store reclassified from the individual's point of view, according to him, was more convenient for that individual and also a more liberating place to shop. By encouraging more autonomy, he argued, more things would eventually be sold.

Pennell also picks up on another recurrent theme of the time: that going 'self-service' needs to be 'scientific'. He suggests that its implementation cannot be half-hearted or it is bound to fail. Indeed, extensive advice was available from a range of sources including the numerous trade journals – such as *Shop Review*, *Self-Service and Supermarket*, *Shop Equipment News* – devoted to spreading the word about 'self-service'. These focused on everything from store design, shop layout and promotional techniques to technological developments in the area of cash registers, refrigeration, and packaging materials.[5] The widespread development of prepackaging, for instance, was regularly represented as allowing for a greater individualization of merchandise. It was also seen to provide an enhanced opportunity for what we would today call 'branding' of the merchandise itself – the use of particular colours, images, logos, promotional spiels and so on and so forth on the goods – including the opportunity for multiple retailers to go 'own branding' to a degree hitherto unknown. At the same time, the spatial management of the store and the temporal habits of the shopper were also considered to be of considerable significance. All the main trade journals stressed the need for careful attention to be paid to the layout of the shelves and the product selection displayed therein. Goods were to be grouped together in meaningful clusters, where their relationship to one another could spark off associations in the minds of consumers thus leading to more 'impulse buys', a favourite catchphrase of the time (Galvani and Arnell, 1952: 20–83). Some of the most common advice concerns the importance of placing high-volume goods at strategic points throughout the store – thus enticing customers into the shop and ensuring they circulate – and of situating goods most likely to be bought on impulse – chocolates, sweets, razor blades, hairbands, cigarettes and so forth – at the end of gondolas and at the checkouts, thus taking some more money from the customer prior to them leaving the store (Zimmerman, 1955). Clearly, we are not talking about complete consumer autonomy here, but regulated freedom. The consumer is encircled within the mechanics of the shop, its intrinsic ordering directing them around its perimeters and through its aisles in a particular manner. But this concern with spatial management is also coupled with a more abstract concern with the ease and pleasure of the shopping experience and therefore with time spent in the store. One issue on which many trade journals focused was the practice of 'wandering'. Wandering was considered to result in more purchasing and therefore encouraging wandering, directed wandering, naturally, became a priority. One way to encourage this activity was to give the store as one 'practical guidebook' put it 'a unity in design which carries the theme of the shop beyond the limits of the shopfront' (Galvani and Arnell, 1952: 39). This 'unity' was to give the shop a feel, a mood, and to present an image that fostered immediate recognition even before the shopper entered. Once the housewife felt at home in store, she would wander more freely and buy more. As Alan Sainsbury wrote in 1967, 'we design our stores so that our goods may be displayed in an ordered, logical and tidy way making it as easy as possible for the customer to see what she is getting and to compare alternatives before making her choice ... We think our design will have failed if our customers have to read the name of the shop they are entering' (JS 100, 1969).

A unity of theme was all very well once consumers were used to the self-service environment and were at least partially acclimatized to shopping for themselves. The biggest problem was getting them into the stores in the first place. Promotional campaigns, run through the local media, accompanied by the leafleting of adjacent residential areas, were frequently conducted prior to the opening of a self-service store. Attempts would be made to build up a sense of anticipation among the local populace trading, in particular, on the sense of being part of something new and 'modern' (Humphrey, 1998: Ch. 6.). Once the store was open and shoppers were enticed to its doors, the promotional and the educational would be fused.

Such was the fear among retailers that shoppers would feel alienated by their new surroundings (they assumed to be so unused to exercising their individual freedom within the stores) that they regularly deployed staff to assist shoppers around the store gradually introducing them 'by example' to the arts of shopping for oneself. While some stores (Sainsbury's, for instance) used retired branch managers to assist the newly individualized shopper get their surroundings, others deployed what was known in the trade press as 'the hostess'. This category of person would either stand at the front of the store greeting customers and offering assistance or stroll around the store offering her services as and when she spotted a customer in distress. The aim, again, was to alleviate the anxiety and alienation of 'being alone' and being responsible for one's conduct inside the store and to show, through example, the proper exercise of individual shopping liberty (Zimmerman, 1955; Towsey, 1964).

Much as today, the presumed impersonality of the self-service system was a constant source of concern to retailers throughout the 1950s and 1960s. The need to preserve the element of human contact – the social side of shopping – while gaining the efficiencies of self-service, was emphasized by R.G. Magnus-Hannaford, Principal of the College for the Distributive Trades, at the first national conference on self-service shopping held at the college in London in 1955. He warned delegates that too keen a focus on the economies of self-service could undermine what he considered to be the inherently social side of the retail experience for customers. This could switch them off this form of shopping. He stressed that although shoppers would in reality have no one to blame but themselves if they bought too much or bought the wrong things they would invariably end up blaming the retailers rather than themselves. In order to ensure that adequate attention was being paid to the place of the self-service store in the community, retailers were again encouraged to facilitate wandering as wandering was thought to spark sociality; they could provide pram parking places within their stores and car parks next to the stores, and consider, size permitting, very American developments (mostly associated with large supermarkets) such as customer cloakrooms and customer lounges where refreshments might be purchased (*The Gazette of the John Lewis Partnership*, 21 May 1955, p. 387).

The impersonality that accompanied 'individualization', for want of a better term, was not a simple problematic for British retailers. Despite the negative connotations that the term 'self-service' carried with it – what one trade journal described as 'an image of complete impersonality' whereby 'the inexperienced shopper pictures a "horrible" wire basket, finding everything oneself and not knowing how much one has spent until one is on the way out, when it is too late to do anything about it' (*Shop Review*, 1955: 35), survey after survey of the self-service shopper during the 1950s reported the characteristics of impersonality as one of the positive aspects of the emergent technology that those women who went self-service associated with it. Rather than romanticizing the ideal of 'personal service' as against the impersonal aspects of 'self-service', surveys reported a sense of liberation among some shoppers from the shackles of class-based status and ascription associated with 'personal service'. From this customer's point of view, for instance, 'personal service' was frequently associated with:

1. A reluctance to ask for cheaper articles. 2. Customers are often embarrassed to ask to see certain lines which they would like to consider buying, for fear of being made to feel an obligation to buy and for fear of others waiting behind them observing their purchases. 3. The assistant spends so much time collecting items that the customer has specifically asked for, taking the money, bringing change and wrapping, that valuable time is wasted and there is also little opportunity to introduce new lines or explain the relative advantages of alternative items. 4. Customers are often kept waiting in a queue. 5. Customers are entirely at the hands of someone else and are affected by their defects, bad manners, lack of understanding and incompetence. (Self-Service Retailing summary of surveys for *Self Service and Supermarket*, 1964)

In contrast to these defects, self-service shoppers highlighted the benefits of self-service as including:

1. Being able to inspect the goods themselves and to be able to chose what and when to purchase them. 2. Wide range of goods to choose from. 3. Convenience. 4. Not having to wait to be served and thus saving time. (*Mrs. Housewife and Her Grocer*, 1957)

The surveys conducted frequently found a greater popularity for self-service among younger people of all classes and a greater scepticism among older people of all classes (*Shopping in Suburbia*, 1963). Popularity was also greater among working-class than middle-class shoppers, for example those with less to lose and most to gain, perhaps, from a freeing of the class-based shackles. Interestingly, the perceived impersonality of self-service is also cited as a reason for the gradual emergence of men in the shopping arena. As the Australian sociologist Kim Humphrey (1998: 136) notes: 'If ... self-service began to provide the ground on which to attract men into the shop, either alone or in the company of women, then perhaps this was due to the sense of independence self-service shopping encouraged.' For complex reasons, he continues, self-service seemed to be slightly less feminized than everyday shopping in its pre-self-service form. Similarly, as 'self-service' grew in the 1960s it became increasingly *déclassé*, at least in terms of the people that frequented self-service environments. According to Humphrey:

> Class demarcations remained evident, of course. Yet as self-service spaces became larger and more numerous, class divisions between customers came to be seemingly irrelevant, mirroring the increasing separation of the product from its conditions of production, and the increasing separation of people within the self-service store. (1998: 67)

The impersonality of 'self-service' therefore has some interesting effects, and these extend to retail employees as well as consumers. Although concerns were expressed within the media about the death of personal salesmanship, the effects of self-service upon retail employment were neither uniform nor entirely predictable (*The Gazette of the John Lewis Partnership*, 14 February 1956). In response to Edgar Pennell's 'letter from America' about the benefits of 'self-service', for instance, the chairman of JLP, O.B. Miller, indicated that:

> The Partnership should be as rapid as possible in adjusting its own methods accordingly. It cannot be a very quick business and to a great extent it ought to be possible to retain with an appropriate change of work all really conscientious Partners who otherwise would be displaced ... any development of self-service should not mean that present Partners should have to be dropped but only that additional Partners are not required. (*The Gazette of the John Lewis Partnership*, 6 May 1950)

While one can be sceptical about the ability of retailers to maintain staff levels over time, given the sort of economies that self-service could potentially engender, there was a widespread belief, not limited to special cases like The John Lewis Partnership (a mutual, unlisted on the Stock Exchange), held not only by employers but by many workers that self-service didn't have to lead inevitably to deskilling, rationalization and cost-cutting. This optimistic view may look remarkably naive, from the vantage point of the present, but, seen in context, such optimism is not so surprising. The passing of personal service was not universally mourned by retail workers. In contrast to the sometimes rosy picture of personal service work painted by some social scientists, retail workers often viewed this regime as a form of 'servitude'. Seen in this light, the impersonality of self-service could be seen as something of a relief.

This more upbeat message about self-service work, as opposed to counter service work, finds expression in the first report on employee responses to self-service undertaken by USDAW (Union of Shop, Distributive and Allied Workers) in 1955. While there are clearly problems in generalizing from this less than representative survey conducted among workers in only one major and less than typical British retailer, the findings are nonetheless of interest as they do not give support to those who would argue that self-service was an unpopular imposition, disliked by all workers who experienced it. Here, a large survey of workers in the Co-Operative Society's self-service stores found that two-thirds of employees preferred operating under self-service rather than counter service systems.[6] Among the many reasons given for this preference were:

- The assistant is relieved of constant walking
- Better distribution of duties
- Less weighing up
- Easier to know the stock
- Better working conditions
- Shop is easier to clean
- Customers are pleasanter through having to wait less time
- Staff can get away on time

(USDAW, 1955)

USDAW's endorsement of self-service was framed by the following caveats. That there should be:

- No dismissal or redundancy as a result of conversion
- No undue replacement of men by women assistants
- No undue replacement of older and more experienced staff by younger, less experienced people at lower rates of pay
- No unreasonable or excessive intensification of the work to be performed
- An improvement in the wages or earnings of employees as a result of the savings made by conversion
- That before embarking on a policy of self-service, Management should extend to employees the opportunity for full consultation.

(USDAW, 1955)

For a number of shop workers, therefore, the impersonality of self-service was seen as something of a liberation. Indeed, *The Gazette*, the house journal of the John Lewis Partnership, reports that the first two conversions to self-service undertaken by partnership stores in the early 1950s were greeted enthusiastically by those working in them. Indeed, the journal reports that in both cases workers at the stores volunteered to work around the clock to ensure that the store was fully converted in time for its grand opening (*The Gazette of the John Lewis Partnership*, 18 August 1951, p. 350; 5 July 1952, p. 292; 15 November 1952; 3 December 1955, p. 1108; 23 November 1957, p. 955; 16 January 1958, pp. 1154–5). Being part of something modern and different could be as appealing to retail workers as it could also be for some retail consumers.

**concluding comments**   What can we learn about consumption and personhood from this brief and rather anecdotal trawl through some historical materials on 'self-service' retailing in Britain? First, that organizational changes designed to promote consumption are context specific and contingent. 'Self-service' was not a singular system but a loosely connected set of technologies, many of which had been in existence for some time in various parts of the world, and which could be lashed together, more or less coherently, to adapt to local demands and circumstances. 'Self-selection' and 'exposed selling' were often euphemisms for partial or assisted forms of self-service that retailers found themselves adopting to accrue what benefits they could without scaring away their customers. Many of the assumed benefits of going self-service that pertained in the North American and Scandinavian contexts, for instance, could not be realized in the British context. Retail price controls, for example, ensured that retailers adventurous enough to operate the system could not, as one trade journal put it, 'give back to the public any results that might obtain by increased efficiency in the form of lower prices' (*Stores and Shops*, 1956, reprinted in *The Gazette of the John Lewis Partnership*, 11 November 1956, p. 35). With strict planning regulations, high property prices and rents, and tight labour market conditions to boot, the economies to be realized from going self-service might be outweighed by the potential costs, particularly in terms of customer reaction to having to do for oneself. Caution and pragmatic appropriation therefore ruled the day. Self-service was not a revolution. Its success neither immediate nor total.

Secondly, 'self-service' entered a world where existing understandings of the conduct of shopping, for instance, were often at odds with those informing self-service practices. As we have seen, established class- and gender-based understandings about shopping and consumption were, to some extent, antithetical to the impersonal and individualized demands of self-service. In particular, middle-class assumptions about who did what for whom in the shop, about the relations between service and work, were challenged by the tenets of self-service. This potential and often actual antagonism between retail technology and consumer practice goes a long way towards explaining the cautious and experimental approaches to the technology adopted by some of the big high street names in Britain. In the United States and parts of Scandinavia, by contrast, the idea that self-service could be seen as a bad thing because it effected a transfer of work from the retail employee to the consumer was almost entirely absent. The huge amount of material–cultural–economic work retailers engaged in in Britain to convince the public to go self-service suggests that there was not a massive latent demand for the technology among consumers, simply waiting to be activated by the canny retailer. The self-service shopper had to be 'made up'. Existing habits had to be broken and different ones put in their place. A new consuming persona were therefore created, and individuals were encouraged to adapt/adopt this status and role. A huge network of agents – marketers, shop-fitters, psychologists, packagers, shopping trolley manufacturers and so on – were enrolled to assist in this endeavour, to the point where self-service gradually became the only game in town.

Finally, seen from the vantage point of hindsight, self-service certainly effected a change in both the nature of the job of retail sales assistance (and management) and the social characteristics of those performing that work. However, that shift was effected over time, quite a considerable period of time, in fact and not immediately. That many retail workers could see self-service as a liberation not as a device that would fundamentally undermine the conditions of their existence for the worse again attests to the importance of context and culture. Self-service could seem easier work, cleaner and safer work, less servile work for those used to personal service. Only once personal service has almost disappeared can it then be re-imagined as an ideal – as a lost 'golden' age of skill and control for the retail worker. Seen in a cultural–economic context, the generally favourable view of self-service held by retail workers comes as no surprise. It may well be that they were in effect 'the brilliant allies of their own gravediggers', to use Milan Kundera's phrase from another context (1993), but that can only be considered a fault if they were assumed to possess a god's eye view of the world, which they, like the rest of us, simply didn't and couldn't possess.

## notes

1   Notable exceptions include the work of Kim Humphrey (1998) and Rachel Bowlby (2000).
2   Though their share of total trade was more substantial, being estimated at 32.7% by 1964 (Towsey, 1964: 6).
3   By 'person' I am not referring exclusively to human beings. Rather, as outlined in Chapter 1, I am using the term to refer to any entity, human or non-human (a corporation, an association), that is capable of being allotted rights or duties. In legal terms, persons are nothing but the subjects or substances of which rights

and duties are the attributes. Thus, not only may non-humans be 'persons' but not all humans will be 'persons' in all contexts and circumstances. See, for instance, the classic discussion in Cousins (1980).

4   Even by 1960, 48% of all self-service stores in the UK were operated by the Co-Operative society (Towsey, 1964).

5   For a detailed sociological study (from an actor network theoretical perspective) of packaging and its relationship to self-service see Cochoy, 2002. Space does not permit the sort of detailed delineation and discussion of these various devices and technologies and their contingent assemblage into a shopping regime that the argument of the chapter suggests is essential to understanding self-service. For recent work that does just this, see Leymonerie (2006) and Grandclément (2006).

6   The USDAW questionnaire was sent to 209 Co-Operative Societies which, between them, operated 1,112 self-service branches. A response rate of more than 80% was achieved. It should be remembered that at this time, 1954/55, it was The Co-Operative Society alone that ran the majority (about 75%) of the self-service stores operating in the United Kingdom.

2

# re-instating an ethic of bureaucratic office: office, ethos and persona in public management

> But the law is the law, duty is duty, and a man defrauds his own name if he but once neglects his office.
>
> (Ronan Bennett, *Havoc In Its Third Year*)

Notions of personae and role-playing have enjoyed considerable usage in sociological and social theoretical discourse, being deployed to provide organizational and explanatory models for understanding diverse aspects of social life (Burkitt, 1992). What is meant by persona, though, as I indicated in Chapter 1, can be quite variable. At one extreme, as Conal Condren (2004: 1) has suggested, 'it is little more than a performed role and presupposes an inner but ultimately accessible moral and decision-making agent who decides when to adopt a persona and when to put it aside. The inner "self" is thus a postulated *explanans* for conduct.' At another extreme, however, is the idea of the persona as a manifestation and representative of an office, an embodiment of moral economy. Here, office denotes an assemblage of duties, responsibilities, rights of action for their fulfilment, necessary attributes, skills, and a register of virtues, vices and failures. The determinants of office include its purposes and its limits: assertions as to end and limit thus operate as axes for the definition of a particular sort of persona, and the qualities that best fitted the purposes and recognized the limits of office (Condren, 2004: 2). As I argue below, the world of offices – political, administrative, legal and so forth – has recently begun to attract renewed attention, though it must be said that the correlate that people in office – office-holders – be seen as persona rather than as individual 'selves' has, with honourable exceptions, been the road less travelled. This notion of persona as an expression of office offers a useful antidote to contemporary social scientific reductions of persona to notions of 'self' and 'role'.

In Part II of the book, attention is focused upon a particular 'persona' – the state bureaucrat, public administrator or career civil servant – and upon recent and ongoing politico-organizational attempts to transform the conduct of this persona. The essays in this section therefore offer both an attempt to develop the approach to person, persona and personae introduced in Part I, and a defence of a particular persona whose status-conduct enthusiasts for change – many armed with expressivist ideas about individual liberty and self-constitution – find so difficult to appreciate. The chapters in this section represent something akin to a plea to the politically enthusiastic and the organizationally impatient to consider, in detail, what their own dreams and schemes presuppose and express, in terms of the daily consequences of the practices and conducts they advocate. I begin, in this chapter, by attempting to make a case for the continuing indispensability of office-specific conceptions of moral agency in the realm of governmental and political action.

In recent years there has been a considerable upsurge of interest in the concept of 'office' within the social sciences, humanities and among scholars of public law and public management (Thompson, 1987; Minson, 1993, 1998, 2004; Orren, 1994; Uhr, 1994, 2001; Condren, 1997, 2004; Dobel, 1999; du Gay, 2000a; Geuss, 2001; Sabl, 2002; Loughlin, 2004). Although there are a number of disparate, often discipline-specific, factors contributing to this renewed focus, two rather more general aspects of the 'turn' to office stand out. First, a rekindled interest in the moral attributes of public agency inspired not only by a number of well-publicized political controversies – from the sexual scandals that beset the Clinton administration in the USA, to the Hutton and Butler enquiries in the UK into events surrounding the decision to go to war in Iraq – but also by growing ethical uncertainties attendant upon a rapid and equally controversial series of managerial reforms of a wide range of public institutions. Secondly, a historical, philosophical and practical concern with the manner in which certain prominent contemporary conceptions of moral agency presume a dichotomy between moral autonomy, on the one hand, and subordination to higher authority, on the other, such that to hold a subaltern status and to exercise moral agency are represented as fundamentally incompatible (Schneewind, 1990).

Although it would be somewhat problematic to conjoin both of these strands into something akin to a unified field, there are nonetheless clear points of connection between them. One crucial area of overlap concerns the forms of moral agency appropriate to the performance of political and governmental offices.

Thus, in his remarkable study of the language of 'Office' in seventeenth-century political argument, the historian Conal Condren (1997) indicates how and why it is difficult, if not impossible, to make defence of office in early modern political argument register in terms of modern expressivist understandings of liberty and resistance. Rather, he is careful to show how early modern conceptions of 'liberty, discipline and submission to authority' were entirely 'compatible, closely related notions' (1997: 462). In arguing that liberty of office presupposes subordination to a higher authority, Condren also suggests, with Hobbes foremost in mind, that the modern depiction of subaltern status and moral autonomy as mutually exclusive, and the consequent dismissal of the ethics of office as morally bankrupt, is politically disabling, particularly so when it comes to exploring civil ethics of state (Condren, 2002: 70–2). This is an important point, one with much contemporary relevance, as I will indicate towards the end of the chapter. For Condren (2004) ethics of office may well involve the exercise of judgement but such judgements are not personal in the sense of being about the free and full exercise of an individual's authentic moral conscience or 'self'; rather, they are choices facing individuals as the embodiment of a distinctive persona – an official. When it comes to office, Condren suggests, 'allowable liberties are the functions of obligations' (1997: 472), including obligations to specified authority.

This chapter seeks to make a case for the continuing indispensability of office-specific conceptions of moral agency in the realm of governmental and political action. Its main focus of concern, however, is with the office of the state bureaucrat, career civil servant or public administrator. This category of 'person' has been the object of significant practical reform over the last two decades, and serious debate continues concerning whether such incessant reform has undermined key aspects of the role and function of the office to which this persona is attached. Indeed, rhetorics of office have played and continue to play an important part in framing debates about the status of recent reforms of the state administration as an institution of government.

In seeking to show the continued relevance of office-based conceptions of moral agency to the practice of state administration and to the status conduct of the public administrator I will have cause to question some of the assumptions underpinning contemporary reforms of state bureaux and the norms of conduct they advocate. I suggest that many of the experiments in public management that have been foisted upon state bureaux over the last two decades have had the effect of undermining the 'core business' of public administration: running a state. I begin, however, by introducing the idea of the state as a structure of offices and by focusing, in particular, on the purposes and status of the office of state bureaucrat.

**offices of state**    According to Quentin Skinner (1989, 2002), among many others, the idea of the modern state was developed slowly and with some difficulty to facilitate the construction of a single integrated system of authoritative political and legal decision-making over a given territory and subject-population, and to offset the continuing subversive or anarchistic potential of the long-standing viewpoint that derived political authority, in one way or another, from the people over whom it was exercised. At the centre of this novel idea was the concept of sovereignty, of ultimate worldly authority over people and territory, and its firm location within specific institutions and decisions: the right to be obeyed without challenge. 'The entity in which that right inhered', as John Dunn indicates, was no longer envisioned as a particular human being

> but as a continuing structure of government, decision-making, legal interpretation and enforcement, which was sharply distinct from its current human incumbents. Such a structure could take in or lose subjects or territory without altering its identity. It could change its system of rule or legal adjudication almost beyond recognition, and yet remain intractably itself. (2000: 80)

And, as Udo Wolter (1997: 18), for instance, has argued, a central feature of this sovereign entity is the institution of office. According to Wolter (1997), the sovereign state is an abstract structure of offices endowed with all manner of powers, warrants and resources that are to be sharply distinguished from the contingent human occupants of these offices. Office is therefore an institution that the state and other juristic bodies of public law make use of in order to accomplish certain purposes. Sovereign and fiscal tasks are delegated to a persona – the 'office-holder' – for a portfolio of responsibilities that is delimited, amongst other things, by norms of competence. These persons – state functionaries or bureaucrats – are subject to official duties that result, *inter alia*, from legislation, constitutional dictat or official instructions, 'as for example concerning due execution, incorruptibility, or impartiality' (Wolter, 1997: 19).

For Wolter (1997: 19–21), the concept of office can be delineated and analysed along two axes. First, organizationally, in terms of the office as instituted competence. Here, the modern state accomplishes its tasks and objectives through a division of labour. Therefore, the idea of office presupposes the existence of a large number of offices that work together in something akin to a 'permanent structure of offices' (1997: 19). The definition and distribution of the functions of an office result from the establishment of specific competencies. In so far as the office fulfils a function of state, it is defined in relation to competencies and therefore made independent in an abstract sense. This requires, first, a fixed definition of responsibilities and, secondly, the coordination of offices in a hierarchy. Because the office is a function of state, it is also equipped with authority. If the office fulfils duties on behalf of the state, the state has to grant to the office those means that are qualitatively equivalent to those of the state. In other words, the office has the 'official authority' to order and enforce everything that is necessary to fulfil its duties as bound by the limits of its competence (1997: 19–20).

Secondly, Wolter traces the concept of office in relation to the persona of the office-holder, in terms of the regulation of status and duties. The abstract existence of the office, he argues, makes it qualitatively different from any natural person. It is constructed precisely in order to make the activity of the state independent of the insufficiency of any human being, and to achieve substantive effects despite the individual imperfections of any particular office-holder (see also Kallinikos, 2004). The office is therefore a fundamentally impersonal institution. This means, negatively expressed, that the office cannot be treated as a personal possession or tradeable good. More positively it means, for instance, that the maintenance of the office-holder has to be secured independently of the income of the office, and that the 'depersonalization' of the execution of official duties has to be ensured through the regulation of official duties (Wolter, 1997: 19–20).

Thus, in his classic dissection of the vocation of bureaucratic office-holding, Max Weber writes:

> Legally and actually, office holding is not considered ownership of a source of income, to be exploited for rents or emoluments in exchange for the rendering of certain services, as was normally the case during the Middle Ages ... nor is office holding considered a common exchange of services, as in the case of free employment contracts. Rather entrance into an office ... is considered an acceptance of a specific duty of fealty to the purpose of the office (*Amtstreue*) in return for the grant of a secure existence. It is decisive for the modern loyalty to an office that, in the pure type, it does not establish a relationship to a *person*, like the vassal's or disciple's faith under feudal or patrimonial authority, but rather is devoted to impersonal and functional purposes ... The political official – at least in the fully developed modern state – is not considered the personal servant of a ruler. (1978: II, p. 959)

For Weber, the institutional and moral responsibility of the different officers of state – rulers, political leaders, bureaucrats – is to be understood in terms of their quite distinct duties attached to their particular responsibilities of office.

According to Weber (1978: II, p. 958ff.), the state bureaucrat or administrative official, on the one hand, and the politician or ruler, on the other, have very different purposes and forms of responsibility. Such differences are not to be deduced from the relative 'interest' or 'complexity' of the tasks each performs, nor from a mechanistic distinction between policy and administration, but, rather, from the demands made upon them by the distinctive offices they occupy.

'Officials' too are expected to make independent decisions and show organizational ability and initiative, not only on countless individual cases but also on larger issues. It is typical of littérateurs and of a country lacking any insight into its own affairs or into the achievement of its officials, even to imagine that the work of an official amounts to no more than the subaltern performance of routine duties, while the leader alone is expected to carry out the 'interesting' tasks which make special intellectual demands. This is not so. The difference lies, rather, in the kind of responsibility borne by each of them, and this is largely what determines the demands made on their particular abilities. (Weber, 1994a: 160)

Weber is clearly referring to 'responsibility' in a very specific sense. The term as he deploys it does not pertain to a simple division of organizational labour, in which bureaucratic officials are allocated the sole responsibility for administration, and politicians the sole responsibility for policy. Rather, 'responsibility' refers to a division of ethical labour in which official and political leader are subject to specific imperatives and points of honour and develop quite different capacities and comportments as a result of the demands of their respective 'offices' – their placement within what Weber describes as different 'life-orders'.

In his classic account of the 'persona' of the bureaucrat, Weber (1978: II, p. 978ff.) treats the impersonal, expert, procedural and hierarchical character of bureaucratic conduct as elements of a distinctive ethos. According to Weber, the bureau comprises the socio-technical conditions of a distinctive organization of the person. Among the most important of these are, first, that access to office is dependent upon lengthy training, usually certified by public examination; and second, that the office itself constitutes a 'vocation', a focus of ethical commitment and duty, autonomous of and superior to the bureaucrat's extra-official ties to kith, kin or conscience (see also, Hunter 1994a). In Weber's discussions of bureaucratic office-holding as a vocation, these conditions mark out the office as a particular sphere of life and provide the office-holder with a distinctive ethical bearing or status-conduct. In particular, Weber (1978: II, p. 983ff.) stresses the ways in which the ethos of bureaucratic office-holding constitutes an important political resource because it serves to divorce the administration of public life from private moral absolutisms. Without the historical emergence of the ethos and persona of bureaucratic office-holding, Weber argues, the construction of a buffer between civic comportment and personal principles – a crucial feature of liberal government – would never have been possible. Indeed, without the 'art of separation' (Walzer, 1984) that the state bureau effected and continues to effect, many of the qualitative features of government that are regularly taken for granted – for instance, reliability and procedural fairness in the treatment of cases – would not exist.

As Weber makes clear, the crucial point of honour for bureaucrats is not to allow extra official commitments to determine the manner in which they perform the duties associated with their office:

> On the contrary, he (sic) takes pride in preserving his impartiality, overcoming his own inclinations and opinions, so as to execute in a conscientious and meaningful way what is required of him by the general definition of his duties or by some particular instruction, even – and particularly – when they do *not* coincide with his own political views. (Weber, 1994a: 160)

Without this 'supremely ethical discipline and self-denial', the whole apparatus of the state would disintegrate (Weber, 1994b: 331).

It is the relationship between extra official commitments, broadly defined, and the independent obligations of office that has preoccupied many of the contemporary critics of state and bureaucracy. It is to the work of these critics that I now turn.

**contemporary challenges to state and bureaucracy**  As Richard Chapman (2000: 4) has reported, the original Society of British Civil Servants had as its motto (when mottoes, as opposed to visions, were in vogue) 'We serve the State'. It is indicative of how far we have travelled that it is impossible to imagine a similar body today choosing to deploy the 'S' word to frame its 'core business' (Walker, 2004). A document produced by the UK Cabinet Office (1999b) entitled *Vision and Values* provides the more appropriate contemporary comparator. Here we find the Civil Service's mission defined thus: 'to make the UK a better place for everyone to live in, and support its success in the world. We want to be the best at everything we do.' A more vacuous statement it is hard to imagine, but a more telling example of the eclipse of the state in contemporary public management discourse it would be difficult to find.

Given the contemporary obsession with 'society' as the source of public policy, most notably in contemporary theories and programmes of 'network governance'(Rhodes, 1996, 2000a; Stoker, 1998, 2000a), it seems that reasons of state are always bad reasons (Kriegel, 1995). This gradual occlusion of the concept of the state in recent political and public management thought, most especially but not exclusively its ethical component, has condemned a whole body of practical thinking concerning the problems, purposes, techniques and comportments appropriate to the responsible running of a state, if not to oblivion, then certainly to a shadowy existence in the interstices of various machineries of government adopted by many actually existing states (Minson, 1998; Geuss, 2001). In particular, it has condemned the ethos of bureaucratic office to the dustbin of history, representing it not only as morally bankrupt but also as organizationally redundant.

Exactly why the state and bureaucracy find themselves in this position is not too difficult to discern. After all, opposition to the idea of 'the state' and to 'bureaucracy' has long been a feature of a wide variety of political discourses. Over the last 30 years or so, however, it has enjoyed a remarkable resurgence in popularity. One of the most prominent of the many recent criticisms directed at the 'cold monsters' of state and bureaucracy concerns their presumed negative consequences for personal liberty. Whether couched in predominantly managerialist or economistic terms – states and their bureaucracies hinder the unique virtue and efficacy of a capitalistic organization of production – or in relation to populist criteria of political right – only governments that are responsive to, and thus accurately and sensitively express, the opinions and judgements of their own citizens can be fully entitled to their obedience – states and bureaucracies are seen as undermining freedom.

Underlying the first of these conceptions, we might contend, is the assumption that economic freedom, and the efficiency of governmental policy, is a function of the state's subordination to the laws of the 'free' markets. For the second, the guiding assumption is that the justness of governmental policy is directly related to the degree of the bureaucracy's subordination to the popular will. Both strands of critique can be easily traced in recent and ongoing experiments in reforming state bureaux, most particularly but not exclusively, in their Anglo-American variants. So, for instance, contemporary demands for more 'responsive' public management and the mechanisms devised to achieve this end frequently contain two distinctive elements. On the one hand, the 'unresponsiveness' of which many democratic populists complain often appears to be based upon the assumption that it is impossible to justify substantial governing power being allotted to unelected officials. Thus the ceaseless demands for 'modernization' and 're-invention' of state bureaux made by advocates of enhanced democratic rule are based on the belief that bureaucracies should be more 'responsive' to the wishes of their political superiors and to the people they ostensibly serve. When applied to the machinery of government, this understanding of 'responsiveness' is thought, for instance, to entail the development of policies and practices that remove 'obstacles' between government and governed ('sunshine' laws requiring that governmental deliberations be conducted in public; increasing 'deliberative democracy' and 'client participation' in agency decision-making).

On the other hand, the 'unresponsiveness' of which many managerialist or economistic critics of state bureaucracy complain centres on the presumed 'inefficiency' of grant-incomed state bureaucracies as compared with organizations exposed to the vicissitudes of market competition. When applied to the machinery of government, this understanding of 'responsiveness' entails, *inter alia*, the development of market-type mechanisms ('internal-markets', quasi-autonomous agencies, and Public Private Partnerships (PPPs)) that will help stimulate efficiency, competition and profitability (in no matter how opaque a manner) in and among state bureaux, or by passing those bureaux entirely in the pursuit of what has been popularly termed 'entrepreneurial governance' (Osborne and Gaebler, 1992; Osborne and Palstrik, 1997). In contrast to the democratic impulse, this approach to responsiveness highlights the need for managerial autonomy from political control so that services can be delivered to customers with maximum efficiency, as in any other business context.[1]

As indicated earlier, both strands of critique can be traced in recent and ongoing experiments in reforming state bureaux. The question that arises, though, concerns the effects of such demands on the character of bureaucratic office. What impact have attempts to institute more 'responsive' forms of government had upon the capacity of state bureaucrats to live up to the obligations of their office? In particular, what effects have programmes designed to enhance 'responsiveness' had upon what Weber characterized as the separation of office and self?

**populist democratic critiques and the ethos of bureaucratic office** There are, of course, many different forms of populist democratic critique of state bureaux. Some critics approach the issue of enhanced 'responsiveness' by stressing the bureaucrat's independent obligation to act on the basis of their sense of individual and/or social responsibility. Here, bureaucrats are represented as influential participants in the policy process, who should be encouraged to act more freely on the dictates of their own consciences to ensure socially equitable outcomes (for a discussion, see Uhr, 2001). Others encourage the adoption of relatively direct ways for members of the public to influence the behaviour of public bureaucrats, through the deployment of citizen/consumer charters for instance, or through associated devices such as the creation of various user groups that function as virtual boards of directors for public organizations (for a discussion, see Peters, 2000b). Yet others propose the enhanced use of political appointees and special advisers in an increasing number of government positions, thus ensuring that the will of the government can be enthusiastically promoted and its priorities enforced in the face of the perceived inertia represented by the 'forces of conservatism' inherent in state bureaucracies (for a discussion, see Jones, 2001).

What each of these critiques shares is an assumption that the justness of bureaucratic policy and practice is a function of the degree to which it is subordinate (i.e. 'responsive') to a conception of the 'popular will'. On the one hand, this may be achieved through mechanisms such as the increased use of political appointees, in which the 'popular will' is effectively mediated through political elites of some sort. Responsiveness here is conceptualized as being to political leaders as representatives of 'the people'. On the other hand, mechanisms such as 'citizen/consumer' charters or client 'virtual boards of directors' suggest a more direct – though still mediated – form of popular control.

The idea of the bureaucrat acting on his or her own conscience in the service of individual moral and/or social responsibility appears at first sight to sit uncomfortably with either of these notions. However, the inculcation among bureaucrats of an office-independent, socially responsible muscle of the spirit suggests that the bureaucrat is in some sense re-imagined as a representative of the people, continually conducting an inner moral audit, measuring their conduct not so much against the demands of their office, but against a wider conception of moral principle and socially beneficial outcomes. The 'responsiveness' here is to the bureaucrat's own conscience as evidenced in their moral conception of 'socially responsible' conduct. Only insofar as role or office-based obligations are represented in terms of morally justifiable higher purposes – engendering social justice and civic renewal – should public bureaucrats regard them as an altruistic 'personal' responsibility (Minson, 1998).

While it often seems difficult to argue against populist, democratic mechanisms for holding bureaucrats to account – however they are understood – given the normative power associated with the democratic signifier, nonetheless there may be some significant problems with the practical operation of such mechanisms when it comes to maintaining the separation between 'office' and 'self' that Weber characterized as a fundamental component of the operation of the state as a state. As we saw earlier, Weber's understanding of bureaucratic office is framed in opposition to theological or otherwise pre-modern understandings of office as divine right, personal possession or private property. It is also clearly distinguished from certain doctrines of popular sovereignty. As he makes clear in *Economy and Society* and 'The profession and vocation of politics', for instance, when you have a state as your form of political organization, and especially if you are living in a world of basically competitive states, the preservation and flourishing of your state gives rise to an independent set of reasons for action: those pertaining to the security of the state as its own *raison d'être*. Or what we have come to know as *raison d'état*. If, in certain forms of populist democratic thought, 'public' means all that pertaining to the concerns of all the people, then when state officials come to take care of these public concerns it is clear that a transmutation of meaning and ethos is effected that is of fundamental significance (Geuss, 2001). For under these circumstances the term 'public' comes to refer to the offices themselves rather than the 'common concerns' or, more specifically, the latter come to be seen exclusively in terms of the former. It is precisely a reversal of this development that I argue can be seen at work in the contemporary populist democratic critique of bureaucratic office.

Such thinking is evident when considering that loose form of populist 'direct democracy' associated with the mobilization of the citizen/consumer, for instance. Here, there is an attempt to enable the 'public', conceptualized as consumers of public services, to exert some influence over the public policies and institutions that act upon them. One of the most pervasive of contemporary attempts to 'democratize' state institutions has been the instrument of the 'citizen/consumer' charter. That initial populist element in the 'responsiveness' regimen has been followed, *inter alia,* by the mechanisms of the Complaints Task Force (Peters, 2000b: 131). The assumption guiding these experiments is that consumers of public services are not only capable of assessing the performance of many public organizations, but are the persons best placed to undertake this task. Not only this, they are also the persons most able to transform those assessments into enforceable decisions that will, in turn, help reform governmental operations and policies.

A related aspect of this democratization agenda is the creation of various user groups that function as virtual boards of directors for public sector institutions (Peters, 2000b: 131–2). This form of democratic control has been particularly influential in areas such as housing, education and healthcare where governmentally constituted 'virtual consumers' are held to 'demand' greater control over the activities of service providers. The groups that function as the mechanisms of accountability are often elected from the relevant 'consumer' group – or client base – thereby possessing, it is argued, a democratic mandate for enforcing responsiveness over state providers (Peters, 2000b; Runciman, 2005).

One problem, as a number of commentators have indicated (Plowden, 1994; Peters, 2000b), is that a small, vocal and socially distinctive segment of the population can become the reference group for enforcing certain forms of accountability and judging aspects of official performance. That is, those citizen/consumers who feel that they have been wronged, or who have the requisite skills to complain effectively, become the measure of good and bad administration, rather than a professional or legal standard of some sort fulfilling this role. Here, the demands of office are transcended or trumped by the normative power of the direct democratic mandate. As Plowden (1994), for instance, has argued, respect for citizen/consumers preferences in this populist, direct democratic manifestation is a tiger that, when taken by the tail, can pull governments and their officials in uncomfortable and sometimes undesired directions. He cites a classic case from the 1990s, when the then Conservative administration in the UK allowed some schools, still publicly funded, to opt out of control of elected authorities and to come under the jurisdiction of local boards of governors (mainly parents), subject to ultimate final control by the then Department of Education. This was wholly in line with Conservative thinking about 'responsibilization', 'responsiveness' and, centrally, 'consumer choice and satisfaction'. Great, then, was their concern when a school in a particularly deprived part of east London, largely populated by recent immigrants from the Indian subcontinent, fell under the control of some strident Muslim governors who were soon in conflict with the head teacher at the school, whose day-to-day activities they tried to control. The situation was only resolved when the Secretary of State for Education directly intervened (Plowden, 1994: 307). Controversies such as this associated with experiments of this sort in various social policy fields indicate precisely what can happen when small and strident sections of the 'user' population are able to gain undue influence in decision-making (Bishop and Davis, 2001; Evans, 2003).

The danger with these sorts of programmes, and the assumptions informing them, is that an ethic of responsibility associated with an ethos of bureaucratic office is transmuted by mechanisms of populist participative democratic rule into an acceptance of private interest as the means, *inter alia*, of evaluating performance, of deciding when there has been a failure of administration, or of what particular policy objectives should be given greater or lesser organizational weighting. In other words, while more traditional approaches to institutional accountability, for instance, tend to focus on official failure to meet bureaucratically constituted – office-based – goals of equality and fairness, standards built into more populist participative democratic mechanisms, especially where participation is by an 'active' minority, may well lead to the acceptance of arbitrary standards and thus of greater levels of inequality, except for those from the participating segment. They may also, over time, lead to the re-emergence of patronage and other forms of direct partisan involvement in administrative life, which the development of an ethos of bureaucratic office had helped to expunge (Chapman, 2004). According to Dobel (1999: 41), for instance, the adoption of these mechanisms can undermine the independent status of office so that the latter once again becomes something akin to a possession – in this case subject to 'consumer capture'.

Concerns about the erosion of an ethos of bureaucratic office also arise when discussion turns to the increased use of political appointees and special advisers in official positions within state bureaux. Here, as I indicated earlier, another form of a populist, democratic impulse can be seen at work.

The last three decades have witnessed a concerted attempt by governing parties in many different political contexts to strengthen their control over state bureaux. These moves have been framed in terms of enhancing the responsiveness of the bureaucracy to the political will of those with a democratic mandate. One aspect of this particular trend has been the erosion of the powers of centralized staffing agencies that safeguarded public service recruitment and promotions from political or official interference; strengthening ministerial control of top departmental appointments by removing the need to consult an independent staffing agency; substituting short term contracts for security of tenure in top official posts; and generating the general attitude that party-political governments should not have to tolerate obstruction or inertia from conservative bureaucrats, and should instead surround themselves with enthusiastic, committed leaders who would champion their policies and ensure they were 'delivered' (Chapman, 2004). In attempting to achieve these ends, however, politicians and their advisers have arguably weakened the legitimate role of officials in government by undermining the ethos of bureaucratic office (Parker, 1993; du Gay, 2000b; Chapman, 2004).

The increasing use of external appointments to senior civil service positions and, in particular, the appointment of those with known prior policy enthusiasms gives rise to two particular problems.[2] The first is that of ensuring that standards in state service are maintained – that the obligations of office are lived up to; the second is that distinctions between office and self are not so blurred that the state service becomes a politically partisan institution.

In the United Kingdom, for instance, the political neutrality, or party political impartiality, of the British Civil Service, has flowed in no small part from its career basis (Bogdanor, 2001; Chapman, 2004). Career civil servants are expected to serve successive governments of differing party political hues. The key to being able to do this, as Weber indicated, is to cultivate a degree of indifference to the enthusiasms of all political parties; to display, in effect, party political impartiality. Traditionally, at least, civil servants have been trained to conduct themselves in such a manner. Indeed, in Britain, as elsewhere, people with strong party political or single issue interests have – until recently – been unlikely to be appointed to senior Civil Service positions or to present themselves for consideration as candidates in the first place (Chapman, 1988). As a result, civil servants have been likely to greet the panaceas of all political parties with caution, if not scepticism. Inevitably, this leads them to embrace party political programmes with less fervour than party political enthusiasts would like. But this is part of their job, one assigned to them by the constitution. And in fulfilling this role they may be seen as servants of the state. It is precisely this statist/constitutional role – an obligation of office – that is being affected by the appointment of political enthusiasts or loyalists to senior positions in the bureaucracy. New recruits coming from outside – whether from commercial organizations or social enterprises – will generally lack the traditional patterns of experience, such as those gained by being a private secretary to a minister, which help inculcate in civil servants those very conducts of impartiality (Bogdanor, 2001: 276). Moreover, someone recruited from outside the service by virtue of relevant knowledge and approved commitments is likely to arrive with all sorts of partisan baggage derived from their previous situation. That is almost inevitable, if 'new' civil servants are expected to be cheerleaders for government and act as committed champions of specific policies. It is not easy, however, for those same people to both fulfil such a role and, at the same time, conform to traditional practices of subordination and lack of constitutional personality, their views being those of their minister, and not their own (Bogdanor, 2001: 296).

As Bogdanor (2001: 296) has suggested, it is not clear, therefore, how far outside recruitment to senior policy positions in the Civil Service can avoid the dangers of politicization or at least a degree of prior policy commitment, incompatible with traditional notions of 'political neutrality'. The problem here, in effect, is that office and self become blurred, with the committed champion coming to see the office as an extension of themselves, thereby effecting a confusion of public and private interests and identities. Dobel (1999: 131) calls this 'zealous sleaze', a process whereby individuals come to see public office as an extension of their own will and ideological commitments. The introduction into state bureaux of too many people with prior policy commitments and enthusiasms sympathetic to the government of the day could therefore easily undermine the traditional obligations of office framing the conduct of the Civil Service as an institution of government. Similar objections accompany the increased use of special advisers, especially when, as in some well known cases in the UK, this category of actor has been allotted extraordinary powers to issue orders to civil servants, or has, through its gatekeeper role with ministers, effectively been able to negate the influence of civil servants in the area of advising on policy issues (Jones, 2001; Daintith, 2002; Oliver, 2003).

'Zealous sleaze' also arises as a problem when attention turns to the demand that state bureaucrats act 'outside of role', heeding their own consciences in the service of individual 'personal' or 'social responsibility'. Here, a long-standing critique of the one-sided instrumentalism of bureaucratic conduct joins hands with the neo-Aristotelian revival in the field of applied ethics. Encouragement is given to public officials to cultivate an independent mindset and commitments based upon wider moral considerations that transcend the office-specific obligations of their given institutional milieu (Longstaff, 1994).

If the only bona fide kind of moral agency is vested in the idea of the morally autonomous, 'whole' person, then it is not difficult to see how the office- or role-based mentality of the bureaucratic ethos is deemed to fall considerably short of the ethical mark. The problem with this approach is twofold. The first problem concerns its conception of 'the person', in the singular (see Chapters 1 and 2). Clearly, there is not simply one way in which values, for instance, may be personal. For example, values may be personal in the sense of issuing from processes of moral reflection that individuals, rightly or wrongly, identify with their own inner conscience. But values might also be personal in the sense of providing a focus for individual moral commitment and ethical action. These two senses are not identical. Individuals can and do find a (personal) focus for moral life in an ethos – of office, say – which derives from impersonal ethical institutions, rather than their own individual moral reflections. It is in this sense that state bureaucrats should be personally committed to the ethos of their office, even though that ethos lies outside their own individual moral predilections or principles.

Second, and relatedly, this approach reduces matters of public accountability and authority to matters of individual accountability and morality. This, of course, leaves the door wide open for people to see their institutional obligations in terms of their own moral predilections and thus to blur the distinctions between their sense of self and the obligations of the office they happen to occupy. As John Uhr (1994: 166; 1999) has argued, ethics in government is about meeting the demands of public, not individual accountability. While ethics can certainly be about individual choice, that choice is not the individual's own one, but an official one: a choice facing him or her in their role or office as a professional public servant. He concludes that the primary ethics question for public servants is not: what is my individual moral preference as to this or that course of action, 'Rather it is: "what is my duty or responsibility as a public official in relation to this or that course of action"' (Uhr, 1994: 166). We need only think for a minute about what might happen if policemen were allowed to decide for themselves what rules to follow and which to set aside on the basis of their individual moral predilections, or if civil servants in departments of state had individual moral discretion concerning what forms or types of authority to comply with or not.

Since discussions about the ethics of bureaucratic conduct inevitably focus upon the ethics of an office or role, then clearly the ethical template, if that is the right phrase, needs to be tailored to the demands of that limited role, rather than expanded to cover the multiple ethical 'personas' that any individual human being can be implicated in. As Weber (1994b: 362–3) famously put it, 'we are placed in various orders of life, each of which is subject to different laws'. Is it then possible, Weber asked, 'that any ethic in the world could establish substantively identical commandments applicable to all relationships, whether erotic, business, family, or official, to one's relations with one's wife, greengrocer, son, competitor, with a friend of an accused man?'(p. 357). Obviously, state bureaux are no less in need of human beings who are in some basic sense 'sorted out' than any other institutions, but if, as John Rohr (1998: 21) puts it, 'specific questions for government administrators must be postponed until they have first become well-integrated human beings, we may never get on with our work'.

The idea that the state bureaucracy is a substantive ethical domain in its own right, and the associated notion that individuals are involved in multiple ethical personas, obviously seems strange from the perspective of a personalist morality committed to the generalization of populist democratic participation. However, this attempt to 'democratize' state bureaux, like the other populist impulses outlined above, may in fact undermine a rare and important ethical resource: the bureaucracy's 'official' capacity to separate administration of public life from moral absolutes and zealous principle. Something similar is at work in managerially framed demands for 'responsive' government. It is to those demands that attention now turns.

### managerialist critiques and the ethos of bureaucratic office

Underpinning both democratic populist and managerialist demands for 'responsiveness' is an assumption that politicians and bureaucrats have lost sight of their legitimate and effective roles in governance. As we have seen, some critics have framed this problem as one of a democratic deficit and have sought measures whereby elected representatives or citizen/consumers might tame the power of 'officials', enhancing their own status within government, and that of democratic rule more generally, as a result. Others have focused upon the need to exclude elected representatives from the day-to-day operation of state bureaux, thus enabling bureaucrats, reclassified as managers, to get on with the 'core business' of delivering services to customers with maximum economy and efficiency.

While it is undoubtedly true that this managerial imperative, like its democratic relation, is a multifaceted rather than monochromatic creation, there is nonetheless a general consistency and style to the various impulses one might usefully gather under its umbrella heading. In no small part, this is due to the leitmotif animating managerial reforms: the ideal of making government more businesslike.

The rhetoric and imagery of business discourse has had a profound effect on the ways in which state bureaux are conceptualized and their purposes and performances assessed. For over a century, it has been customary for politicians and state bureaucrats to speak fondly and freely of running government on a businesslike basis. By this, though, little more has normally been meant than the salutary aspiration that state bureaux should work more effectively. Recent enthusiasms for 'new public management' have had a rather different intent. Here we see the ideal of 'being like a business' given a much more literal spin, one in which differences between administration as governance and management as delivering services to customers are elided. The conduct of government, in all its manifestations, is represented first and foremost as a particular sort of managerial enterprise. Here, the statist and constitutional dimensions of the work of public officials disappear from view entirely. This contemporary managerial ideal has a number of components, but three in particular stand out. We might label them: market creation; entrepreneurial conduct; and performance measurement (see Goodsell, 2004: 150–61).

A key feature of recent reforms of state bureaux has been the use of market-type mechanisms to reform working practices and ethics, and to create competition within government itself. Internal markets, agencification, contracting out, market testing, and private finance initiatives are but some of the techniques deployed by government to make the provision of public services more businesslike. Each, in their particular ways, involves the establishment of a system for the delivery of public services modelled on a conception of market relations (what we might term an 'imagined' or 'virtual' market), and thus has (in no matter how artificial a manner) the production of profit as one of its basic organizing principles (Scott, 1996).

Justifications for contracting out or 'outsourcing', for instance, frequently begin by invoking the purported failures of in-house systems of provision based on hierarchies of public offices (Painter, 2000). In assuming that office-holders are self-interested and opportunistic, public choice theories of bureaucracy, for example, on which much of the justification for contracting is based, turned traditional virtues of office-based governance into their opposites: permanency was an invitation to complacency, the combination of 'purchaser' and 'provider' roles was regarded as being inevitably accompanied by inefficiency and ineffectiveness as incentives to perform were absent, and so on and so forth. One obvious remedy, given the assumption of inherent 'economic' self-interest and opportunism, was to harness these capacities more productively through the use of competitive tendering and contracting out, or the development of internal markets again based on a contractualist logic (Le Grand, 2003). Contracting not only would reduce costs, due to downward pressure on prices from competitive tendering, but would result in continuous quality improvement as providers sought to outdo each other in meeting service specifications (Painter, 2000: 180).

However, it is clear that when the language of office-holding is replaced by that of market creation, in the form of contracting and competitive tendering, a number of profound consequences can flow for the structural and institutional integrity of public administrative activity, and the ability of public officials to live up to the demands of their office (Painter, 2000). First, in the name of (a distinctive understanding of) economy, efficiency and delivery, public offices and officials in many areas of activity have been replaced by contracted private agencies or businesses. Thus, public officials begin to lose many intrinsic aspects of their role, not least of which is their status as 'authorities'. As government contracts out more and more of its activities, its constituent office-holders really do begin to lose competence in the areas covered by contractors, areas within which until now public office-holders have had unrivalled expertise. As Crouch (2004: 100) has argued, 'as they become mere brokers between public principals and private agents, so professional and technical knowledge passes to the latter. Before long it will become a serious argument in favour of private contractors that only they have the relevant expertise.' Attempts by public officials to write codes of ethics that both defend traditional public service conduct and celebrate market-mimicking conduct, clearly testify to the nature of the choices that contractualization brings in its wake. Attempts by contract mangers to adapt contracts to incorporate the more complex dimensions of public office-holding responsibilities, for instance, highlight both the difficulties of attempting to have your cake and eat it, and, perhaps more importantly, the inappropriateness of such instruments to the tasks in question. These tensions are made evident in the manner in which traditional forms of political accountability are mostly bypassed or supplanted by narrow, one-dimensional mechanisms of contract enforcement and service delivery (Plant, 2003).

In sum, the replacement of the generic, comprehensive forms of supervision, accountability, regulation and teamwork inherent in a system of state service based on a structure of interrelated public offices, by the particularistic, task-specific and often privatized forms inherent in the contract, represents 'a threat to the basis of ethical conduct in the mangement and delivery of public services' (Painter, 2000: 181). This threat refers, primarily, to the ways in which the expert tasks, powers and responsibilities of government in a sovereign state – that forgotten 'core' business of public administration – are irreducible to business terms alone, much as they are to democratic terms. Such reductionism is often attractive – particularly to partisan reform enthusiasts – and clearly not impossible, but its costs are apt to be quite high. The point is that there are limits; limits that is, to the extent to which the complex oscillations and balances between different ethical capacities within a given bureaucratic life-order can be pushed in one direction towards any single vision of ordering without significant, perhaps pyrrhic, costs attaching to such an endeavour: whether that push is framed in terms of the demands of 'audit', 'modernisation', 'governance' or 'managerialism' (du Gay, 2000b; Strathern, 2001). In the case of contracting out, such costs include not only the loss of public expertise and authority – a diminution of office-based competence – but vastly increased scope for patronage and private influence, as well as enhanced opportunities for and temptations to corruption – the blurring of office and self, and the re-emergence in suitably modern guise of office as a tradable good (Doig and Wilson, 1998; Chapman, 2004; Crouch, 2004).

A second central feature of the business management model is the role allotted to enterprise and entrepreneurialism when discussing the changing ethics required of 'new' public managers as opposed to that of public officials. Much like the discussion of 'markets', the enterprise evoked and praised in new public management discourses is of a hybrid or 'virtual' sort. It has little to do with business start-ups or the model habiti of successful entrepreneurs. Rather, the signifier 'Enterprise' functions here as a rhetorical move in a political polemic, 'sexing up' the content of what was, until comparatively recently, a largely non-emotive subject: namely public administration. Thus the category of entrepreneur, when applied to public management, functions itself as an umbrella term for a range of measures deemed necessary to making state bureaux more businesslike. 'Leadership', 'innovation', 'creativity', 'risk-taking', 'experimenting' and so on and so forth are all attached to the signifier to evoke new ideals of conduct to be embodied and expressed in the activities of public officials.

In recent years, the issue of 'executive leadership', for instance, has emerged as a hot topic within the field of public management. The British New Labour Government's White Paper *Modernising Government* (Cabinet Office, 1999a) and its related policy documents, for instance, places considerable emphasis upon the capacity of executive leadership to help change the culture of 'risk aversion' that it considers endemic to the British Civil Service. Thus, the White Paper states that officials must 'move away from the risk-averse culture inherent in government' and that this is to be achieved through removing 'unnecessary bureaucracy which prevents public servants from experimenting, innovating and delivering a better product'. As with a previous attempt to inculcate 'real qualities of leadership' amongst senior civil servants (Efficiency Unit, 1988: para. 35), quite what this means in the British constitutional context, where ministerial accountability is still assumed to be a crucial constitutional convention, is not at all clear. The business of a government department must, inevitably, be scrutinized in a different way from that in which shareholders of a public company judge the operations of a firm. As Bogdanor has argued:

> In the latter case, the net financial outcome of all the firm's operations over a period of time will be evaluated at the annual meeting of shareholders. Parliament, however, may scrutinise any single operation carried out by government at any time, and may do so some considerable time after the operation in question has occurred. This has obvious implications for record-taking and for the avoidance of risk. It makes it difficult for civil servants to be 'creative', or to display the 'leadership' so beloved of the management consultants – indeed, it might be argued that under ... [this] constitution it is for politicians and not for civil servants to display leadership. (2001: 298)

Seen in this light, the creativity and innovation demanded of public officials looks like an invitation to set aside the constitutional obligations of their office. Creativity is represented as something that is blocked by bureaucratic constraint and therefore bureaucracy must bow to its demands. The cases of WorldCom and Enron come to mind, where creativity was exhibited precisely by supplanting or subverting bureaucratic procedure. Public accountability also looks like one of the victims of this managerial demand. By encouraging all senior civil servants to become leaders and to take individual responsibility for their decision-making the managerialist impulse seems to wish to turn them into politicians. This makes accountability enforcement rather difficult. With so many people being 'leaders' in the system, where would the buck stop exactly? It also encourages, contra Weber, individuals to identify the goals of office with their own sense of self.

A third key feature of the business model is the issue of performance and performance evaluation. In Britain, the current Labour government's obsession with 'delivery', combined with non-too-subtle distaste for the traditions of state bureaucrats – that other governing profession – led it quickly to demand changes in the 'ethos' governing the conduct of civil servants. As the former Home Secretary Charles Clarke put it in 2002, 'what I think we'd benefit from is a more effective managerial quality at the top, and I'd say put the "just do it" ethic in, is the change that's needed' (BBC Radio 4, 25 July 2002). Once again, the civil servant as part of an institutional 'gyroscope of state' and bulwark against, what Walt Whitman once called, 'the never ending audacity of elected persons', was to be reconfigured as something akin to an energetic and entrepreneurial 'yes-person'. In order to be able to 'just do it', though, the variety of duties and obligations that bureaucrats were traditionally expected to fulfil had to be transmuted into, or reduced to, the more modest activities of generic management.

In order for managers to 'really' be able to manage, a space had to be created permitting freedom from day-to-day supervision. This distance could not be total, however, only partial and this is where targets, audits and the other paraphernalia of 'responsibilization' come into play. The increased use of devolved budgets, targets, performance evaluation and audit attest to managerial independence at the same time as channelling managerial freedom and shaping managerial action in specific directions (Power, 1997; Rose, 1999; Strathern, 2001).

One of the main features of the contemporary passion for 'performance' is its distinctive reductionism. The language of performance requires relatively simple, mainly quantitative measures to be created so that evaluation of success or failure can be unambiguously reached. But what if certain, perhaps crucial, aspects of a complex and contingent office-based role are simply not amenable to calculation in these terms? What happens to these in the performance mix? According to Power (1997) and Paton (2003), for instance, that which is not amenable to performance 'verification' is simply white noise, at best an irritation, at worst an irrelevance. As Paton puts it:

> The problem is that the language of performance takes no prisoners. Through its lenses, the world is straightforward, situations are or should be controlled, the issues are clear, the criteria unambiguous – and results have either been achieved or they have not. Uncertainty, patchiness, ambiguity, riders and qualifications – all these can be read as excuses, signs of weakness. 'Performance' is categorical – that is precisely its attraction. (2003: 29)

And, some might argue, precisely its weakness. As suggested earlier, office-based obligations tend to be plural rather than singular. A senior civil servant working in the institutional milieu of British central government has, traditionally at least, needed to be, *inter alia*, something of an expert in the ways of the constitution, a bit of a politician, a stickler for procedure and a stoic able to accept disappointments with equanimity (Chapman, 1988; Bogdanor, 2001). As an institution of government, the public administration in Britain therefore reflects and performs not simply bureaucracy but also politics, diplomacy and indeed certain forms of enterprise (clearly, an institution that in the immediate aftermath of the Second World War, under extraordinarily difficult circumstances, succeeded in establishing the National Health Service, a new social security system, the expansion of education at all levels and the nationalization of the major public utilities could hardly be considered to lack the qualities of managerial initiative and enterprise). However, reduction to any one of these various ethical capacities and comportments alone would undoubtedly damage the purposes the public administrator is charged with fulfilling. It would, in other words, have a significant impact upon their ability to live up to the obligations of their office. Such reductionism is not impossible but, as we saw earlier, its costs are apt to be high.

In his classic text *Bureaucracy in Modern Society*, Peter Blau (1956) indicated all too clearly what would happen if performance targets are allotted too much weight in framing the conduct of bureaucratic office. The lessons he outlined appear not to have been learnt. In their text *Re-Inventing Government*, Osborne and Gaebler (1992: 157) commended Arkansas and Florida state administrations for removing funding from adult education programmes if 70 per cent of its graduates failed to get jobs. Blau's argument was that organizations will respond by accepting recruits to the programme on a selective basis. His assumption is borne out in the experience of professionals working throughout the British public sector where, as Power (1997), Miller (2005) and Strathern (2006) for instance, have shown, meeting targets has had a profound impact on the ability of officials to live up to the plural obligations consequent upon their occupation of a given office. In the 1990s, for instance, the British Government's Child Support Agency was held to have found it easier to meet certain financial targets by attempting to gain increased sums from fathers who lived apart from their children but who were already making a contribution to their upbringing, rather than to seek new fathers who were absent and give no assistance (Jordan, 1994: 276).

As the House of Lords Public Service Committee (1998) commented on the increased use of 'performance management' techniques in the British Civil Service, targets and performance 'aren't everything'. Because a system of government requires officials to act as custodians of the constitutional values it embodies, it cannot frame their official role or persona solely in terms of performance, responsiveness and meeting targets. The pursuit of more 'businesslike' management in government, no matter how important it may be in and of itself, has to recognize the constitutional and political limits to which it is subject (Johnson, 1983: 194).

As I argued earlier, the managerial imperative, like its populist democratic relation, is a multifaceted rather than monochromatic creation. It is probably best not to overstate its singleness of purpose or its technical homogeneity. Nonetheless, the transparency it demands in all its manifestations is more troubling than it might at first appear. It is certainly possible to view constructs such as 'customer satisfaction' – in both a managerialist and a populist democratic manifestation – as relatively banal devices for increasing the efficiency and effectiveness of governmental departments and agencies by ensuring that officials include new calculations in the performance of their role. However, the language of the 'customer', as part and parcel of a distinctive way of conceiving of the activity of state service – that of a commercial enterprise – not only has clear limits in the public administrative context, but also has clear and present dangers for the ethos of office traditionally conceived. For the languages of managerialism, with their demands for explicit distinctions – between policy and management, and autonomy and authority, for instance – override and thus, in a sense, occlude many of the virtues of bureaucratic office, because the latter simply cannot be registered in the language managerialism insists on using. As John Rohr (1998: xi), for instance, has argued, this is a 'forest and trees problem of the first order ... and underscores one of the most fundamental problems with the public management movement', namely its diminution of the statist and constitutional character of public bureaucratic office through the substitution of a language of political administration by a managerialist lexicon.

**the ethos of bureaucratic office and state interest**   Clearly, political circumstances change, and so should the machinery of government. After all, too narrow a focus on the inviolability of a set of pre-existing commitments can be just as problematic, politically and administratively, as too abstract a fixation on the imperatives of epochal change. Institutions must be allowed to adapt from their original purposes if the circumstances in which they operate have changed. This, though, begs a very large question. Have political circumstances changed so fundamentally that we can do away with office-based conceptions of ethical agency?

To judge by the comments of some advocates of entrepreneurial government, or social governance, for example, many of the problems the state evolved to address have been solved; the only issues left to deal with concern better management of contracts, or how to make decision-making more 'deliberative' or 'participative'. These may be the 'parish pump' concerns of what has been epochally characterized as a fundamentally 'anti-statist' age (Mulgan, 1994; Gamble and Wright, 2004), but are such assumptions warranted? Has the state and its hierarchically structured domain of offices been transcended?

We have been here before. Early in the twentieth century we find Max Weber railing against the various political romanticisms – anarchists, socialists, armchair littérateurs – who would do away with bureaucracy, law and other detritus of the liberal state in pursuit of their own radical 'visions'. Weber was quite clear that the ethos of bureaucratic office constituted a virtue that a liberal regime, with a parliamentary democracy and market economy, could not do without. As we saw earlier, he was adamant that 'without this supremely ethical discipline and self-denial the whole apparatus would disintegrate' (Weber, 1994b: 331).

To reiterate. For Weber, the state bureau comprises the social and cultural conditions of a distinctive and independent comportment of the person, one that is basically non-sectarian in character. Among the most important of these conditions is that the office constitutes a 'vocation' (*Beruf*) – a focus of ethical commitment and duty, autonomous of and superior to the holder's extra-official ties to kith, kin, class or conscience. For Weber, this marks out the bureau as a specific *Lebensordnung* or 'life-order', and provides the bureaucrat with a distinctive ethical bearing and status-conduct. The ethical attributes of the good bureaucrat – strict adherence to procedure, acceptance of sub- and super-ordination, *esprit de corps*, abnegation of personal moral enthusiasms, commitment to the purposes of the office – are to be seen as a positive moral achievement requiring the mastery of definite ethical techniques and routines – declaring one's 'personal' interest, developing appropriate professional relations with one's colleagues, subordinating one's 'self' to the dictates of procedural decision-making – through which individuals come to acquire the disposition and ability to conduct themselves according to the ethos of bureaucratic office (Weber, 1978: Vol. II; Minson, 1993; Hunter, 1994a; du Gay, 2000a).

In addressing the different kinds of responsibility that particular 'offices' make on those subject to their demands, Weber is insisting on the irreducibility of different orders of life and on the consequent necessity of applying different ethical protocols to them. Forged in the party system and tempered by the organizational adversarialism of the parliament, the politician belongs to an order of life quite unlike that of the state bureaucrat. The party leader possesses the political abilities and ethical demeanour required by the unremitting struggle to win and regain power. As Weber makes clear, it is not the trained expertise and impersonal dedication of the official that equips the politician to pursue the worldly interests of the state in the face of hostile and unpredictable economic and political environment. At the same time, however, those very same capacities that enable the bureaucrat to live up to the demands of their office also enable him or her, in their different but no less essential way, to serve the interests of the state. The key to the 'self denial' that Weber recognized as a crucial feature of the performance of bureaucratic office, was a trained indifference – *sine ira et studio* – to party or partisan creed, combined with an attachment to the authority of the state, political order or regime. In other words, official indifference meant not being committed, by convictions guiding one's official actions, to the creed and platform of a political party, while being able without a crisis of conscience to further the policies of any current governing party. In this way, state bureaucrats were likely to greet the panaceas and enthusiasms of all political parties with caution. This was part of their job and in performing that role they could be seen as servants of the state. As Weber makes clear, it is the honour of bureaucrats not to allow extra-official commitments to determine the manner in which they perform the duties associated with their office.

More recently, Michael Lind (2005: 34–7) has written of the how the bureaucratic 'mandarinate' – that other governing profession – having helped to deliver the state from the dangers of 'mobocracy' in the early twentieth century now finds itself scapegoated by a range of powerful forces: managerialist, populist, libertarian and religious. To the managerialist, the bureaucrat is an amateur; to the libertarian, a statist; to the populist, an elitist; and to the religious fundamentalist, a heathen. Lind (2005: 37) asks the rhetorical question: 'What could be worse than a society run by such people?' His answer is simple: 'a society without them. The contemporary US, and to a lesser extent Britain, shows the consequences of turning a modern democracy into a mandarin free zone.' Lind is referring, in particular, to the vast social experiment with managerialism and populist democratic mechanisms that has taken place in these and other liberal regimes, an experiment 'as audacious in its own way, as that of Soviet collectivism' (p. 37). Referring explicitly to developments in America Lind writes:

> The US ship of state veers now in one direction, now the other. From a distance, one might conclude that the captain is a maniac. But a spyglass reveals that there is no captain or crew at all, only rival gangs of technocrats, ideologues, populists and zealots devoted to Jesus Christ or Adam Smith, each boarding the derelict vessel and capturing the wheel briefly before being tossed overboard. (2005: 37)

For both Weber and Lind, in their rather different ways, something important is being registered: the crucial role of the ethos of bureaucratic office as a sort of 'gyroscope of state', helping to provide, for example, the stability, continuity and institutional memory that were once deemed crucial to the realization of responsible and effective governance. It is precisely this *etatiste* role and status-conduct that constitutes the distinctiveness and virtue of the ethos of bureaucratic office, and yet is also exactly this, as we have seen, which cannot be registered in the pervasive languages of managerialism or democratic populism.

How then do we recover and rehabilitate these 'virtues' in the context of the ongoing 'audacious' social experiment? Clearly, both Weber and Lind offer some important lessons. Another important source we might mine is that early modern tradition of political thought known as *prudentia civilis* or civil prudence, which sought to develop an ethic of state in the far from fertile context of enduring religious strife in early modern Europe. I turn to this strand of thought for two reasons. First, because it offers a distinctive and coherent conception of the detheologized sovereign state as a structure of offices. Secondly, because it indicates how official non-sectarian comportments of the person can be formed, and outlines the positive political and governmental ends they can serve.

Civil prudence is associated with a strand of natural law, ethics and political thought that developed most forcefully in seventeenth- and eighteenth-century German states, through the work of Samuel Pufendorf, Christian Thomasius and others, but which has obvious (and acknowledged) antecedents in the work of, *inter alia*, Jean Bodin and Thomas Hobbes (for an overview, see Hunter, 2001). It was a practical ethic, a form of training in the arts of good government offered to princes, political advisers or counsels and other categories of governmental person, and provided a certain way of thinking about the purposes of government, forming a type of public conscience and professional character suited to hold office within a civil state. The precepts and practices of civil prudence offered princes, officers and political advisers an immanent ethic of state, one reminiscent, *avant la lettre*, of Max Weber's 'ethic of responsibility', based as it was on an awareness of the existence of rival yet ultimate moral ends, and thus of the costs of seeking to pursue any one of them at the expense of the others (Weber, 1994a; see also Larmore, 1987). In so doing, civil prudence contributed to the early modern proto-liberal settlements that, in the wake of the Peace of Westphalia, helped to becalm the European wars of religion.

In civil prudential thought the civil state was conceived of as a structure of offices – sovereign, political advisor, public official – each of which had its own purposes, modus operandi and associated register of vices and virtues. Individuals placed in different offices would need to learn to comport themselves appropriately and to 'regionalise their conscience' accordingly (Saunders, 2002). For instance, they would need to learn to distinguish their responses to questions facing them in an official capacity from other commitments they might have, whether in relation to clan, kith or religious belief, for example. In their official capacity, therefore, they had to learn to adopt a more or less finely honed posture of neutrality or impartiality towards controversial religious or moral matters.

According to civil prudential thought, the state should be indifferent to the private morality and beliefs of its citizens; it should be concerned only with their public conduct. However, if civil peace was threatened, the state reserved unto itself the right and duty to intervene by whatever means necessary to impose peace upon its subject population. It was the responsibility of the state, not the subject's own right, to judge the degree of jeopardy in every case. The state carried (and must carry) the authority of its subjects' own will and choice to make that judgement on their behalf, and to act decisively upon it. Indeed, each subject had a right against every other subject that it should do just this.

Early modern civil prudence therefore provided a series of axioms concerning the necessity for, and organization of, something approximating to the structure of the modern state as a free-standing, independent entity. It indicated why and how the 'state' was an entity which can claim for itself a distinctive, overriding, civil authority. This authority is distinctive in three ways. First, the authority of the state is both binding and content-independent. It is by no means the authority of the people who happen to constitute the subjects of the state, either individually or collectively. The conception of the state promoted by civil prudence therefore sets its face against civic republican doctrines of popular sovereignty. Secondly, the authority of the state is not congruent with the individual authority of the holders of the great offices of state. In this sense, civil prudence sets its face against theological and feudal conceptions. Thirdly, the state is conceived of as an abstract structure of offices, and associated with these offices are a vast array of powers, resources, mechanisms and techniques that are not really under the individual control of the human being who happened to occupy the office at any given time, but which inhered in the very purposes and habitus of the office itself (Geuss, 2001).

This de-transcendentalized conception of the state as a structure of offices offers some useful tools for challenging the arguments made by populists and managerialist reformers. With regard to the former, for instance, civil prudence enables us to immediately point out that one of the main reasons for having a free-standing coercive structure called a state is precisely that it be devoid of popular control. The authority of the state and its office-holders cannot be the authority of 'the people' deemed to constitute the subjects of the state. Indeed, the basic fact of independence means that there 'is always going to be a gap between the political power of the state and the effective powers of the populace, and, on this argument, that is a good thing' (Geuss, 2001: 129). Put more bluntly, the concept of the state is an invention designed to oppose the doctrine of popular sovereignty. Thus, while some of the institutions of representative democracy may serve some very useful purposes – as information exchange fora, for instance – and some forms of democratic rhetoric might function as 'a useful social-psychological emollient'(Geuss, 2001: 129), helping to reconcile people to their de facto subjugation to an entity that has much greater power than they do, and which doesn't always do or give them what they want, 'the hope that state-power could ever really be "our" power or fully under collective control is completely misplaced' (p. 129). More importantly, what Unger (1986) terms (and demands) the 'cracking open of everything to democratic politics' is potentially disastrous for security and social peace – the raison d'être of the state. For instance:

> One of the points of having police is that they can face down the local lynch mob. The police serve *this* function perfectly well even if they are the agents of a highly authoritarian and non-democratic central government. That means, though, that if the state as an institutional coercive apparatus which is beyond the control of its members has a rationale at all and is going to continue to exist, then the moralising ideal of full Rousseauean political autonomy is illusory ... (Geuss, 2001: 129)

One lesson civil prudence offers to populist democratic reformers of state bureaux is that the sovereign state as an independent, abstract structure of offices retains pre-eminent value. It, and it alone, provides the conditions under which subjects can enjoy civil rights and freedoms. Attempts to democratize state bureaux may therefore, as Weber too pointed out, undermine a rare, reliable and important ethical resource: the state bureaucracy's capacity to divorce the administration and 'management' of civic life from moral absolutes and zealous principle. The dreams and schemes of managerialist reformers similarly fail to register the statist character of public bureaucratic office and so civil prudence has some useful correctives to offer them, too.

In seeking to recast bureaucratic office-holders as generic managers, managerialists constrict their role in governance. They do so by evacuating the bureaucratic role of much of its determinate content. By conceiving of state bureaux as predominantly 'delivery' mechanisms, for instance, some of the crucial *etatiste* responsibilities of office become literally 'inconceivable'. In Britain, for example, the Blair government's informal 'all on one team' approach, combined with its singular focus on 'delivery' and its experiments with fostering a 'just do it ethic' among civil servants, has had some unfortunate consequences for the ethos of bureaucratic office, and thus for the effective management of the state and for the provision of effective and responsible governance.

The revelations elicited by the Hutton Inquiry, into events surrounding the death of the government weapons expert, Dr David Kelly, of the extent to which, under the 'New' Labour administration, the traditional bureaucratic practices of careful and precise note-taking and writing of minutes, had fallen into abeyance were both striking and deeply worrying. It was revealed most vividly when Jonathan Powell, the Prime Minister's (partisan) Chief-of-Staff, disclosed to Hutton that of an average 17 meetings a day in Downing Street, only 3 were minuted. When role-specific differences between politicians, special advisers and career state bureaucrats, for example, are elided, then detailed record-keeping, it would appear, can be deployed more flexibly; perhaps, because it's assumed that everyone is obviously singing from the same hymn sheet, the need for things like minutes is less obvious. What the Butler report into the use of intelligence in the lead up to the invasion of Iraq famously described as 'the informality and circumscribed character of the Government's procedures' seriously risked 'reducing the scope for informed collective political judgement'. As a former cabinet secretary (Lord) Richard Wilson (2004: 85) commented in relation to this point, formal meetings and minute-taking, for instance, might seem overly 'bureaucratic' and thus very un-modern technologies, yet they play a crucial practical role in ensuring good government and provide a necessary underpinning for the realization of constitutionally sanctioned accountability requirements – of ministerial responsibility to parliament, for example – by ensuring a proper record of governmental decision-making exists and that agreed actions are clearly delineated.

Linked to this, Michael Quinlan (2004) has shown how the government's zealous managerialist focus on 'delivery' has occurred at the expense of attention to bureaucratic due process. As he puts it, a singular focus on delivery can easily 'slide into a sense that outcome is the only true reality and that process is flummery. But the two are not antithetical, still less inimical to one another. Process is care and thoroughness; it is consultation, involvement … legitimacy and acceptance; it is also record, auditability and clear accountability. It is often accordingly a significant component of outcome itself; and the more awkward and demanding the issue – especially amid the gravity of peace and war – the more it may come to matter' (Quinlan, 2004: 128). Too exclusive a focus on delivery can therefore have the effect of undermining other aspects of the role that an official is charged with undertaking.

What we see here is a managerialist agenda constitutionally incapable of registering the statist – non-partisan – character of public bureaucratic office-holding. By casting reasons of state and public administration in term of its own 'business' model, managerialist reforms have assisted in the politicization of state service. In focusing so determinedly – and simplistically – on 'delivery', such managerial reforms have enabled the governing political party to buttress its own power and influence at the expense of the proper exercise of sovereignty. The managerialist approach to government can therefore have deleterious consequences for the maintenance of the 'independent' state-oriented obligations of office, and for what Dobel (1999: 41) describes as a 'prized accomplishment' of modern political existence, the separation of public office and 'self'. It is in this latter aspect of the authority of the state – the distinction between an office and its human occupant – that we encounter the crucial distinctions between individual and persona that preoccupy civil prudential discussions of the moral and ethical aspects of office-holding.

One of the central figures of *prudentia civilis*, Samuel Pufendorf (1691/2003), formulated a distinctive ethic of office through a doctrine of 'moral entities'. For Pufendorf, as Saunders (2002: 2182–3) has made clear, moral entities are artificial sets of duties and capacities enabling human individuals to organize a particular civil existence. And moral 'personae' are the central 'moral entities'. A moral persona is thus the individual or individuals to whom a moral entity, or status, has been 'superadded' or attached, 'to develop the life of man and to reduce it to order'.

[T]he way in which moral entities are produced can scarcely be better expressed than by the word imposition. For they do not arise out of the intrinsic nature of the physical properties of things, but they are superadded, at the will of intelligent entities, to things already existent and physically complete, and to their natural effects, and, indeed, come into existence only by the determination of their authors. (Pufendorf, quoted in Saunders, 2002: 2182)

As Saunders (2002: 2182) indicates, the notion of moral entities, for Pufendorf, 'detaches attributes designed to order civil existence from pre-existing theological essences … In this way, Pufendorf can formulate an ethics of civil conduct within the terms of natural law, re-conceptualised on the basis of juridical concepts of persona and office'.

As a result of this disaggregation of individual and persona, 'one and the same individual may sustain several persons together, provided that the various functions which attend such persons can be simultaneously met by the same person [individual]' (Pufendorf, quoted in Saunders, 2002: 2182). So the one physical individual cannot be 'both a master and a slave or a husband and a wife at the same time, but can be the head of a family, a senator in parliament or at the king's court a counsellor' (Saunders, 2002: 2182–3). Furthermore, this pluralization of personae in relation to their specific purposes is given an extra spin by Pufendorf when he suggests that 'the obligations attached to any one state [status] may in their parts be derived from different principles' such that 'he who has gathered from the Sacred Scriptures the parts of the duties of priests, assuredly cannot deny that those priests are also obliged to perform such duties as are required by the constitutions of individual governments' (Pufendorf, quoted in Saunders, 2002: 2183). For Pufendorf, then, 'there is no status morally so fundamental – including the clerical – that its rights transcend the rights attaching to all other statuses' (Saunders, 2002: 2183).

Pufendorfian offices are not therefore predicated upon the existence of an integral, trans-contextual moral agency. Rather, in this civil prudential conception of offices, individuals are required to cultivate a plurality of functionally specific moral personae. It is these, and these alone, that form the locus of obligation for individuals qua moral agents. As Pufendorf suggested, it is the duty of citizens not to allow their spiritual zeal to overpower their civic demeanour; and as Weber later made clear, it is the honour of the bureaucrat not to allow extra official commitments to determine the manner in which they perform the duties associated with their office. It is precisely at this nexus, though, that contemporary democratic populist and managerialist programmes have some of their most deleterious effects.

In Britain, the Hutton and Butler inquiries, mentioned earlier, provided a welter of evidence concerning the manner in which partisan conviction, and a populist and managerialist 'pair of spectacles' (Hennessy, 2004) led the New Labour Government to view the British Civil Service simply as a mechanism for delivering whatever it wanted. The demands of a managerialist 'just do it' ethic, combined with suspicion of established – deemed 'conservative' – bureaucratic procedure has been conspicuously displayed in a number of farragoes, from the shambolic attempts to abolish the post of Lord Chancellor and the appellate jurisdiction of the House of Lords, up to and including more recent parliamentary debacles over hunting with dogs, 'living wills' and 'control orders'. What Hutton and Butler suggested is that this was not simply a reflection of the 'normal' complexities of governing, but rather a widespread feature of a New Labour 'style' of governing; a product of attempts to bypass established machinery of government, and the rules and procedures they gave effect to. It is reminiscent of what Jane Caplan (1988) in another context described as the nightmare of 'government without administration'. In Michael Quinlan's words, Hutton and Butler clearly indicated that the Labour Government had

> little interest in or tolerance for distinctions of function and responsibility between different categories of actor within the Government machine (except perhaps when political defences needed to be erected, as over the purported 'ownership' of the September, 2002 dossier). Not only in the interface with the intelligence structure and in the way Alastair Campbell operated within and beyond No. 10, but also in matters such as the saga of Jo Moore and Martin Sixsmith in the Department of Transport, there was sense of all participants – ministers, civil servants, special policy advisers, public relations handlers – being treated as part of an undifferentiated resource for the support of the central executive. (2004)

Civil prudence required states to develop ideologically neutral judiciaries and bureaucracies – within the limits of the possible – and Weber stressed the importance of these institutions being protected from party capture once states acquired democratic electoral systems. What Quinlan's comments suggest is that a partisan ideological and managerialist approach to these institutions can quite easily undermine their 'independent' state-oriented obligations of office. When a governing party exhibits no tolerance for distinctions between different offices of state, and the particular functions they fulfil, and sees them only in terms of what they can deliver for the party, then those offices are but a small step away from capture. Here 'office' is regarded as an extension of the governing party's own will and ideological commitments – even if that ideology describes itself as non-ideological and supremely pragmatic, in the New Labour jargon 'what works is what's best'. This sort of capture has serious repercussions for the ability of a range of personae to live up to the demands of their particular offices, and therefore for those offices to fulfil their designated purposes. The treatment by a governing party of all manner of state offices as 'an undifferentiated resource' suggests a paradigmatic instance of what Weber (1994b: 357) termed 'unworldliness' – the desire to 'establish commandments of identical content' across different life-orders.

Similarly, as we saw earlier, such 'zealous sleaze' also arises from the demand that state bureaucrats act 'outside of role', heeding their own consciences in the service of individual 'personal' or 'social' responsibility. Here, officials are encouraged to develop an independent mindset and commitments based upon wider – trans-contextual or even universal – moral considerations that transcend the 'instrumental', 'one-sided' obligations of their given official milieu. Rather than separating out extra official obligations from the conduct of official duties, bureaucrats are expected to incorporate such obligations into their official thinking. Neutrality or impartiality is registered as an impossible conduct, and indeed as a fundamentally unethical one.

Underpinning this demand is a conception of the human being as a morally autonomous 'whole' person whose ultimate arbiter of the true and the good is its own conscience. For Pufendorf, though, as we have seen, there is no status morally so fundamental, that its duties and rights transcend those attaining to other statuses. The 'person of conscience' does not, then, trump all other personae. Indeed, if it did, the functions that other personae were forged to fulfil would find no means of expression. They would simply disappear. Are we really ready to live without the ethos of bureaucratic office and the persona that it gives rise to, for instance? The littérateurs or political romantics chided by Weber, and whose 'visions' for the body politic are still alive and well today, may well answer with a loud 'Yes'. But for those with less metaphysical inclinations, attempts to moralize, democratize or otherwise 'elevate' or transcend state bureaux might well appear to undermine an important ethical resource: the bureaucratic persona's 'official' capacity to separate the administration of public life from moral absolutes and ideological principle.

As I have attempted to show, civil prudence provides an ethical rationale for the pre-eminent authority of the state, and a role-ethical deportment whereby officers of the state responsibly exercise their various governing powers through adhering to the purposes and limits their offices bestow upon their persons. It is an immanent ethic in that it specifies normative limits for state action: the civil state binds itself to pursuing purposes and observing limits that are internal to its concept– securing social peace and the conditions for sociality – rather than defined by ideals of moral expressivism – an all pervading sense of community or an inalienable right to personal autonomy, for example (Larmore, 1987; Holmes, 1995; Minson, 2004).[3]

The lesson of civil prudentialism is that the sovereign state as a structure of offices retains a pre-eminent value. It, and it alone, provides the conditions under which subjects can enjoy civil rights and freedoms (including the right and freedom to sketch managerialist fantasies and populist democratic dreams in which the ethos of bureaucratic office has been superseded). Attempting to turn such dreams and schemes into practice is fraught with many dangers, as the foregoing analysis has testified. The central hazard, though, is that unworldly attempts to move beyond sovereignty and its offices can risk reproducing the very – unpredictable, hostile and insecure – conditions the state was first instituted to avoid.

**concluding comments**   In this chapter I have sought to make a case for the continuing indispensability of office-specific conceptions of moral agency in the realm of governmental and political action. In particular, I have attempted to provide a number of arguments in support of the continued relevance of the ethos of bureaucratic office to the practice of state administration. In so doing, I have suggested that many of the audacious experiments in public management – whether couched in populist democratic or overtly managerialist terms – that have been foisted upon state bureaux over the last two to three decades have had the effect of undermining the 'core business' of public administration: running a state as a state and operating a constitution. Slogans about the state being the servant not the master of 'the people' (Mulgan and Wilkinson, 1992) or those that espouse the managerial line of 'businesslike is best', have a way of trapping minds. And for such trapped minds, state bureaux can only be viewed as a profound disappointment, ripe for transcendence or radical reform.

How one seeks to deal with such disappointment is the crucial question. For democratic populists and managerialists this involves imagining the state and its offices as something other than they are. In particular, they want the state and its bureaux to conform to or express some sort of principle. In so doing, as I have attempted to show, they serve to evacuate state or public administration of its determinate content. The work of Max Weber, and of that tradition of thought known as civil prudence, offer an alternative way of dealing with such disappointment. At heart, this means coming to terms with the state's imperfection and accepting it as an inevitable part of its positivity. After all, as Pufendorf's work indicates, the state is born imperfect, for to be born it had 'to renounce perfection, its own and that of its subject population, making do instead with its capacity to enforce social peace and their capacity to act civilly' (Hunter, 2005: 9). It is also imperfect because it is nothing more than a bundle of offices – political, legal, bureaucratic, military, police – reliant on contingent funding, fallible (or, as we have seen, worse) management, and prone to varying degrees of dissolution arising from a host of sources (corruption, incompetence, ideological conflict, military disasters, etc.) (p. 5). And yet, what else can do its job? Certainly nothing sketched in the dreams and schemes of populist democratic critics and/or their managerialist counterparts. So, while they and the advocates of other visions – of global cosmopolitanism or of religious fundamentalism, for instance – seek to move beyond the state and its structure of offices, for others it might be useful to follow in the footsteps of John Dewey for whom it was 'always important to rediscover the state'.

## notes

1   Interestingly, though, while both conceptions of 'responsiveness' are distinctive and non-reducible, they have often fed off one another in specific programmes of administrative reform. Thus proponents of increased democratic control have often advocated managerialist measures to achieve their desired ends, while managerialist critics have themselves cited enhanced consumer choice as one of the 'democratic' outcomes of their favoured reform measures (du Gay, 2000a; Peters, 2000b).

2   In the United Kingdom, the current government has indicated its desire to open up more and more senior public positions to external competition. It wants to do this not only to attract the requisite talent able and willing to deliver its reform agenda, but also because an 'open' civil service is deemed to be preferable to a 'closed' civil service. As Bogdanor puts it:

> [T]his argument would seem at first sight to be unanswerable. Yet, if the Civil Service is, as some former heads such as Warren Fisher and Edward Bridges believed, a genuine profession, ought it not in fact to be closed? It would not, after all, be very sensible to suggest to someone who objected to unqualified doctors or lawyers that he or she favoured a 'closed' medical or legal profession. For professions are, almost by definition, closed. (2001: 295)

The big issue is whether the Civil service as a profession devoted to running a state and operating a constitution, based on its own particular expertise and obligations of office, is to survive or whether it is simply set to become a politicized vehicle for enthusiastically delivering the government's agenda.

3  By 'expressivism' I am referring to those critics who require a political order or institutional regime to express certain moral ideals – such as an all pervading spirit of community or an inalienable right to personal autonomy. Such critics assume that these domains should express the highest ideals of its members, and thus refuse to envision the possibility that the political and institutional realms and other areas of life 'may heed different priorities' (Larmore, 1987: 93).

# the tyranny of the epochal: change, epochalism and organizational casuistry

> The romantics transform ... every instant into a historical moment ... But they do even more than this. Every moment is transformed into a point in a structure ... so every point is a circle at the same time, and every circle a point. The community is an extended individual, the individual a concentrated community. Every historical moment is an elastic point in the vast fantasy of the philosophy of history with which we dispose over peoples and eons.
>
> (Carl Schmitt, *Political Romanticism*)

> The one thing that does not change is that at each and any time it appears there have been 'great changes'.
>
> (Marcel Proust, *Within a Budding Grove*)

As I indicated in Chapter 5, 'change' in today's management terminology, is frequently represented as an unalloyed good. Indeed, it has become a matter of serious criticism to accuse an institution or an individual of being incapable of adjusting to – or, better still, 'thriving on' – change, or of failing to grasp its multitudinous 'opportunities'. Change, here, means transformation, not piecemeal reform, but radical transmutation (perhaps 'transubstantiation' captures it best): those who cannot or will not accede to its demands are 'history'.

In this chapter, I focus on this discourse of organizational 'change' as it has appeared in a specific context, the contemporary field of public administration, and, in particular, I explore its role as a rhetorical device in reshaping the identity of public service. I do so, first, by seeking to indicate the epochalist bent of much contemporary theorizing about contemporary economic and organizational change – in both its academic and its more commercial manifestations. I highlight its reliance on a logic of over-dramatic dichotomization that establishes the available terms of debate and critique in advance, in highly simplified terms either for or against, and offers no escape from its own categorical imperatives. Secondly, I show how a particular discourse of organizational change mobilizes support for attempts for the 're-invention' or 'modernization' of the public administration as an institution of government. Finally, I seek to offer a few words in support of the seemingly unfashionable art of 'piecemeal reform', as Popper (1944/1985) famously put it, or what I refer to as case-based organizational reasoning or 'organizational casuistry'.[1]

**all or nothing at all: the extremism of 'change'**  What is striking about much contemporary organizational theorizing – whether critical or more commercially purposeful – is the epochalist terms in which it is framed. By 'epochalist' I refer to the use of a periodizing schema in which a logic of dichotomization establishes the available terms of debate in advance, either for or against. As Tom Osborne has indicated with reference to contemporary social theories, epochal accounts

> are those which seek to encapsulate the *Zeitgeist* in some kind of overarching societal designation; that we live in a postmodern society, a modern society, an information society, a rationalised society, a risk society … Such epochal … theories tend to set up their co-ordinates in advance, leaving no 'way out' from their terms of reference. (1998: 17)

Whether the theorizing in question is being conducted by Zygmunt Bauman (2000 – 'liquid modernity'), Scott Lash and John Urry (1994 – 'economies of signs'), Manuel Castells (2000 – 'the network society'), Tom Peters (1992 – 'chaos' or 'crazy times') or Charles Leadbeater (1999 – 'the knowledge-driven economy'), the interpretation proffered bitterly pessimistic or dizzyingly optimistic, the common denominator is an epochalist emphasis. A couple of examples should suffice to illustrate this argument.

In recent years, certain arguments have been advanced within the realm of social theory – often associated with terms such as 'economies of signs', 'the network society' and 'the knowledge economy' – that we are living in an era in which economic and organizational life has become thoroughly 'culturalized'. One of the most sustained attempts to make this argument is contained in Lash and Urry's *Economies of Signs and Space*. Here, it is argued that:

> Economic and symbolic processes are more than ever interlaced and interarticulated; that is … the economy is increasingly culturally inflected and … culture is more and more economically inflected. Thus, the boundaries between the two become more and more blurred and the economy and culture no longer function in regard to one another as system and environment. (1994: 64)

In attempting to back up this claim that the economy is now more than ever 'culturalized', Lash and Urry point to a number of developments. For instance, they claim that organizations whose business involves the production and distribution of cultural hardware and software have become the most innovative and creative economic actors in the world today. The 'creative' or 'culture' industries broadly defined and other 'soft' knowledge intensive industries not only represent the most important economic growth sectors but also offer paradigmatic instances of the generalized process of 'de-differentiation' of economy/culture relations (Lash and Urry, 1994: 108–9).

At the same time, Lash and Urry argue that a fundamental shift has taken place in the extent to which meaning is attached to products and services. They argue that more and more of the goods and services produced for consumers across a range of sectors can be conceived of as 'cultural goods', in that they are deliberately and instrumentally inscribed with particular meanings and associations as they are produced and circulated in a conscious attempt to generate desire for them among end-users. As such, 'what is increasingly produced is not material objects but *signs*' (Lash and Urry, 1994: 4). They assert that there is a growing aestheticization or fashioning of, often seemingly banal, products where these are marketed to consumers in terms of particular clusters of meaning, often linked to 'lifestyles', and this is taken as an indication of the radically increased importance of 'culture' to the production and circulation of a multitude of goods and services. This process, they argue, has been accompanied by the increased influence of what are often termed the 'cultural intermediary' occupations of advertising, design and marketing.

Lash and Urry's account of contemporary economic and organizational change can be described as epochalist in that it is both founded upon and sustains a dualism that is also a periodization. A dualism is posited, for instance between 'use-value' and 'sign value', which is then used to frame two loosely periodized epochs – the less culturally inflected past (Fordism, as they have it) and the thoroughly culturalized present (aesthetically reflexive post-Fordism/postmodernism). In so doing, they reduce a range of economic, social and organizational changes to one or two 'overarching' and fundamental characteristics. Clearly reductionism is necessary to any periodization – otherwise we are in danger of reproducing the 'one damn thing after another' approach to historical explanation. However, it is important to note that the empirical significance of these epochal claims does need careful consideration. After all, authors working in fields as diverse as organization studies, the social anthropology of economic life and the history of advertising, for example, have indicated just how empirically unsubstantiated are the exemplary oppositions – between a more 'use-value'-centred past and a more 'sign-value'-centred present – that run through epochalist accounts such as this (Douglas and Isherwood, 1979;

Miller, 1995; du Gay, 2000a; McFall, 2002). Perhaps much of the hyperbole surrounding epochal claims of 'increased culturalization' can be explained by the fact that those taking the 'cultural turn' in the field of economic and organizational analysis are busy finding culture where none was thought to exist. However, they also tend, perhaps, to work against the grain of 'cultural economic' analysis, as an emergent form of inquiry concerned with the practical material–cultural ways in which 'economic' and 'organizational' objects and persons are put together, by, as Osborne (1998: 19) has it, setting up their co-ordinates too far in advance and thus leaving 'no way out' from their terms of reference.[2] This has the effect of rendering certain potentially significant, if (seen from the heights of the epochal mindset) often seemingly banal, contextual details unimportant or invisible (Law, 2002; McFall and du Gay, 2002). After all, techniques of economic and organizational management rarely come ready-made; they have to be invented, implanted, stabilized and reproduced. This involves much hard, frequently tedious, work, whose success and effects cannot be taken for granted 'in advance'. Thus the emergence of such techniques is probably not best explicated in terms of large-scale transformative processes – transitions from Fordism to post-Fordism or organized to disorganized capitalism, and so on – beloved of epochal theorizing, but rather cry out for the 'grey, meticulous and patiently documentary' forms of analysis recommended by Foucault (1986c: 76) among many others (Law, 1994, 2002; Callon, 1998). This should not be taken to imply an out-and-out rejection of all claims of 'increased culturalization'. Clearly, there are any number of substantive developments in organizational life – such as the recent obsession with 'culture' amongst the senior managers of many enterprises – that might conceivably be explicable in terms of some suitably situated 'culturalization' hypothesis. However, it is important that such claims be assessed with care and on more of a case-by-case basis – through a more casuistic form of organizational analysis – rather than simply being assumed or asserted. As Paul di Maggio (1994: 27), for example, has argued, in relation to the upsurge of interest in all things 'cultural' in the field of economic and organizational analysis, 'the price of the insights and explanatory power that a cultural perspective can generate is an enduring scepticism towards "culturalist" accounts that claim too much or generalise too broadly'.

If Lash and Urry's account is epochalist – tending towards an over-dramatic dichotomization that not only renders important contextual details insignificant if not entirely invisible, but also makes the changes they outline appear largely inevitable and hence incontrovertible – then the work of Tom Peters (1987, 1992, 1994) is the same, but much more so.

Clearly, Peters is not involved in the same practice as Lash and Urry. His work is not primarily academic but explicitly hortatory. It is attempting to mobilize practising managers around a new image of their role and how they should conduct themselves at work (and outside work, too). It pursues its distinct purpose in a profoundly evangelical manner, one designed to challenge and subvert the 'established church' (now fallen, in Peters's eyes) of what is described as 'traditional' management (Hopfl, 1992; Pattison, 1997). The key dichotomy is between the ossified 'old', which is in need of urgent 're-invention', and the 'visionary' new, whose demands must be heeded or disaster will result. The dominant metaphors are 'discontinuity', 'instability', 'fluidity' and 'chaos'. Radical transformation is seen as inevitable and as potentially disturbing, as it is in Lash and Urry's epochal schema, but with an added twist (as befits the difference in purpose and hence narrative style): transformation is ultimately good for everyone, even if not everyone can see that, yet. The basic narrative informing all of Peters's many works is that organizations and their management are operating in an increasingly chaotic environment. This chaos has the capacity to destroy businesses and managers if left unconfronted. The 'threat' in the form of global competition, is at the gates and threatens to lay waste the promised land which has been betrayed by inflexible, complacent and 'amoral' bureaucracy. If managements and organizations are to survive and flourish in a world turned upside down, they need to completely alter their modes of conduct. For the old order is passing away, the old ways cannot work and there is a need for total transformation and, through that, regeneration. However, salvation is at hand if, and only if, the old ways are abandoned and the prophet's commandments obeyed to the letter and with total commitment – hence the call to develop 'a public and passionate hatred of bureaucracy'. You must receive the spirit whereby you, too, 'face up to the need for revolution' and 'achieve extraordinary responsiveness' (Peters, 1987: 3–4). If you do this then the future might just be yours. You, too, will be in tune with ultimate reality and will be able to manipulate the creative/destructive forces of chaos – which are a bottom-line inevitability – to your own advantage. You'll be 'liberated', 'emancipated', 'free' because you've learnt to 'thrive on chaos'. The alternative, which doesn't bear thinking about, is sure-fire death. So choose life, choose 'maximum businessing'.[3]

Deploying this evangelical strategy, Peters sets up a dynamic of fear, anxiety and discontent amongst his would-be followers. An atmosphere of total, but non-specific, threat is evoked – what could be more threatening but unspecific as 'chaos'? This threat is then blamed on and used to problematize the authority of the present order – the 'rational' bureaucratic culture (Pattison, 1997). Recasting specific circumstances into polarities that construct polemical comparisons out of non-comparable terms is a favoured 'technique of negation' deployed by Peters. He conjures up an aggressively polarized world in which businesses are either conspicuously successful – entrepreneurial organizations thriving on chaos – or total failures – formal, hierarchical bureaucratic dinosaurs. There is nothing in between. Peters then reveals his simple message of salvation that people must follow if they are to avoid annihilation and, more positively, become fully developed human beings able to turn the unavoidable chaos to their own advantage. Damnation/irrelevance is not inevitable, but it will be if you don't become that which you have a duty to be – a 'businessed' person.

As Stephen Pattison (1997: 137) has indicated, this constitutes something like Peters's basic 'religious system', within which the underlying metaphor for contemporary managerial reality is that of 'chaos'. This understanding is total and unquestionable, as was, Pattison argues, the Old Testament prophets' understanding of God. As Pattison (1997: 137) continues, 'to de-personify the transcendent by getting rid of any overt deity, as Peters does, is not to dispose of its transcendent nature, though it may make it less obvious'. The statement that the world is 'chaotic' is a remarkably religious assertion, one whose veracity cannot be questioned or tested: it can only be accepted or rejected. Acceptance of this basic reality is acceptance of an overarching moral order within which all events, meanings and experiences can be situated and explained. It is the gateway into Peters's unified view of the world. Indeed, Peters acts as the channel or voice for the transcendent chaos that communicates its essence through him. Like a prophet, he issues a number of commandments that will guide his followers to organizational and personal salvation. These culminate, as Pattison (1997: 138) indicates, in an injunction to intensive and ceaseless effort on the part of every individual member of an organization, no matter what their status or standing.

But this wilful and continuous change and transformation on the part of organizations and persons is not represented as a painful burden or tedious obligation, nor is it to be undertaken simply for instrumental purposes. Above all, it is a means to self-fulfilment and complete development. The wholeness that the bad old bureaucratic past rent asunder is to be recovered, the disenchantment it brought in its wake reversed, through 'maximum businessing', through living life like a business of one. As Peters (1992: 755) put it, 'life on the job is looking more like life off the job for a change. ("For a change?" For the first time in a couple of hundred years is more like it.)'

The tone of his commands is direct, didactic and highly moral. Peters is a charismatic leader, in Weber's terms, attempting to organize life 'on the basis of ultimate principles' (Weber, 1978: I.467). Indeed, Peters (1987: 149) is quite explicit that adopting his epochal world view is akin to a 'religious conversion'. In this way, the 'management revolutionary' as charismatic religious prophet enthrones himself as moral judiciary. His claim is to unify, through the strategy of 'maximum businessing', that which 'bad old bureaucracy' is held to have set apart as separate spheres of existence: work and leisure, reason and emotion, public and private. For the epochalist prophet, this 'vision' or unified view of the world offers the route to salvation.

As Charles Turner (1992: 12) has argued, epochal accounts such as those offered by Peters, and Lash and Urry depend upon 'the extrapolation from one set of predicates to the set of all possible predicates, upon the globalisation of a local phenomenon, in which the one-sidedness of a specific problematic becomes the universality of a general problem'. The more they seek to offer a systematic or 'totalizing' account of the epoch, the more abstract that account becomes: the systematicity promised by the epochal formulation (Fordism/post-Fordism, bureaucracy/enterprise, modern/postmodern) being brought at the cost of a denial of locatedness and of specificity. In other words, rather than offering an account rooted in an empirical analysis, they deploy instead an abstract hermeneutics whose formulation of the character of 'the epoch' has the necessary effect of drowning out or making invisible the specificity of empirical history. In so doing, they express what Weber (1948: 55) termed 'the speculative view of life' and Schmitt (1986: 74–5) the romantic attitude of 'fanciful construction'.

Schmitt's acerbic comment suggests that epochal diagnoses should not be taken seriously. Yet, from the point of view of developments in many contemporary organizational domains, it is Schmitt's perspective which appears as 'fanciful'. In the life-order of government across the liberal-democratic world, for instance, regimes of many different political hues are home to prestigious exponents of the 'epochal arts'. Epochal theorists, such as Anthony Giddens, Geoff Mulgan and Charles Leadbeater, have all been involved, either implicitly or explicitly, with the development of public policy in Britain's New Labour Government and the epochal formulations and designations they or their compatriots are associated with ('the Third Way', 'connexity', 'the knowledge-driven economy' and so on) can be seen to structure reforms in many areas of governance – not least in the field of public administration.[4] It is to developments in this latter field that I now turn.

**epochalism in administrative reform**  The epochalist schemas briefly sketched above are established in large part through sets of dualities and oppositions in which the discontinuity between past and future is highlighted.[5] While the narratives proffered are meant to be taken as empirical descriptions of reality, the oppositions they rely upon and through which they are framed are highly prescriptive in orientation (this is true of academic- as well as consultancy-oriented epochalisms). In epochalist discourse, 'change' is presented as homogeneous and uni-linear, making objects and persons that may be different in quality and kind, seem all bound up in the same global process. In the field of public administration, for instance, such representations make change appear the inevitable outcome of abstract, non-locatable, impulses and imperatives (the ICT revolution, the changing consumer, globalization) rather than the result of specific (and traceable) political choices (Clarke and Newman, 1997).

In the highly influential tract, *Re-Inventing Government*, for example, Osborne and Gaebler (1992) found their demand for a complete transformation in the ways in which government conducts itself, and in which people conduct themselves within government, on just such a loose agglomeration of abstract imperatives. Amongst many other things, a generalized crisis in governmental authority, the dislocatory effects of an increased deployment of new information and communication technologies, and the logics of 'globalization' are all lumped together to constitute what the authors term 'an environment characterised by uncertainty'. It is this environment that is allocated agency when it comes to public administrative reform, rather than the choices of politicians or, heaven forbid, the management consultants from whom they frequently seek advice.

> Today's environment demands institutions that are extremely flexible and adaptable. It demands institutions that deliver high-quality goods and services, squeezing every more bang out of every buck. It demands institutions that are responsive to the needs of their customers and, offering choices of non-standardized services; that lead by persuasion and incentives rather than commands; that give their employees a sense of meaning and control, even ownership. It demands institutions that empower citizens rather than simply serving them. (Osborne and Gaebler, 1992: 15)

What this 'environment demands' then, when it comes to public administration, is 'entrepreneurial government'. It is the latter, and the latter alone, which is held to offer the only viable means through which a 'broken' public administration can be effectively 're-invented'. Unsurprisingly, the key tenets of this 'new entrepreneurialism' are the absolute opposite of those bad old bureaucratic practices held to have got government into such trouble in the first place.

> Entrepreneurial governments promote *competition* between service providers. They *empower* citizens by pushing control out of the bureaucracy, into the community. They measure the performance of their agencies, focusing not on inputs but on *outcomes*. They are driven by their goals – their *missions* – not by their rules and regulations. They redefine their clients as *customers* and offer them choices – between schools, between training programs, between housing options. They *prevent* problems before they emerge, rather than simply offering services afterward. They put their energies into *earning* money, not simply spending it. They *decentralize* authority, embracing participatory management. They prefer *market* mechanisms to bureaucratic mechanisms. And they focus not simply on providing public services but on *catalysing* all sectors – public, private and voluntary – into action to solve their community's problems. (Osborne and Gaebler, 1992: 19–20)

While such epochalist narratives and oppositions provide a simple and easily digestible set of slogans through which to catalyse the demand for 'change', problems invariably arise when it comes to the nitty-gritty of actually effecting practical changes within governmental institutions based on such gestural categories. After all, I would suggest, judgements about the wisdom of certain forms of organizational change, arrived at in the concrete circumstances of a practical case, can no more be abstracted from their detailed circumstances than can medical judgements about the present condition of individual patients. As Amélie Rorty (1988: 8) has argued in this regard (see the Introduction to the present volume, p. 11–13), since judgements and contexts are particular, all the way up and all the way down, judgements are given their sense and direction by the particular context within which they arise. Yet, it is precisely the individual circumstances that epochal approaches make invisible or render insignificant and herein lies their practical danger. In so far as they neglect the specificity of circumstances, attempts, such as Osborne and Gaebler's, to generalize 'entrepreneurial principles' to all forms of organizational conduct may well end up serving to incapacitate a particular organization's ability to pursue its specific purposes by redefining its organizational identity and hence what its purposes are (Jordan, 1994; du Gay, 2000a). A brief examination of the Clinton administration's National Performance Review in the USA and subsequent report *From Red Tape to Results: Creating a Government That Works Better and Costs Less* (NPR, 1993), and the Blair government's *Modernising Government* White Paper (Cabinet Office, 1999a) and subsequent initiatives in the UK give a flavour of just how such a slippage can occur when epochal diagnoses form the basis of practical organizational interventions in the area of public administration. While these two are by no means the only examples of epochally framed administrative reform that could have been chosen (developments in New Zealand and Australia offer clear parallels), they are often represented as 'exemplars' that other governments should emulate if they are to stay at the 'leading edge' (Pollitt and Bouckaert, 2000: 59).

**re-inventing government: the national performance review**   The centrepiece of public administrative reform under the Clinton presidency in the USA was the National Performance Review (NPR) chaired by then Vice-President Al Gore. In launching the NPR in April 1993, Gore indicated that 'our long term goal is to change the very culture of the federal government'. This was to be achieved through a process coined 'Re-Inventing Government'. The origins of this phrase are not hard to trace. Osborne and Gaebler's bestseller is entitled *Re-Inventing Government* and their epochal pronouncements and diagnoses clearly inform the philosophical premise and practical goals of the NPR. Indeed, David Osborne played a major part in drafting the NPR's final report *From Red Tape to Results: Creating a Government That Works Better and Costs Less* (1993).

As we have seen, Osborne and Gaebler's text picks and mixes ideas from a number of different discursive locales – from the voluminous privatization literature of the 1970s and 1980s, to the populist business motivation literature of the 1980s and early 1990s. The result is a heady brew that could appear acceptable to liberals and democrats who wanted to save government from the worst excesses of the New Right but who also wanted a more 'responsive' government that catalysed all sectors of society and, importantly, cost less to run. Such a government was realizable, Osborne and Gaebler argued, if there was a cultural shift away from what they call 'bureaucratic government' and towards what they termed 'entrepreneurial government'. This epochal opposition was taken up by the NPR and constitutes something like its basic organizing framework.

The NPR indicates that 'Re-Inventing Government' rests upon 'four bedrock principles' of entrepreneurial management (1993: 6–7). These are remarkably similar (indeed, pretty much a distillation of) Osborne and Gaebler's 'ten principles for entrepreneurial government' (1992: 19). So, first, effective entrepreneurial managements cast aside red tape and move away from systems where people are accountable for following rules to ones where people are accountable for achieving results. Secondly, entrepreneurial managements are customer-focused and insist on customer satisfaction. Thirdly, entrepreneurial managements transform their cultures by decentralizing authority. They empower those working on the frontline to make more of their own decisions and to take responsibility for solving their own problems. Finally, entrepreneurial managements constantly seek to do more for less, through 're-engineering' their work systems and processes. 'These are the bedrock principles on which the federal bureaucracy must build' (NPR, 1993: 7).

These 'principles' are not presented as propositions subject to disproof but simply asserted. Objections and questions concerning the wisdom of these assertions – is being against red tape (e.g. bureaucratic regulation) really a useful organizing principle for the administration of government given its politico-legal role? – are suppressed in advance through the continuous invocation of the impossibility of the status quo. 'Change' is the given; it is simply not able to be challenged within the terms of reference of the Gore report. In this sense, it has acquired, as Moe (1994: 113) indicates, 'a theological aura'. It rejects

> the traditional language of administrative discourse which attempts, not always with success, to employ terms with precise meanings. Instead, a new highly value-laden lexicon is employed by entrepreneurial management enthusiasts to disarm would-be questioners. Thus, the term 'customer' largely replaces 'citizen' and there is heavy reliance upon active verbs – reinventing, reengineering, empowering – to maximise the emotive content of what otherwise has been a largely nonemotive subject matter. (Moe, 1994: 114)

This epochal schema in which 'bureaucracy' or 'administration' is reduced to a simple and abstract set of negativities contrasted with an equally simple and abstracted, but positively coded, set of 'entrepreneurial' principles systematically evacuates the field of public administration of any of its characteristic content. How could anyone be for bureaucracy if it is defined simply as a dysfunctional, outdated and inefficient form of organization? Who could not be supportive of a form of organization that shares none of those deficiencies and guarantees a better future? However, when attention is focused on the specific purposes of public administration and its particular political and constitutional embeddedness, the generalized articulation of bureaucracy with the outmoded and dysfunctional is less obvious and the generalized superiority of 'entrepreneurial principles' much more problematic.

As a number of commentators in the US have argued, the implementation of the NPR's proposals raised a host of constitutional issues and yet the Gore report is characterized by an almost complete absence of the language of constitutionalism (Moe, 1994; Rohr, 1998). At one level this seems shocking, given the role of the public bureaucracy as an institution of government, yet it is not that surprising when one remembers the epochalist manner in which the NPR reduces the field of public administration to a conflict zone between the abstractions of bureaucratic and entrepreneurial management, thus evacuating the constitutional and political from view. Since the NPR is adamant that the status quo cannot hold, that wholesale re-invention is the only way forward, then it follows that everything that is currently done should be problematized and that implicitly includes contemporary constitutional practice. Because the government is broken and 'entrepreneurial management' is the only way to fix it, then redefining, for example, the roles and authorities of the institutional presidency and the central management agencies in accordance with these 'entrepreneurial principles' is an unquestionable necessity.

Thus, the NPR sought to institute a highly pluralistic organizational and management structure upon the executive branch of government in keeping with its model of best 'entrepreneurial' practice. Congress was represented here as a relatively unimportant and, indeed, largely negative factor in this new paradigm. The President, in turn, was seen more as a catalytic policy entrepreneur than as the legal agent of sovereign power. Thus the entrepreneurial management paradigm sought to reverse the thrust of prior constitutionally based organizational management initiatives in government, in which the institutional presidency was considered central to the management of the executive branch of government, and to devolve management responsibility to the lowest practicable levels (Moe, 1994: 117). As a consequence, primary accountability would no longer be to the President through departmental lines and central management agencies, but to the customer. This was a shift of remarkable constitutional importance and yet its merit was taken for granted simply because it conformed to 'good' entrepreneurial management.

Working toward a quality government means reducing the power of headquarters vis-à-vis field operations. As our reinvented government begins to liberate agencies from over-regulation ... all federal agencies will delegate, decentralise, and empower employees to make decisions. This will let front-line and front-office workers use their creative judgement as they offer service to customers to solve problems. (NPR, 1993: 70–1)

The central discourse of the NPR was thus an 'entrepreneurial' managerialist one rather than a political or constitutional one. As such it reinterpreted the latter through its own epochal prism, or cluster of concerns, altering the rationales of the field of public administration in the process. There are clear and present dangers here. For, if the key terms of an institutional or professional enterprise are no longer defined specifically by reference to one another but are fundamentally redefined in terms of the concerns of some other enterprise, then that institution or profession will begin to lose the distinctiveness of its purpose or project. In reinterpreting the role of the institutional presidency, for instance, with its traditional 'reliance upon public law and the President as Chief Manager' exclusively through the prism of 'entrepreneurial principles', Moe (1994: 117) argues that the NPR 'constituted a major attack' on a key aspect of the constitutional practice of public administration in the USA.

The constitutional and political dangers of epochally oriented programmes of organizational 'change' are not restricted to reforms of the public administration in the USA; they are also discernible in recent and ongoing attempts to modernize the Civil Service in New Zealand and the UK, for instance. It is to developments in Britain, most particularly the New Labour Government's 'Modernizing Government' programme that we now, briefly, turn.

**modernizing government**    As Nikolas Rose (1999: 476), for example, has argued, one key organizing presupposition linking programmes and strategies for the re-formulation of social governance under the Thatcher and Major administrations with those currently being developed and espoused by the Blair administration is a widespread scepticism concerning the powers of 'political government' to know, plan, calculate and steer from the centre. The state is no longer to be required to answer all of society's needs for health, security, order or productivity. Individuals, firms, organizations, 'communities', schools, parents, and housing estates must themselves take on – as 'partners' – a greater proportion of the responsibility for resolving these issues. This involves a double movement of 'responsibilization and autonomization'. Organizations and other agents that were once enmeshed in what are represented as the 'bureaucratic' lines of force of the 'social' state are to be made more responsible for securing their own future survival and well-being. Yet, at one and the same time, they are to be steered politically from the centre 'at a distance' through the invention and deployment of a host of techniques which can shape their actions while simultaneously attesting to their independence – techniques such as audits, devolved budgets, relational contracts and performance-related pay.

Embedded in these contemporary programmes and strategies for the reformulation of social governance is a particular ethic of personhood – a view of what persons are and what they should be allowed to be. Thus a certain 'ethic of personhood' that stresses autonomy, responsibility and the freedom/obligation of individuals to actively make choices for themselves can be seen to infuse New Labour's attempts to 'modernize' the British Civil Service as much as it permeated successive Conservative attempts to 're-invent' that same institution (Cabinet Office, 1999a). Indeed, the similarities are perhaps even more striking than that. As Tony Blair put it, New Labour's 'modernising government' programme is fundamentally concerned with 'stimulating more entrepreneurship' within the British Civil Service (*Guardian*, 1999a) through, for instance, making civil servants more individually responsible for achieving specific policy outcomes. Such a shift would only be accomplished, it was further observed, through instilling more of a 'private sector work culture' (*The Observer*, 1999) within Whitehall. The political stripe of the government may have changed but the 'mentality of governance' appears to exhibit considerable continuity. So, while commentators frequently point to New Labour's preoccupation with 'community', 'partnership', 'participation' and 'stakeholding' in order to highlight the present government's distinction from the Conservative's entrepreneurial ethos of public sector reform (Elcock, 2000), they often do so without indicating how key elements of that latter ethos – the modes of authority and subjectification they idealize, for example – are held in place within New Labour's project of governmental 'modernization'.

'Modernization', just like 'Re-Invention', relies on a series of epochal oppositions and dualities in which the discontinuity between past and future is highlighted. A White Paper, Our Competitive Future: Building the Knowledge Driven Economy (DTI, 1998), highlights the inevitability of change and the important role of 'enterprise' in managing its effects and securing a 'modernised' future. Tony Blair, in the foreword to the above, writes:

The modern world is swept by change … In Government, in business, in our universities and throughout society we must do much more to foster a new entrepreneurial spirit: equipping ourselves for the long-term, prepared to seize opportunities, committed to constant innovation and improved performance. (DTI, 1998: 5)

A crucial feature of this discourse of 'modernization' is the assumption that no organizational context is immune from the uncertainties of unrelenting change and that, as a result, all organizations – public, private and voluntary – need to develop similar norms and techniques of conduct, for without so doing they will not survive (du Gay, 2000b: 78). Thus all organizations need to look to current 'best practice' so they can equip themselves accordingly to meet the challenge of change head-on. For the public administration, the first place it is encouraged to look is a familiar one. As the White Paper, *Modernising Government*, puts it, 'we need to make sure that government services are brought forward using the best and most modern techniques, to match the best of the private sector' (Cabinet Office, 1999a: 5). So while the government points out that it, unlike successive Conservative administrations, 'will value public service, not denigrate it' (p. 6), this certainly does not mean 'an unchanging public service, a public service at any price' (p. 55). What it means is a public service that must move away from a 'risk averse culture' and 'unnecessary bureaucracy' towards inculcating and stimulating the qualities of innovation, responsiveness, creativity and enterprise, which are represented as essential to meeting 'the challenges of the 21st century' (p. 61).

These 'entrepreneurial' dispositions and capacities are positively contrasted with current practices and forms of conduct that, as we have seen, are represented – bizarrely given the constant 're-inventions' of the last two decades – as 'deeply resistant to change', and hence as preventing 'public servants from experimenting, innovating and delivering a better product' (Cabinet Office, 1999a: 5). Consequently, in order to ensure that the sorts of capacities and dispositions the government regards as essential to 'modernisation' will flourish 'there has to be a change of culture. This needs to be led from the top and driven throughout the organization' (p. 60). It will involve revising 'the core competencies for staff and appraisal systems to reflect the qualities we seek' (p. 56). Overall, everything possible will be done to 'encourage the public sector to test new ways of working by suspending rules that stifle innovation. It will encourage public servants to take risks, which, if successful, will make a difference' (p. 61).

While the White Paper continually draws implicit distinctions between pro-private sector, anti-public service, market-mad Tories and the more public-service-oriented, 'what matters is what works' New Labour 'vision', one could nonetheless be forgiven for thinking that many of the tropes of 'modernization' sound remarkably familiar. Consider the particular example of what the White Paper refers to as 'risk aversion'. It states that 'the cultures of Parliament, Ministers and the civil service create a situation in which the rewards for success are limited and penalties for failure can be severe. The system is too often risk averse. As a result, Ministers and public servants can be slow to take advantage of new opportunities' (Cabinet Office, 1999a: 11). The government therefore proposes removing 'unnecessary bureaucracy' in order to encourage public servants to 'experiment with new ways of working' so that they might become 'as innovative and entrepreneurial as anyone outside government' (p. 11).

These sentiments echo those expressed by the authors of *The Next Steps* report (Efficiency Unit, 1988), which paved the way for the agencification of the Civil Service under the last Thatcher government. For example, the report said there was in government 'a lack of clear and accountable management responsibility' (para. 14); and that senior managers must be prepared 'to show real qualities of leadership and to take and defend unpopular decisions' (para. 35). When *The Next Steps* report was published questions were asked about what exactly these sentiments meant and about their degree of fit with constitutional practice – with the convention of ministerial responsibility, for example (Chapman, 1988; Bogdanor, 1996). In the event, these serious questions received no satisfactory answers but they acted as markers for what became real problems associated with agencification.[6] Some enthusiasts, not only from the major political parties but also amongst civil servants themselves, seemed somewhat muted or changed their views when the main difficulty that emerged from the creation of the *Next Steps* agencies was precisely this point about risk and accountability in the context of British constitutional 'regime values' (Chapman, 1999: 15).

Like the Conservatives before them, and in the manner commended by the premiere advocates of 'entrepreneurial governance', Osborne and Gaebler, New Labour wants 'to foster a new entrepreneurial spirit' amongst public servants. *The Modernising Government* White Paper says that 'through bureaucracy and an attachment to existing practices for their own sake', public servants have had their creativity, initiative and enterprise stifled. The assumption here is that 'red tape and established procedure' should be suspended and public servants given the opportunity to experiment to see what works best. These sentiments echo Osborne and Gaebler's *cri de cœur* (1992: 136) for a legitimate permission to fail on the part of 'entrepreneurial public servants'. New Labour, just like Osborne and Gaebler, come perilously close here to opening up the door to corruption. And they do so precisely because the oppositions they set up between 'bureaucracy' and 'enterprise', a bad old past and a bright innovative future, have the effect of evacuating public administration of its determinate content. New Labour rails against the alleged 'inefficiency' and 'red tape' of bureaucratic regulations in government from the perspective of 'entrepreneurial' principles but without seeing what politically and constitutionally productive role those very regulations are performing. While it is not their only target in this regard, their criticisms of 'red tape' are often associated with financial controls in government. The point is, though, that the public administration as an institution of government operates within a political context in which principles governing the use of public money are minutely detailed and where the use of such funds is rigorously monitored. And this for very good reasons. Public funds possess a unique status: in large part they have such a special status because abusing them is held to eat away at the foundations of representative government. Rigid criteria for deployment and use of public funds – the 'excessive red tape' and bureaucracy beloved of critics – is a price that the political system is prepared to pay to safeguard its own integrity. For instance, exceedingly tight and 'bureaucratic' controls are in place to keep the political system from turning into an instrumentality of private profit for those in its employ. After all, the temptations facing officials can be enormous. Through the use of elaborate procedural safeguards – as well as formal training and learning by example – corruption and other forms of malpractice have gradually been squeezed out of the system. For years, though, the cry has been heard that prevention costs more than the ailment itself. And yet, as I indicated above, the governmental domain does not conform to the same 'regime values' or ethos of other life-orders. Businesses may be tempted to ditch costly bureaucratic procedures whose benefits are not easily weighted but government and hence public administration is different. Here, as Herbert Kaufman (1977: 53) put it, it is no contradiction at all to argue that governments should 'spend $20 to prevent the theft of $1'. In the political environment within which public administration operates, highly value-laden matters of process – concerned with qualitative issues about the manner in which results are achieved – will always intermingle and frequently compete with the so-called 'bottom-line' issues of costs and quantities of outputs. Consequently, accountability and efficiency in public administration may be more nuanced and intricate in practice than accountability and efficiency in other sectors, where the management and organizational challenges may be no less demanding but less complex, more easily graspable and, most importantly for our argument, less bureaucratic.

**concluding comments**    As we have seen, epochal schemas have considerable intuitive appeal. The stark disjunctures and oppositions they deploy offer an easily graspable narrative that can act as a catalyst for 'transformation'. However, in their belief in a managerial algorithm – a universal and invariable recipe of managerial procedures and techniques providing answers to all organizational problems – they tend towards an approach to management that has proven, historically, at best questionable, and at worse disastrous. For even if one accepts that there may be some generic management principles that are 'universally' applicable (and that is a very big 'if') they are always applied in a specific context, including a value context. The nature of the management task, and the appropriateness of the management method deployed, can be defined only in relation to the particular objectives of the organization being managed, the values to be upheld by its

**152**

managers as determined by its constitution or 'mission' and the status of its relationships with its users, whether as citizens, clients, consumers or customers. In this sense, as Rohr (1998: 167) indicates, management is best understood as a 'function of regime' and not as a universal panacea.

As the examples in the two previous sections indicate, epochal approaches to organizational and managerial reform engender proposals for sweeping solutions ill-suited to the environment within which they are meant to take place. The NPR exhibited just such a tendency by, for instance, failing to pay adequate attention to the characteristics of the political and constitutional environment within which public administration takes place, when advocating its reform measures (Moe, 1994; Rohr, 1998; Pollitt and Bouckaert, 2000). Ongoing attempts to 'modernise' the British Civil Service by the New Labour government suffer from similar lacunae (Chapman, 1999; du Gay, 2000b) as do many of the experiments in public sector reform gathered together under the umbrella heading of 'governance' (Peters, 2000a) (see also Chapter 7, this volume).[7] This does not mean to say that all of the techniques associated with such reform agendas should be ruled out of court. Rather, as Rohr (1998: 104) has argued, instead of renouncing 'entrepreneurial government', for example, and all its works and pomp in its entirety (thus replicating the very absolutism one seeks to criticize), we would do well to 'tame its excesses by subjecting it to the discipline of constitutional scrutiny'. Some carefully targeted 'entrepreneurial' interventions may then still prove useful in crafting better public administration, others may not.[8] Therefore, I would suggest, casuistry not epochal absolutism would prove a more appropriate reform mentality.

This is not an uncontroversial conclusion, despite the powerful lines of argument with which it is associated in the social sciences and humanities.[9] For instance, it might plausibly be claimed that the abstract theories of the kind espoused by 'epochalists' are nothing more than 'forms of rhetorical appeal which make use of certain quasi-propositional fragments' (Geuss, 2001: 157). In this view, to espouse such an epochal theory does not amount to, and shouldn't be understood as, the assertion of a set of sober propositions that are to be taken as literal truths. Rather, it can be better understood as a form of discursive mobilization, designed to highlight issues and directions in which people are trying to focus interest and attention. This is all well and good in some respects. It is clearly not possible to know antecedently at what level of generality an appropriate solution to a problematic situation will be found. Therefore it makes no sense to assume that abstract or general theories have no explanatory purchase or practical use per se, as Richard Rorty (1989), for instance, can sometimes appear to suggest. In making such a move, Rorty sometimes comes perilously close to endorsing a version of the metaphysics of presence that he (rightly) criticizes in the work of others (Geuss, 2001: 158). The fact that the fit between general theory and practical action can sometimes be loose or tenuous does not mean that general theorizing is of absolutely no use. We simply don't know in advance. As Geuss (2001: 159) puts it, 'the practically significant choice ... is not whether or not to have a general view, but whether to have a more sophisticated, reflective, and more empirically informed view rather than a less reflective and informed general view'. It is my contention that epochalist variants of 'general' or 'abstract' theorizing are precisely unable to live up to the demands Geuss would make upon them, being neither reflective, sophisticated nor empirically informed. Rather, epochal theorizing tends instead towards an unattractive admixture of self-referentiality, teleology and circularity. Epochalists always seem to know what's needed in advance.

Some of the debates about organizational change, in general, and public administrative reform, in particular, become intractable when the concerns of one context are imported into another, in the premature interest of constructing a unified theory, or as a rhetorical move in a political polemic. When there are seemingly irresolvable debates about the primacy of competing concepts of 'change' – as there are, for instance, in the debates about the manner in which state bureaux should be managerially reformed – the first move should be to formulate, in casuistic or case-based fashion, the issues that lie behind the dispute, specifiying the distinctive sources and conflicts of competing representations of an organization's purpose and modus operandi. As Amélie Rorty (1988: 7–8) has indicated, 'apparently irreconcilable opponents are often interested in different issues, asking different questions, each assuming that the answer to one question determines the answer to the others'. In assuming a congruence between public administration and all other organizational domains, epochal theories ignore the milieu-specific character of organizational arrangements in state bureaux. As I have attempted to indicate in this chapter, ethical and constitutional problems can and do arise from misguided attempts to drive through 'change' in organs of the state based on an epochally framed (and illicitly decontextualized) concept of organizational 'best practice'. When it comes to 'change' the differences between organizations – their distinctive purposes, varying social and political obligations, and typical ways of specifying and addressing ethical concerns, for instance – are as vital as their similarities. Respect for general principles that require similar cases to be treated alike also necessitates that dissimilar cases be treated differently. This is the casuist's rule of thumb.

Casuistry – or case-based reasoning – is not currently popular, whether in philosophical or organizational analysis.[10] In the latter field, rather more prestige and standing seems to flow to the theoretically grand and the managerially visionary than to practitioners of the art of 'piecemeal social engineering', to use Popper's (1994/1985: 304) phrase. This is a pity. For it appears clear, from the cases outlined earlier, that whereas the casuist would approach an organizational problem with a relatively open mind as to the scope of the reforms that might be necessary – Geuss's more sophisticated, empirically informed and reflective 'general theorizing – the epochalist cannot do this; for they have decided, in advance, that a complete re-invention and reconstruction is necessary and possible. The coordinates are set up in advance and there is no escape from their terms of reference. As a result we are faced with a set of forced options. And forced options usually prove to be false options.

## notes

1   'Casuistry' or case-based reasoning has been much abused. It is frequently regarded as synonymous with 'sophistry' and carries a range of sinister connotations. However, when seen for what it is – a practical art, concerned with the analysis of moral, ethical and legal (and we might add organizational) issues and dilemmas in terms of cases and circumstances, such negative coding becomes difficult to maintain. After all, not only is the common law system the product of a prolonged exercise in casuistry, in that the study of cases has been the principal means through which a person has come to rank as a learned lawyer and indoctrinated into the 'artificial reason of the law', but people confront many of the practical quandries of everyday life through the implicit use of 'case analysis'. Friends and colleagues, parents and children, 'agony aunts' and psychotherapists; anyone who has occasion to consider moral questions in practical detail knows that morally significant differences between cases can be as vital as their similarities. Respect for general principles that require similar cases to be treated alike also necessitates that dissimilar cases be treated differently. One crucial instrument for helping to resolve moral questions in practice, therefore, is a detailed and methodical mapping of morally significant likenesses and differences: a moral taxonomy (Jonsen & Toulmin, 1988: 14). Such taxonomic mapping is an essential element of the casuist's art. For a complete statement see Jonsen and Toulmin (1988).

2   For an introduction to this emergent form of 'cultural economic' inquiry see the contributions to du Gay and Pryke (2002).

3   'Businessing' represents individuals and groups as 'units of management', and requires that they adopt a certain 'entrepreneurial' form of relationship to themselves as a condition of their effectiveness and of the effectiveness of this sort of strategy. As Peters (1994: 73) explains, to be businessed is to be given responsibility and to be held accountable for 'running one's own show inside the organization'.

4   Anthony Giddens is an internationally renowned sociologist and former Director of the London School of Economics. His epochalist political tracts *Beyond Left and Right* (1994) and *The Third Way* (1998), have led to him being labelled 'intellectual guru' of the British 'New' Labour Government. Geoff Mulgan and Charles Leadbeater came to prominence through their involvement in the 'New Times' project of the influential but now defunct magazine *Marxism Today*. Mulgan went on to help found and then direct the think tank *Demos* before becoming a political adviser to the New Labour Government in 1997. Until recently he was a senior civil servant in the Cabinet Office and Director of the Performance and Innovation and Forward Strategy Units. His characterization of the current

'epoch' is contained in his *Connexity* (1998). Charles Leadbeater is perhaps best known for his populist epochal tome *Living on Thin Air* (1999) in which he argues for 'knowledge' as the driving force of contemporary economy and society. The book cover contains an enthusiastic endorsement by the British Prime Minister, Tony Blair, and Leadbeater's influence on New Labour policy formulation can be detected in a number of areas, most notably, perhaps, in The Department of Trade and Industry's policy document *Our Competitive Future: Building the Knowledge Driven Economy* (1998).

5   Similar arguments to mine have been deployed – without recourse to the notion of 'epochalism' – by writers from a range of different theoretical perspectives. See, for instance, the social constructionist analysis deployed by Clarke and Newman (1997: esp. Ch 3); those advanced from a psychoanalytic perspective by Levine (2001); and the broadly ANT (Actor Network Theory) inspired arguments of Munro (1998).

6   As Mark Freedland (1996: 28) has indicated, the *Next Steps* programme transmuted and fragmented the integrality of the political-administrative process within departments of state. In place of the doctrine of political ministerial responsibility for all aspects of departmental decision-making there arise instead two 'distinct accountabilities each of which is primarily a financial accountability'.

> The agency will have a primary decision-making role – and will often play this role within a central policy making area of the parent department – and will in that sense be responsible for the decision-taking. But its responsibility in the sense of answerability is conceived of and expressed in terms primarily of financial accountability, that is to say in terms of a liability to show that there has been efficient financial management and adherence to targets and budgets ... The parent department retains ... a kind of responsibility for the decision-making which occurs at agency level. But the separation of the agency as a distinct centre of decision-making means that the departmental responsibility has been turned into a secondary and essentially supervisory one ... Moreover, that departmental accountability is in a way that mirrors that of the agency, increasingly conceived of in financial terms – the primary role of the parent department tends to become that of accounting to the Cabinet and to Parliament for the efficiency and good financial management of the departmental operation as conducted through the subsidiary agencies. As if by a conjuring trick, the spell of financial accountability has enabled ministerial responsibility not only to be sawn in half but actually to be spirited off the stage. (Freedland, 1996: 28)

The anti-bureaucratic logic of the *Next Steps* reforms therefore tends towards a situation in which, if the relationship between the executive agency and the parent department of state is working in the way it is meant to work, the decision-makers and decision-making at agency level cannot be seen as part of an integrated bureaucratic institutional structure, an indivisible unity, such as the constitutional convention of ministerial responsibility to Parliament has traditionally been seen to require.

7   It is sometimes suggested that the current craze for evidence-based practice (EBP) marks a shift away from a belief in such algorithms to the sort of context and case-based reasoning I am advocating. This does not seem likely. For an interesting argument about the pragmatic limits to evidence-based medicine, for instance, see Black (1998).

8   This is not the same thing as a (New Labour) belief in 'what's best is what works', for 'what works' cannot simply be a question of performance and outcomes but equally one of process, procedure and constitutionality.

9   There is a 'family' of very powerful lines of argument, instances of which have been developed, *inter alia*, by E. Burke, M. Oakeshott, K. Popper and B. Williams, which is predicated upon a scepticism about the possibility or utility of 'abstract theorizing'.

10  That is not to say that there are not excellent examples of casuistry to be found in either subject area. The work of Sissela Bok (1978, 1982), Michael Walzer (1980) and Amélie Rorty (1988) in philosophy, and John Rohr (1989, 1998) in the area of public management, for instance.

# the trouble with 'governance': state, bureaucracy and freedom

Like the notion of 'change' explored in Chapter 6, 'governance' is a fashionable, if rather polyvalent, term. It has come to prominence over the last two decades or so, most frequently at the expense of the concept of 'government'. Indeed, 'governance' is generally perceived as an alternative to government, that is to a particular form of political ordering by the state under the rule of law. As one analyst has argued, 'current use does not treat governance as a synonym for government. Rather governance signifies a change in the meaning of government, referring to a *new* process of governing; or a *changed* condition of ordered rule; or the *new* method by which society is governed' (Rhodes, 1996: 653).[1] While governance is to be distinguished from government in most usages of the term, this is normally where agreement about the concept's meaning begins to falter. Governance has multiple meanings depending on context of use and preferred project, and there is a remarkable ambiguity in its differential deployment. Nonetheless, as Paul Hirst (2000: 13) has indicated, most usages of the term governance either signal a problematization of conventional forms of political government by the state under the rule of law or they actively propose to sidestep those forms of ordering.

This chapter sets out to consider certain notions of governance and explore some of the issues of political ordering, particularly those relating to sovereignty and authority, they tend to challenge, sideline, or attempt to transcend. It will do so primarily through a brief examination of the way these notions have been deployed to explain and/or endorse reforms in the organization and role of the public administration in certain liberal democratic states, most notably the UK. As Jon Pierre (2000: 7) has noted, public administration has been the governmental life-order where experiments in 'governance' have been most frequently attempted. The chapter concludes with a few observations on the relationship between centralized bureaucratic public administrative capacities, sovereign authority and liberal freedoms. In so doing, many of the conclusions outlined in Chapter 5 are reiterated.

**governance and anti-statism**   Most analysts of governance are keen to indicate that they are not seeking to offer a 'normative theory' but merely an 'organizing framework' for understanding changes in contemporary forms of political ordering (Rhodes, 1996, 1997; Stoker, 1998: 18). Yet discussions of governance are continually dogged by a conflation of analysis and normative evaluation. Analysts of governance in the area of public administration are no exception. According to Rhodes (2000a: 60), for example, 'networks are at the heart of the notion of governance in the study of Public Administration'. Networks are represented here as a form of social coordination involving the management of inter-organizational linkages and partnerships. In this sense they are viewed as a mechanism for coordinating and allocating resources – a governing structure – in the same way as hierarchies and markets. For Rhodes (2000a: 61) 'networks are an alternative to, not a hybrid of, bureaucracies and markets'. They are characterized by 'high levels of trust' between their participants and are 'regulated by rules of the game negotiated and agreed' by those same participants (p. 61). Networks are therefore characterized by autonomy and self-governance. They are not only largely autonomous of, and unaccountable to, the state, but also highly resistant to government steering, developing 'their own policies' and moulding their environments. 'Network governance', Rhodes (1996: 666) argues, 'can blur, even dissolve, the distinction between state and civil society'. The state becomes nothing more than a loose collection of 'interorganizational networks made up of governmental and societal actors with no sovereign actor able to steer or regulate'. It has to be acknowledged at this point that analysts of governance in the field of public administration are very confusing on this latter point. Sometimes networks are represented as unamenable to any form of external control or regulation, at others to imperfect, indirect or light-touch steering by the state and at yet others as constituted by the state as part of a rationality of rule often described as 'government at a distance' (Rose, 1999). Frequently all three assertions are to be found in the same article, sometimes on the same page of an article (see, for example, Rhodes, 2000a: 61, 72). While all analysts agree that 'governance' refers to what we might call 'the mobilisation of society' (Donzelot, 1991), they are not always entirely clear about who or what is motivating the mobilization – the state, network participants or other actants. This makes it very difficult to pin down the nature of the theoretical and substantive claims being made as well as assessing their explanatory reach. Quite obviously, 'government at a distance' is to a very large extent a state-instituted rationality of rule wherein the objects of governance – networks, associations – are mobilized and regulated by state institutions more or less tightly. The attribution of an innate capacity for autonomous self-realization to networks of groups and individuals, making them largely if not totally unamenable to external control or regulation, is another matter entirely. I have chosen to focus mostly on this latter aspect of 'governance', the better to highlight some of the politically romantic, anti-statist normative values attached to this notion by its analysts/advocates.

So, for instance, while Rhodes argues that network forms of political ordering are 'not cost free', being, *inter alia*, closed to outsiders and unrepresentative, frequently unaccountable to anyone but themselves for their activities, and liable to serve private interests over and above the public interest, he nonetheless appears attracted to 'governance' as a narrative of rule (1999: xxiv, 2000a: 54, 66, 2000b: 163). According to John Clarke (2000: 13), for example, Rhodes's analysis of network forms of governance is in fact endowed with 'a strong normative value. In this model "self-governing" seems to denote a condition to be prized above being directed by other authorities or processes.' Rhodes is not alone in this regard. Stoker (1998: 19; 2000a: 14) and Hirst (2000: 18–19), for example, are both conscious of some of the obvious political costs of 'network' governance, but appear to regard it as a potential source of value, whether in challenging the unitary nature of the sovereign state and instigating a more differentiated polity or in stimulating experiments in 'associational democracy'.

Scratch the surface of 'governance' in the study of public administration, then, and it is not long before the figure of the 'self-governing community' appears to greet you. This notion has been a central feature of anti-statist discourse for as long as the state under the rule of law has existed, as Blandine Kriegel (1995), for example, has argued. In tandem with the figure of 'civil society, it has regularly functioned as a vehicle of critique for intellectuals of all persuasions – left, right, liberal, unaligned – keen to unmask the state under the rule of law as a medium of modern forms of moral vacuity or, worse, catastrophe. For advocates of 'governance' it appears in two particular guises. First, in the 'strong' assumption, common to many governance models, that somehow citizens know better what they want and need than does government, and therefore are entirely justified in finding ways to avoid unwarranted incursions of state authority and bureaucracy into their lives. The currently popular and influential communitarian and deliberative democratic critiques of political government, for example, are frequently infused with claims about the capacity of people and communities to identify their own needs and govern themselves autonomously (Bohman, 1996; Etzioni, 1997). Second, in those analyses of governance as 'self-organizing networks', there reside less vehement but nonetheless clearly normative assumptions, as we saw earlier. Here, the normative element is that 'civil society' today is capable of managing its own affairs without need for intervention by the state. Now, the focus on 'today' is important as there are those who argue that state bureaux are made redundant by self-organizing networks precisely because of the former's historic success in equipping the latter with the capacities for self-governance. Their mission accomplished they can now wither away, victims of their own success. For others, however, 'civil society' is always already equipped with the capacities for self-governance and 'today' is only important in that it is now, at last or once again, depending on your point of view, that these capacities are being recognized by government and allowed/encouraged to flourish (Hargreaves, 1998; Botsman and Latham, 2001).

Both versions – whether more communitarian or liberal (it's not always easy to distinguish between them when exploring 'governance') – appear prone to what Charles Larmore (1987: 75) calls 'political expressivism'. They require a political order to express certain moral ideals – such as an all pervading spirit of community or an inalienable right to personal autonomy. In other words, they both assume that the political domain should express the highest ideals of its members and, thus, refuse to envision the possibility that the political realm and other areas of life 'may heed different priorities' (Larmore, 1987: 93) For them both, governance, unlike traditional bureaucratic forms of political government, is capable of constructing forms of political order that enable these ideal human capacities to flourish.[2]

**questions of authority**    It would be foolish to argue that so-called 'self-organizing networks' are incapable of improvising a kind of order – quite obviously they are. However, what that order is will only be known after the event, as a historical fact; there will be no prior, logistical guarantees. The best governance is not always the least government. It is more than possible, for instance, that a structure of minimal constraint that leaves individuals and groups equally free to pursue their equally authorized or unauthorized moral ideals would result in a fatal 'antagonistic pluralism', rather than the more cosy interdependencies assumed by some analysts of governance. The only guarantees come, as Thomas Hobbes knew only too well, when someone or something is prepared to assume the role of sovereign.[3]

Hobbes (1991: II. 94), like all liberals, accepts the fact of pluralism. 'All men', he writes, 'are by nature provided of notable multiplying glasses, (that is their Passions and Selfe-Love).' Moreover, because 'Nature hath made men so equall' in both 'ability' and right, from this 'ariseth equality of hope in the attainment of our Ends' (1991: I.61). However, these ends may not be the same or, even if they are, they maybe such that they cannot be attained equally by both parties, and so, in the absence of an arbiter 'to keep them quiet', they 'become enemies' (1991: I. 61–2). For Hobbes, then, pluralism and equality, rather than being conditions that argue for our freedom from government, are, in fact, conditions demanding absolute government. If society is to endure and perpetual conflict be curtailed there arises the need for 'a common Power to keep them all in awe' (1991: I.62). Famously, Hobbes argues that the only way to erect such a Common Power is, to conferre all their power and strength upon one Man, or upon one Assembly of men, that may reduce all their Wills, by plurality of voices, unto one Will: which is as much as to say, to appoint one Man, or Assembly of men, to beare their Person; and every one to owne, and acknowledge himselfe to be Author of whatsoever he that so beareth their Person, shall Act, or cause to be Acted, in those things that concerne the Common Peace and Safetie; and therein to submit their Wills, every one to his Will, and their Judgements, to his Judgment ... And he that carryeth this Person, is called SOVERAIGNE, and said to have *Soveraigne Power*. (1991: II.87)

Because 'the plurality of voices', if left to its own devices, can result in discord, and because there is simply no mechanism in nature to harmonize it, an artificial mechanism – a pacifying reason of state – must be established and fastidiously maintained. For Hobbes (1991: I. 64), the 'generall rule' is that 'every man ought to endeavour Peace'. If peace cannot be obtained so long as 'masterlesse men' enjoy a 'full and absolute Libertie', then that liberty must be constrained. More importantly, the proper 'liberty of Subjects' only exists in relation to the 'Artificiall Chains' put in place by the Sovereign and the Civil Laws. It is the presence of 'Artificiall Chains' that secures liberty for subjects, not their absence (1991: II. 108–9). For so long as every man is encouraged to 'do anything he liketh ... so long are all men in the condition of Warre'. In the truly autonomous realm, beyond government, there can be no a priori guarantees. Therefore, it 'is very absurd for men to clamor as they doe', for such 'absolute Libertie', Hobbes (1991: II.109) argues, because the proper 'Liberty of a Subject' depends on the presence not absence of an absolute authority. Thus, the idea that 'every private man has an absolute Propriety in his Goods', Hobbes continues, 'tendeth to the Dissolution of a Commonwealth'.

Every man has indeed a Propriety that excludes the Right of every other Subject: And he has it onely from the Soveraign Power; without the protection whereof, every other man should have equall Right to the same. But if the Right of the Soveraign also be excluded, he cannot performe the office they have put him into; which is, to defend them both from forraign enemies, and from the injuries of one another; and consequently there is no longer a Commonwealth.[4] (Hobbes, 1991: II.169–70)

It is hardly surprising that Hobbes's modus vivendi authoritarianism appears illiberal when benchmarked against the standards of contemporary 'expressivist' liberal (and communitarian) thought. Hobbes is negatively coded in the eyes of contemporary expressivist liberals, for example, because he refuses to affirm from the doctrine of equality the *positive* values – autonomy, free choice, free association, individual self-realization – that inform modern liberal thought. As Fish has argued:

> For Locke, Kant, Mills and Rawls (in their different ways), the equality of men and the values they invariably espouse points to the rejection of any form of absolutism: if no one's view can be demonstrated to be absolutely right, no one should occupy the position of absolute authority. For Hobbes the same insight into the pluralism of values and the unavailability of a mechanism for sorting them out implies exactly the reverse: because no one's view can be demonstrated to be absolutely right (and also because every one prefers his own view and believes it to be true), someone *must* occupy the position of absolute authority. (1999: 180)

To counterpose Hobbes's 'authoritarianism', then, with something 'truly liberal' is to misunderstand the historical emergence of liberalism as a form of political ordering (Holmes, 1994; Hunter, 1998). Liberal freedoms – such as religious toleration – were not, as is so often inferred in modern liberal thought, the product of a social delimitation of the state. Rather, they were the contingent outcome of attempts in early modern Europe to de-confessionalize politics and politically pacify rival moral communities engaged in 'Warre' (Hunter, 1998: 260). In this sense, the standard tropes of modern liberal thought, individual rights for example, do not function as transcendental limits on state action but are rather the product of action by sovereign states. As Holmes (1994: 605) puts it, 'statelessness means right-lessness. Stateless people, in practice, have no rights.' Inhabitants of weak or poor states tend to have few or laxly enforced rights. Without central-ized and bureaucratic state capacities, there is no possibility of forging 'a single and impartial legal system – the rule of law – on the population of a large nation. Without a well-organized political and legal system, exclu-sive loyalties and passions' are difficult to control (p. 605). It is not easy, then, to hitch liberalism to anti-statism, without doing considerable damage to the historical emergence of liberalism as a form of political ordering.

And yet this is precisely what happens on a regular basis in what Holmes (1994: 599) calls 'storybook accounts of liberalism' and, as we shall see shortly, in story-book accounts of the emergence of 'governance' – where self-organization, free association, limited government and so on are seen to emerge from a 'critique of state reason' and function as elements of a moral ideal. Here, as we saw earlier, liberalism (and governance) is a form of 'political expressivism'. In expressivist accounts, a particular practice – religious toleration, say – is tied to a profound moral principle – a Kantian respect for the autonomy of free agents, for example. As we have seen, though, not all liberalism is expressivist. Under Hobbesian 'authoritarianism' toleration is enacted from fear of civil chaos and as a means to peaceful coexistence. It does not function as a moral ideal. As John Gray (2000: 3), for example, has indicated, 'nothing in Hobbes suggests he favoured toleration as a pathway to the true faith. For him, toleration was a strategy of peace.'

Hobbes saw that, in its capacity to guarantee social peace, the sovereign state had no need for 'higher' religious or philosophical justifications. The state's indifference to the transcendent beliefs of the rival communities over which it ruled was based neither on an ideal of individual liberty or free agency nor on a commitment to a shared moral consensus amongst its citizens:

> The emergent ethical autonomy of the state meant that the 'citizen' (whose public obedience to the law was a condition of social peace) could no longer be thought of as identical with the 'man' (who might freely follow the light of his conscience as long as this did not interfere with his public duty to the law). (Hunter, 1994a: 41)

The state's indifference to the personal beliefs of those it ruled was therefore grounded in an 'art of separation' of social life into different spheres – political and religious, public and private and so forth. This art of separation was opposed to the idea of society as an organic 'whole' and the associated conception of the human being as a unified moral personality. A pacified civil society required a conception of the human being as the bearer of a differentiated set of *personae*, of which *homme et citoyen* (man and citizen)were two of the most obvious. The persona of the citizen as inhabitant of the sovereign state, and the persona of the practititioner of religious (or other forms of communal) self-governance, now represented two distinct and autonomous modes of comportment, housed in two distinct realms, of 'public' and 'private' conduct (Hunter, 1999). For Hobbes, religious toleration, or the state's indifference to moral identities and transcendent truth claims, is a crucial element in the state's elevation to sovereignty in the political arena, which in turn is the precondition for social pacification.[5]

The expressivist or sacralizing tenets of contemporary 'governance' – the desire for a state capable of realizing the self-governing moral community from which all good things will come, and hence one capable of making itself redundant – and the profound gulf seperating them from Hobbes's de-sacralized state are hard to miss.[6] In the following section, I focus attention on this 'gulf' by exploring in more detail the historical schema developed by analysts/advocates of governance in the area of public administration to account for the latter's emergence as a distinctive rationality of rule. I suggest that this schema – and the epochal arrangement of governmental rationalities underpinning it – offers little more than a set of theoretical distinctions aimed at contrasting perfectly antithetical forms of political ordering. As such it has little to say about contemporary administrative reform, forcing institutional arrangements into a fit with the schema even where it strains the explanatory reach of the schema's typology.

**the tyranny of the epoch**    The emergence of governance in the field of public administration is frequently represented in terms of a series of 'caesural' shifts that, when taken together, are held to pose 'a tremendous challenge to the state's ability to maintain some degree of control over its external environment and to impose its will on society' (Pierre, 2000: 2). So, for example, economic globalization is depriving the sovereign state under the rule of law of many of its traditional capacities of economic management; sub-national governing bodies are becoming more assertive in their demands for self-determination vis-à-vis the state; and regions and cities – frequently propelled by ethnic and other cultural identifications – are themselves represented as active players in the international arena, apparently bypassing state institutions along the way. These and other imperatives of the real are challenging the very foundations of traditional state-based forms of political ordering – including, most importantly, elements of state sovereignty – and are giving rise to new forms of 'governing without government' (Rosenau, 1992).

Alongside these ostensibly powerful changes in the external environment, state institutions are also represented as the subjects of ongoing radical reforms to their internal environments. These have been inaugurated most frequently by those charged with running them and have, whether consciously or unconsciously, it is argued, stripped those institutions of many of their traditional sources of authority and their capacity to exert control over society. The 1980s and 1990s are said to have witnessed the emergence of a new rationality of rule within many of the advanced liberal democracies – neo-liberalism. Here, political government has been restructured in the name of an economizing logic. To govern better the state is to govern less but more 'entrepreneurially'. It is to mobilize 'society' so that society can play an enhanced role in solving problems that have come to be seen as the sole province of the state to manage. This requires the responsibilization and autonomization of a host of actants – individual and collective – as conditions of its effectiveness. As two influential advocates of this 're-invention' of government put it, the state should 'steer' more but 'row' less:

Entrepreneurial governments promote *competition* between service providers. They *empower* citizens by pushing control out of the bureaucracy, into the community. They measure the performance of their agencies, focusing not on inputs but on *outcomes.* They are driven by their goals – their *missions* – not by their rules and regulations. They re-define their clients as *customers,* and offer them choices – between schools, between training programs, between housing options. They *prevent* problems before they emerge, rather than simply offering services afterward. They put their energies into *earning* money, not simply spending it. They de-centralize authority, embracing *participatory* management. They prefer *market* mechanisms to bureaucratic mechanisms. And they focus not simply on providing public services but on *catalyzing* all sectors – public, private and voluntary – into action to solve their community's problems. (Osborne and Gaebler, 1992: 19–20)

If this 'entrepreneurial government' had one overarching target – that which it has most explicitly defined itself against – then it was the impersonal, procedural, hierarchical and technical organization of the traditional, unified state bureaucracy. Put simply, 'bureaucracy' was represented as the paradigm that failed, in large part because the forms of organizational and personal conduct it gave rise to and fostered – adherence to procedure, abnegation of personal moral enthusiasms and so forth – were regarded as fundamentally unsuited to the demands of contemporary economic, social, political and cultural 'reality' (du Gay, 2000b). In an era of constant and profound 'change', it was argued, a new paradigm was required for the public administration if it was to survive at all (see Ch. 6). 'Entrepreneurial government' (Osborne and Gaebler, 1992) was represented as just such a paradigm.

Quite obviously, a key feature of entrepreneurial government was the crucial role it allocated to a particular conception of the commercial enterprise as the preferred model for the institutional organization of public services. However, of equal importance has been the way the term was deployed to refer to particular enterprising qualities on the part of persons, characteristics such as responsiveness to users needs and desires, keener individual ownership of one's work and the wider goals and objectives it contributes to, and the ability to accept greater individual responsibility for securing outcomes efficiently (Keat, 1990; du Gay and Salaman, 1992).

Refracted through the gaze of entrepreneurial governance bureaucratic public administration appeared inimical to the development of these capacities and comportments and hence to the production of enterprising persons. The bureaucratic commitment to (local and specific) norms of impersonality, party political neutrality, 'snag-hunting' and so forth was regarded as antithetical to the cultivation of those entrepreneurial competences which alone were held to guarantee a manageable and hence sustainable future for the public services. Thus entrepreneurial government not only provided a critique of bureaucratic public administration, but also offered a set of solutions to the problems posed by an assumed process of continuous and unrelenting change. It did so through delineating certain principles, which, when taken together, constituted a new method of 'governing' organizational and personal conduct in the public services.

Entrepreneurial reforms, such as the introduction of 'market-type mechanisms' (MTMs) – contracting out, 'purchaser/provider' quasi-market relations, private finance initiatives and so forth – to all manner of public service business in health care, education, social welfare and the machinery of government, are therefore represented as key processes in what has been termed the 'hollowing out of the state' (Peters, 1993; Rhodes, 1994). The upshot of this 'hollowing out' is an institutional landscape marked by tremendous diversity and fragmentation, where the state has effectively been deprived of capacity to exert control (Pierre, 2000: 2; Rhodes, 1997: 48). So, not only has the state shed its 'rowing' role, but its ability to 'steer' has been seriously undermined as well.

While these external and internal environmental changes may have created 'institutional fragmentation' and undermined the conditions of possibility of traditional political government by the state, they are also held to have – somewhat dialectically – provided the conditions of possibility for the emergence of a new narrative of rule, namely 'governance'. As Rhodes (1997: 48), for example, argues, network governance in the field of public administration is 'an unintended consequence of marketisation. Institutional differentiation – whether by contracting out, public-private partnerships or bypassing local government for special-purpose bodies – creates imperatives for interdependent actors to work together and multiply networks.'

This epochal narrative represents the dynamics of public administrative reform in terms of a simple succession whereby one form of ordering or governing is superseded and effaced by its predecessor. Thus, bureaucracy (an integral, unified governing style) is replaced by marketization (both within and beyond government), which is then displaced or superseded by governance (networks, partnerships and alliances), which promises to overcome the limitations of both bureaucracies and markets. Albeit as an unintended consequence of the proliferation of MTMs, governance appears as a much anticipated 'third way', arriving on cue to help return government to society where, advocates of governance argue, it should belong (Botsman and Latham, 2001).

Despite foregrounding a set of transitions in the organization of the public administration that have a certain intuitive plausibility, this narrative is less an institutional history than an abstracted theoretical account. Blocks of abstract 'governing styles' are allotted a clear and unambiguous identity as they overtake and supersede one another in an onward march towards their dominant contemporary manifestation, 'governance'. Once again, though, empirical, analytical and normative dimensions appear to be elided in this account of the dynamics of public administrative reform. First, it is clear that elements of each historically and conceptually distinctive 'block' are to be found within each of the others. So, for example, 'market-type mechanisms' do not do away with but presuppose the presence of elements of bureaucratic conduct to make them operate as intended. In the case of 'internal markets', for example, the flow of bureaucratic command is replaced by the workings of the market's hidden hand, or so it would appear. On closer inspection, however, it is clear that the power of command is not necessarily superseded but actually, perhaps, enhanced by the introduction of internal markets. As Alan Scott, for example, has indicated:

> The power of bureaucratic hierarchy (whether at the local level of a particular organization or at the level of the nation state) is maintained through the mobilization of the remaining regulative authority which is deployed to manipulate opportunity structures by shifting resources and centrally determined pricing. This induces uncertainty and instability into the environment of those released from the kinds of direct bureaucratic domination Weber described. The new autonomy is real but its beneficiaries find themselves in shifting opportunity structures within which they must operate and over which they do not have direct control. (1996: 101)

The crucial point here is that these shifting opportunity structures or 'externalities' are not those of the fate-like workings of the market alone but are to a very considerable extent the result of governmental decision-making and intervention. The environment within which organizational actors find themselves is governmentally constituted. Those at the centre do not relinquish their bureaucratic capacities by constituting newly autonomous subjects as long as they retain control over the environment within which actors act autonomously.

What we have here, then, is neither traditional Weberian bureaucracy nor a free market but a governmentally constituted quasi market. It is the formation of opportunity structures and environmental parameters rather than routine daily decisions that is the object of organizational manipulation. In the public services there is nothing at all subtle about this form of 'government at a distance'. For example, in all those many areas where the state is still paymaster, the price of units of resource is set centrally. By altering those nominal prices the state retains enormous power over those agencies to which it has also granted a degree of real autonomy (Scott, 1996: 101).

Similarly, there are conceptual and empirical problems with presumed distinctions between 'entrepreneurial governance' and 'network governance', with the former belonging exclusively to the 'marketization' block while the latter moves beyond competition, customers and contracting out to a governing style characterized by high levels of trust and cooperation

(Rhodes, 1996, 2000a). The problem here is that most 'entrepreneurial' models are not exclusively concerned with markets but also with many of the processes that 'network governance' would claim as its own – Osborne and Gaebler (1992) highlight the importance of participatory management, decentralization and on catalysing public, private and voluntary sectors in community partnerships, for example. At the empirical level, the contemporary concern with partnerships and collaborative working in British public administration has not resulted in any simple decline in the use of MTMs. As Pollitt and Bouckaert (2000: 274) note, Britain's New Labour Government has reversed little of its Conservative predecessors administrative reforms but has instead built on them in pursuit of 'better governance'. Chancellor Gordon Brown's self-styled 'entrepreneurial welfare' policies, for instance, emphasize the moral demand for civic responsibility characteristic of 'governance', but utilize a range of strategies, including market-based responsibilization techniques, forms of commercial and moral contracting, risk assessment procedures and so forth, to achieve their objectives (Stoker, 2000b). Attempting to divide out the 'market'-based from the 'governance'-based elements of these policies would be a somewhat thankless task.

Secondly, as these examples suggest, the state does not disappear from view in any of the models, it merely shifts its parameters and relocates elements of its authority. So, for example, in the governance model, the greater the emphasis placed on voluntary associations, such as the family as a source of 'social capital' (Wilkinson, 1998), the greater the constraints that come to be placed on the ways those associations can operate. This should come as no surprise, as Clarke and Newman (1997: 29) indicate, because 'an emphasis on the transfer of tasks, roles and responsibilities away from the state risks neglecting the ways in which the dispersal of power in these processes engages ... other agents in the state's field of relationships'. So, for instance, the dispersal of roles, responsibilities and powers for the provision of public services away from the state to different agents – commercial enterprises, trusts, voluntary associations and so on– places considerable constraints and demands on those agents through processes of assessment, contract specification and performance evaluation. The capacities of the agents in question are not their intrinsic property – as the governance narrative would have it – but an effect of their relationship with the state.

The 'partnership' as an organizational form provides a useful example of just such a relationship. 'Partnerships' – organizational arrangements bringing together two or more actants in pursuit of a policy objective – are frequently regarded as a form of 'network governance', characterized by high levels of independence from the state. However, as Lowndes and Skelcher (1998) have argued, partnerships may be a form of network, but contrary to Rhodes's analysis, they are closely linked to and regulated by central government. Their analysis of partnerships in urban regeneration, training, health and other fields suggests that government plays the central role in the formation and structuring of such bodies. It may do so through statutory direction or by inducement through financial incentives. Its leverage is apparent in the programme approval and monitoring procedures with which partnerships must comply in order to gain access to central resources. These create a form of infrastructure that enables the regulation of such collaborative endeavours.

What we see here, then, is not a simple diminution in the state's authority but a reconfiguration of that authority. A different image of the state and its role in relation to 'society' is emerging, the state as enabler or animator (Donzelot, 1991; Rose, 1999). While the practices of political ordering related to this image are not without their own particular problems, as we will shortly see, it is nonetheless the case that if this is governance, then it is not a simple expressivist variant. Certainly, it appears as a form of rule designed to 'mobilize society', and to do so on the assumption that the state cannot answer all of society's needs without endangering its own long-term vitality. This conception of an 'enabling state' certainly depends upon a view of what humans are or should be – active not passive, responsible not dependent and so forth – and in this sense expresses an ideal. But governance in this form does not involve the wholesale supercession of the state and the dispersal of political power to self-governing communities envisaged in some of its communitarian and radical democratic versions. Rather, as Jessop (1998: 39), for example, has argued, governance in this sense is not only a state-sponsored rationality of rule, the state will typically continue to monitor the effects of 'governance mechanisms' on 'its own capacity to secure social cohesion in divided societies. The state reserves to itself the right to open, close, juggle, and re-articulate governance arrangements not only in terms of particular functions but also from the viewpoint of partisan and global political advantage.'

**re-sacralizing government?**   Despite the lack of fit between expressivist conceptions of governance beyond the state and the state-centred nature of most existing governance initiatives, expressivist ideals show no sign of losing their appeal. As Blandine Kriegel (1995: 3) has argued, reasons of state seem always now to be bad reasons, especially among those who do or would govern us. The 'enabling state' may be a 'state' but for many expressivists it is or is on the way to being something very different from a sovereign state under the rule of law. In principle, the enabling state might well be capable of opening, closing and juggling governance arrangements to suit its own purposes. However, the more it is subject to demands to seem 'less like a state and more like a community' (Latham, 2001b: 260), to become 'the servant not the master' of the people (Mulgan and

Wilkinson, 1992: 354), and to engage in the 'dispersal of power to communities and the wiping out of hierarchies at every opportunity' (Latham, 2001a: 34), then the less will it be able to act as a sovereign state in the manner articulated by Hobbes.[7] For expressivists, the more the state becomes part of society, in a sociological and political sense, not something above or beyond it, then the freer people will be to exert 'personal agency' and the more creative, innovative and dynamic all sectors of society will be (Latham, 2001a).

According to Peters (2000a: 49), the demand that 'governance begins with society and not with government itself', even when not formulated in an overtly expressivist way, is a standard trope of contemporary political discourse. As Stoker (1998: 19) puts it, 'the governance perspective challenges conventional assumptions which focus on government as if it were a "stand alone" institution divorced from wider societal forces'. It is an assumption that frames many contemporary experiments in the field of public administration, from the Private Finance Initiative (PFI) and e-government projects to the renewed interest in the role of religious or faith-based organizations in the provision of education and social welfare.[8] There is a significant problem here, though; in making the state simply part of society, the state becomes something different from what it is in its own terms. It stops being a state.

After all, it is a perfectly simple academic move to indicate how the state is a (social) construct – sociologists, political scientists and critical legal scholars have been doing so for years – but that is not something a state itself can be expected to take cognizance of and act upon and still remain operative as a state. The achievements of sovereign 'stateness' – social pacification, individual rights, religious toleration and so forth – flow from the assumption and performance of independence from society and ultimate authority over it. To take an academic insight into the state's reliance on some other – extra-statist – structure of concern in its own self-constitution and then try and make the operations of the state transparently accord with this insight is a recipe for confusion, if not disaster. For example, were the state to deploy its procedures in the company of an analysis of their roots in extra-state discourses and techniques, it would not be exercising but, rather, dismantling its authority; in short, it would no longer be acting like a state but, rather engaging in some sort of academic enterprise. Rather than producing the authority it retroactively invokes, the state would be in the business of continually calling into question the basis of its authority and hence producing uncertainty, one of the very things it was instituted to avoid.

It is a profound mistake, therefore, to assume that the state should be 're-invented' or 'modernized' to accord with the nitty-gritty facts of social and moral life as conceptualized either in 'social constructionist' academic analyses or in expressivist liberal and communitarian conceptions of 'governance'. Both strive to prove that the 'independence' and autonomy of the 'sovereign state' is a fiction. But the fiction with which the sovereign state sustains its role is in fact the assumption (no more or less vulnerable than any other) that constitutes that role; take it away and you remove the role and all the advantages it brings to bear. The reasoning that academic and visionary analyses deploy seems simple; indeed, it is too simple: since the sovereign state is manifestly dependent upon, makes use of, and invokes materials derived from any number of 'social' locations it must itself be part of society and not autonomous of it. But the fact that an institution and set of practices incorporates material, concepts and *modus operandi* from other contexts does not challenge its autonomy. The reasoning that if the state is not really beyond society, then it is not a sovereign but simply another part of society, only holds if state autonomy is conceptualized as a once and for all condition of hermetic self-sufficiency, rather than as a condition continually achieved and re-achieved as the state takes unto itself and makes its own materials that will help it achieve its purposes (Fish, 1994: 141–77). To actively attempt to de-autonomize the state under the aegis of its status as a social 'construct' or the imperatives of moral expressivism is effectively to re-theologize it (Hunter, 1998). One need only point to the rise of democratic and nationalist movements in the nineteenth century armed with similar expressivist concerns to indicate the dangers such re-theologization poses to social pacification, the rule of law and the practise of religious toleration.

**concluding comments**   We are left with an important question: does this incessant critique of the state's 'fictitious' autonomy, neutrality, sovereignty and so forth made in the name of 'governance', help to foster an atmosphere in which the state's capacity to secure its authority, in the field of public administration, for instance, is effectively undermined? There is certainly a wealth of evidence, anecdotal as well as more empirically substantiated, that current enthusiasms in the field in the UK – such as the PFI, or partnership structures – are tinged with expressivist ideals and that these have caused and are likely to continue to cause serious problems of political authority. With regard to PFI projects in the National Health Service, for instance, ministerial accountability is proving a blunt instrument. Once the PFI contract has been signed, the public administration is not in a position to renegotiate it if Parliament considers that the contract does not meet present or future clinical needs. This reveals the dangers of politicians and state administrators assuming a clear identity of interest between public and private government (Freedland, 1998; Pollock and Dunnigan, 1998; Elsenaar, 1999) . Similarly, in relation to partnership structures. These have been stimulated by central government in line with certain tenets of contemporary governance and appear amenable in principle, as we saw earlier, to the opening, closing and juggling that Jessop refers to. However, such is the complexity of many existing organizational and financial arrangements that not only central government but many of the constituent members of the partnership boards have little idea as to who is in fact accountable to whom and for what. Government attempts to steer such partnerships have been represented in terms of pulling 'rubber levers'. Similarly, the complexity of organizational arrangements have been likened to 'byzantium' (Skelcher, 2000: 16–18).

As David Runciman (1999: 264) argues in his analysis of the work of the English pluralists, 'finding reliable authors and convincing settings for the exercise of political authority is the very stuff of politics'. Runciman indicates how the pluralists, in seeking to move away from Hobbesian conceptions of 'state' and 'sovereignty', found themselves having to face a familiar problem – the problem of authority outlined by Hobbes. Expressivist advocates of governance find themselves in a similar position. In seeking to move away from Hobbesian conceptions of state and sovereignty they have yet to find reliable authors and settings for the exercise of political authority.

As we saw earlier, despite proclaiming themselves as the protectors of individual rights and community freedoms, anti-statist advocates of governance cannot be consistent defenders of these rights and freedoms, because rights and freedoms are an enforced uniformity, enforced that is by sovereign states. Not only this, they are rarely guaranteed without the presence of effective, centralized state bureaucracies capable of creating and regulating them. This is a tough lesson for anti-statists to learn, but a vital one. The contemporary love-affair with decentralized and privatized forms of 'governance' in public administration raises serious and far-reaching questions of political authority. It should be clear by now that the analysis I am offering is unconvinced of the redundancy of either Hobbesian conceptions of 'state', 'sovereignty' and 'authority' or of the vices of centralized, bureaucratic forms of public administration. It is, however, far from confident about the alternatives offered by expressivist 'governance'.

## notes

1   Or, as Stoker (1998: 17) puts it, '[T]he essence of governance is its focus on governing mechanisms that do not rest on recourse to the authority and sanctions of government'.

2   Larmore (1987) distinguishes between two types of expressivism. Those involving 'substantial' ideals of the good life and those involving the 'ideals of autonomy and experimentalism'. The former, which he attributes to communitarians, are those ideals embodying a specific structure of purposes, significances and activities: a life devoted to art, a life centred on work, etc. The latter, which he attributes to liberals, concern the way in which 'we ought to assume and

pursue such ideals. They themselves are not so much ways of life as attitudes in which we are to understand our commitment to ways of life' (p. 74). He refers to autonomy and experimentalism as ideals that demand we subject all our ways of life to critical evaluation concerning their relative strengths and weaknesses in relation to other conceivable ways of being. I have to admit to being somewhat less than convinced that such a separation holds in the manner Larmore suggests. Autonomy and experimentalism, every bit as much as more substantive ideals of the good life, involve particular practices of comporting the person based upon certain strongly held values. The radically 'self-questioning life' may be different from the 'radically embedded' one but they are simply optional or equivalent in terms of being value-based practices of self-formation.

3   Hirst (2000), for example, is more than aware that an 'associational society' that is not riven by fatal factionalism is inconceivable in the absence of a *Rechsstaat* equipped with the sovereign authority and means necessary to construct and coordinate the interrelations of associations and regulate their activities. I draw here, in particular, on the perspective developed in Fish (1999).

4   At common law, only the sovereign is said to have an absolute interest in land, for example: ordinary landowners 'hold of the sovereign'. As Holmes and Sunstein (1999: 63) argue, 'this quaint legalism expresses a deep truth. An autonomous individual in a liberal society, cannot create the conditions of his own autonomy autonomously'.

5   As Ian Hunter (1999: 14–15) has argued, the formation of the authoritarian liberal state is incompatible with 'all notions of popular sovereignty; for here supremacy of power is forged solely from the functional end of civil peace, to the exclusion of all concern with will-representation. Consequently, even when a democratic government is the agent of sovereign power it should serve this functional end, rather than the will of the people.'

6   As one leading Australian proponent has argued, the aim is to lay the 'moral foundations of governance' in a new politics which:

> • Recognises the role of civil society in creating trust and moral obligation
> • Follows the communitarian practice of engaging the public in a civic conversation
> • Builds a new citizenship, based on the big tent of multiple identities
> • Above all else, trusts its people
>
> Without trust there can be no shared morality or, for that matter, shared humanity. (Latham, 2001b: 242)

7   That these demands are made by members of parliament – Latham was Leader of the Australian Labour Party – and senior civil servants – Mulgan, unbelievably given his background and enthusiasms, was a senior civil servant and Head of the Performance and Innovation Unit in the British Cabinet Office – as well as the normal proponents of political expressivism suggests that Kriegel's comments are uncomfortably close to the bone.

8   In Britain, the Private Finance Initiative (PFI) or Public Private Partnerships (PPP) as New Labour prefers, is a perfect example of a policy driven by the assumption that the 'mobilization of society' reaps benefits for all. The PFI was launched in 1992 by the UK Treasury. The basic idea was that the private sector should raise the capital investment required for public sector works (including

roads, bridges, schools, prisons and hospitals), in return for owning, designing, building and operating the facilities. The facilities would then be rented by the public sector or paid for through user charges (in traditional government procurement the public sector retains control of the asset and is not tied into a contract for the provision of services). This idea was linked to the popular 'governance' theme that it no longer mattered who owned or delivered services as long as they continued to be free at the point of delivery. In the Foreword to *Partnerships for Prosperity – the Private Finance Initiative* (Treasury Taskforce on Private Finance, 1997), Chancellor Gordon Brown highlighted the redundancy of what he termed 'the old battles', between public and private, state and free market, and indicated that the PFI was a means to mobilizing and incentivizing the private sector to act in the public interest. The document goes on to assert that

> Public Private Partnerships are all about negotiating deals that are good for both sides. The private sector wants to earn a return on its ability to invest and perform. The public sector wants contracts where incentives exist for the private sector supplier to deliver services on time to specified standards year after year. In that, the public sector shares an absolute identity of interest with private financiers whose return on investment will depend on those services being delivered to those standards. (Treasury Taskforce on Private Finance, 1997: 1)

The notion of a common or even absolute identity of interest between public and private or the effective meaninglessness of the distinction between them pervades PFI/PPP policy documentation (HM Treasury, 1993; HM Treasury, Private Finance Panel, 1995).

# bibliography

Abrams, P. (1982) *Historical Sociology*. Shepton Mallett: Open Books.

Bamfield, J. (1980) 'The changing face of British retailing', *National Westminster Quarterly Review*, May: 15–29.

Barthes, R. (1977) 'Death of the authors', in *Image-Music-Text*. London: Fontana.

Bauman, Z. (1993) *Postmodern Ethics*. Oxford: Blackwell.

Bauman, Z. (1998) *Work, Consumerism and the New Poor*. Buckingham: Open University Press.

Bauman, Z. (2000) *Liquid Modernity*. Cambridge: Polity Press.

Bauman, Z. (2004) *Identity*. Cambridge: Polity Press.

Becker. G. (1981) *A Treatise on the Family*. Cambridge, MA: Harvard University Press.

Becker, G. (1986) 'The economic approach to human behaviour', in J. Elster (ed.) *Rational Choice*. New York: New York University Press.

Bennett, R. (2004) *Havoc In Its Third Year*. London: Bloomsbury.

Bishop, P. and Davis, G. (2001) 'Developing consent: consultation, participation and governance', in G. Davis and P. Weller (eds) *Are You Being Served? States, Citizens and Governance*. Sydney: Allen & Unwin.

Black, D. (1998) 'The limitations of evidence', *Journal of the Royal College of Physicians of London*, 32(1): 23–6.

*Blacks Law Dictionary* (1968) St. Paul, MN: West Group.

*Blacks Law Dictionary* (1999) 7th edn. St Paul, MN: West Group.

Blau, P. (1956) *Bureaucracy in Modern Society*. New York: Random House.

Bogdanor, V. (1996) 'A threat to democracy?', in P. Barberis (ed.) *The Whitehall Reader*. Milton Keynes: Open University Press.

Bogdanor, V. (2001) 'Civil Service reform: a critique', *The Political Quarterly*, 72(3): 291–9.

Bohman, J. (1996) *Public Deliberation: Pluralism, Complexity and Democracy*. Cambridge, MA: MIT Press.

Bok, S. (1978) *Lying*. Brighton: Harvester Press.

Bok, S. (1982) *Secrets*. Oxford: Oxford University Press.

Botsman, P. and Latham, M. (2001) *The Enabling State: People Before Bureaucracy*. Annandale: Pluto Press.

Bourdieu, P. (1987) 'The biographical illusion', in P. du Gay, J. Evans and P. Redman (eds) (2000) *The Identity: A Reader*. London: Sage (originally printed in Working Papers and Proceedings of the Center for Psychosocial Studies, University of Chicago).

Bowlby, R. (2000) *Carried Away: The Invention of Modern Shopping*. London: Faber & Faber.

Brown, V. (1994) *Adam Smith's Discourse*. London: Routledge.

Buchanan, J. (1978) 'From private preferences to public philosophy: the development of public choice', in J. Buchanan (ed.) *The Economics of Politics*. London: Institute of Economic Affairs.

Burkitt, I. (1992) *Social Selves*. London: Sage.

Butler, J. (1993) *Bodies That Matter: On the Discursive Limits of 'Sex'*. London: Routledge.

Cabinet Office (1999a) *Modernising Government* (Cm. 4310). London: HMSO.

Cabinet Office (1999b) *Vision and Values*. London: Cabinet Office.

Callon, M. (1998) 'Introduction: the embeddedness of economic markets in economics', in M. Callon, (ed.) *The Laws of the Markets*. Oxford: Blackwell.

Callon, M. and Muniesa, F. (2005) 'Economic markets as calculative collective devices', *Organization Studies*, 26(8): 1229–50.

Caplan, J. (1988) *Government Without Administration: State and Civil Service in Weimar and Nazi Germany*. Oxford: Clarendon Press.

Castells, M. (2000) *The Rise of the Network Society*, 2nd edn. Oxford: Blackwell.

Chapman, R. (1988) '"The Next Steps": a review', *Public Policy & Administration*, 3(3): 3–10.

Chapman, R. (1999) 'The Importance of *Modernising Government*', *Teaching Public Administration*, 19(1): 1–18.

Chapman, R.A. (2000) 'Ethics in public service for the new millenium', in R. A. Chapman (ed.) *Ethics in Public Service for the New Millenium*. Aldershot: Ashgate.

Chapman, R.A. (2004) *The Civil Service Commission 1855–1991: A Bureau Biography*. London: Taylor Francis Routledge.

Clarke, J. (2000) 'Governing welfare: systems, subjects and states', paper presented at the Social Policy Association Annual Conference, July.

Clarke, J. and Newman, J. (1997) *The Managerial State*. London: Sage.

Cochoy, F. (1998) 'Another discipline for the market economy: marketing as a performative knowledge and know-how for capitalism', in M. Callon (ed.) *The Laws of the Markets*. Oxford: Blackwell.

Cochoy, F. (2002) *Une Sociologie de packaging, ou l'âne de Buridan face au marché*. Paris: Presse Universitaires de France.

Cochoy, F. (2003) 'On the "Captation" of publics: understanding the market thanks to Little Red Riding Hood', Workshop on Market(-ing) Practice in Shaping Markets, Stockholm, June 14–16.

Condren, C. (1997) 'Liberty of office and its defence in seventeenth century political argument', *History of Political Thought*, XVIII(3): 460–82.

Condren, C. (2002) '*Natura Naturans*: Natural Law and the Sovereign in the Writings of Thomas Hobbes', in I. Hunter and D. Saunders (eds) *Natural Law and Civil Sovereignty*. Basingstoke: Palgrave.

Condren, C. (2004) 'The Persona of the Philosopher and the Rhetorics of Office in 16th and 17th Century England', paper presented to The Office of the Philosopher Conference, Centre for the Study of European Discourses, University of Queensland.

Cousins, M. (1980) 'Men's Rea: a note on sexual difference, criminology and the law', in P. Carlen, and M. Collison, (eds) *Radical Issues in Criminology*. Oxford: Martin Robertson.

Cousins, M. and Hussain, A. (1984) *Michel Foucault*. Basingstoke: Macmillan.

Crouch, C. (2004) *Post-Democracy*. Cambridge: Polity Press.

Daintith, T. (2002) 'A very good day to get out anything we want to bury', *Public Law*, Spring: 13–21.

Davies, R. and Howard, E. (1988) *The Changing Retail Environment*. London: Longman/Oxford Institute of Retail Management.

Department of Trade and Industry (DTI) (1998) *Our Competitive Future: Building the Knowledge Driven Economy* (Cm. 4176). London: HMSO.

di Maggio, P. (1994) 'Culture and economy', in N. Smelser and R. Swedberg (eds) *The Handbook of Economic Sociology*. Princeton: Princeton University Press.

Dobel, P. (1999) *Public Integrity*. Baltimore: The Johns Hopkins University Press.

Doig, A. and Wilson, J. (1998) 'What price new public management', *The Political Quarterly*, 69(3): 267–76.

Donzelot, J. (1991) 'The mobilization of society', in G. Burchell, C. Gordon and P. Miller (eds) *The Foucault Effect: Studies in Governmentality*. Brighton: Harvester.

Douglas, M. and Isherwood, B. (1979) *The World of Goods: Towards an Anthropology of Consumption*. Harmondsworth: Penguin.

Ducatel, K. and Blomley, N. (1990) 'Rethinking retail capital', *International Journal of Urban and Regional Research*, 19(2): 207–27.

du Gay, P. (1996) *Consumption & Identity at Work*. London: Sage.

du Gay, P. (2000a) *In Praise of Bureaucracy: Weber/Organization/Ethics*. London: Sage.

du Gay, P. (2000b) 'Entrepreneurial governance and public management: the anti-bureaucrats', in J. Clarke, S. Gerwirtz and E. McLaughlin (eds) *New Managerialism, New Welfare?* London: Sage.

du Gay, P. (2002) 'How responsible is "responsive" government?', *Economy & Society*, 31(3): 461–82.

du Gay, P. and Pryke, M. (eds) (2002) *Cultural Economy: Cultural Analysis and Commercial Life*. London: Sage.

du Gay, P. and Salaman, G. (1992) 'The Cult[ure] of the Customer', *Journal of Management Studies*, 29(5): 615–33.

Dunn, J. (2000) *The Cunning of Unreason*. London: HarperCollins.

Efficiency Unit (1988) *Improving Management in Government: The Next Steps*. London: HMSO.

Elcock, H. (2000) ' Management is not enough: we need leadership!', *Public Policy & Administration*, 15(1): 15–28.

Elias, N. (1968a) 'Homo Clausus', in P. du Gay, J. Evans and P. Redman (eds) (2000) *Identity: A Reader*. London: Sage (originally printed as 'Appendix I' in Elias, N. (1968) *The Civilizing Process Vol.I*. Oxford: Basil Blackwell).

Elias, N. (1968b) *The Civilizing Process Vol. I*. Oxford: Basil Blackwell.

Elias, N. (1983) *The Court Society*. Oxford: Basil Blackwell.

Elsenaar, M. (1999) 'Law, accountability and the Private Finance Initiative in the National Health Service', *Public Law*, Spring: 35–42.

Etzioni, A. (1997) *The New Golden Rule: Community and Morality in a Democratic Society*. New York: Profile Books.

Evans, J. (2003) 'Vigilance and vigilantes: thinking psychoanalytically about anti-paedophile action', *Theoretical Criminology*, 7(2): 163–89.

Falk, P. and Campbell, C. (1997) *The Shopping Experience*. London: Sage.

Featherstone, M. (1991) *Postmodernism & Consumer Culture*. London: Sage.

Fish, S. (1994) *There's No Such Thing As Free Speech ... And It's A Good Thing Too*. Oxford: Oxford University Press.

Fish, S. (1995) *Professional Correctness*. Oxford: Clarendon Press.

Fish, S. (1999) *The Trouble with Principle*. Cambridge, MA: Harvard University Press.

Fish, S. (2003) 'Truth but no consequences: why philosophy doesn't matter', *Critical Inquiry*, 29 (Spring): 389–417.

Force, P. (2003) *Self-Interest Before Adam Smith: A Geneaology of Economic Science*. Cambridge: Cambridge University Press.

Foucault, M. (1971) *The Order of Things*. London: Tavistock.

Foucault, M. (1979) *The History of Sexuality Vol.I*. Harmonsworth: Penguin.

Foucault, M. (1984) *The Use of Pleasure: The History of Sexuality Vol. II*. Harmondsworth: Penguin.

Foucault, M. (1985) 'Introduction to *The Use of Pleasure*', in P. du Gay, J. Evans and P. Redman (eds) (2000) *Identity: A Reader*. London: Sage (originally printed in Foucault, M. (1984) *The Use of Pleasure: The History of Sexuality Vol. II*. Harmondsworth: Penguin).

Foucault, M. (1986a) 'Nietzsche, genealogy, history', in P. Rabinow (ed.) *The Foucault Reader*. Harmondsworth: Penguin.

Foucault, M. (1986b) *The Care of the Self: The History of Sexuality Vol. 3*. Harmondsworth: Penguin.

Foucault, M. (1986c) 'On the genealogy of ethics: an overview of work in progress', in P. Rabinow (ed.) *The Foucault Reader*. Harmondsworth: Penguin.

Foucault, M. (1988) 'Technologies of the self', in L.H. Martin, H. Gutman, and P. Hutton (eds) *Technologies of the Self: a Seminar with Michel Foucault*. London: Tavistock.

Foucault, M. (1993) 'About the beginnings of the hermeneutics of the self', *Political Theory*, 21(2): 198–227.

Freedland, M. (1996) 'The rule against delegation and the *Carltona* doctrine in an agency context', *Public Law*, Summer: 19–30.

Freedland, M. (1998) 'Public law and private finance – placing the Private Finance Initiative in a public law frame', *Public Law*, Winter: 288–307.

Galvani, P. and Arnell, A. (1952) *Going Self-Service? A Practical Guide to Self-Service Grocery Retailing*. London: Sidgwick and Jackson.

Gamble, A. and Wright, T. (eds) (2004) *Restating The State*? Oxford: Blackwell.

Gardner, C. and Sheppard, J. (1989) *Consuming Passion: The Rise of Retail Culture*. London: Unwin Hyman.

Gaukroger, S. (1995) *Descartes*. Oxford: Oxford University Press.

Geuss, R. (2001) *History and Illusion in Politics*. Cambridge: Cambridge University Press.

**179**

Giddens, A. (1979) *Central Problems in Social Theory*. Basingstoke: Macmillan.

Giddens, A. (1991) *Modernity and Self-Identity*. Cambridge: Polity Press.

Giddens, A. (1994) *Beyond Left and Right*. Cambridge: Polity Press.

Giddens, A. (1998) *The Third Way*. Cambridge: Polity Press.

Glazer, N. (1993) *Women's Paid and Unpaid Labour: The Work Transfer in Healthcare and Retailing*. Philadelphia: Temple University Press.

Goodsell, C. (2004) *The Case for Bureaucracy*, 4th edn. Washington, DC: CQ Press.

Grandclément, C. (2006) 'Les marketing des similarités. Les produits à marque de distributeur', *Réseaux*, 24 (135–6): 221–252.

Gray, J. (2000) *The Two Faces of Liberalism*. Cambridge: Polity Press.

Green, L. (1988) *The Authority of the State*. Oxford: Clarendon Press.

*Guardian* (1999a) 'Blair berates Old Labour "snobs"', 7 July, p. 2.

*Guardian* (1999b) 'Top jobs to go in big Whitehall shake-up', 16 December, pp. 1–2.

Habermas, J. (1972) *Knowledge and Human Interests*. London: Heinemann.

Habermas, J. (1981) *The Theory of Communicative Action Vol. 1*. Boston: Beacon Press.

Habermas, J. (1986) *The Philosophical Discourse of Modernity*. Cambridge: Polity Press.

Habermas, J. (1991) *Communication and the Evolution of Society*. Cambridge: Polity Press.

Habermas, J. (1997) *Between Facts and Norms: Contributions to a Discourse Theory of Law and Democracy*. Cambridge: Polity Press.

Hacking, I. (1999) *The Social Construction of What?* Cambridge, MA: Harvard University Press.

Hadot, P. (1992) 'Reflections on the notion of "the cultivation of the self"', in T. Armstrong (ed.) *Michel Foucault, Philosopher*. Brighton: Harvester Wheatsheaf.

Hadot, P. (1995a) *Philosophy as a Way of Life*. Oxford: Blackwell.

Hadot, P. (1995b) 'Reflections on the idea of the "cultivation of the self"', in P. du Gay, J. Evans and P. Redman, (eds) (2000) *Identity: A Reader*. London: Sage (originally printed in Hadot, P. (1995) *Philosophy as a Way of Life*. Oxford: Blackwell).

Hargreaves, I. (1998) 'A step beyond Morris dancing: the third sector revival', in I. Hargreaves and I. Christie (eds) *Tomorrow's Politics*. London: Demos.

Hennessy, P. (2004) 'The lightning flash on the road to Baghdad: issues of evidence', in W. G. Runicman (ed.) *Hutton and Butler: Lifting the Lid on the Workings of Power*. Oxford: Oxford University Press.

Hennis, W. (1988) *Max Weber: Essays in Reconstruction*. London: Allen & Unwin.

Hennis, W. (2000) *Max Weber's Science of Man*. Newbury, Berks: Threshold Press.

Hirschman, A. (1977) *The Passions and the Interests*. Princeton: Princeton University Press.

Hirst, P. (2000) 'Democracy and governance', in J. Pierre (ed.) *Debating Governance*. Oxford: Oxford University Press.

Hirst, P. and Woolley, P. (1982) *Social Relations and Human Attributes*. London: Tavistock.

HM Treasury (1993) *Breaking New Ground*. London: HMSO.

HM Treasury, Private Finance Panel (1995) *Private Opportunity, Public Benefit – Progressing the Private Finance Initiative*. London: HMSO.

Hobbes, T. (1969) *The Elements of Law Natural and Political,* 2nd edn., ed. Ferdinand Tonnies, introd. M.M. Goldsmith. London: London University Press.

Hobbes, T. (1990) *Behemoth or The Long Parliament.* Chicago: Chicago University Press.

Hobbes, T. (1991) *Leviathan.* Cambridge: Cambridge University Press.

Hochschild, A. (1983) *The Managed Heart.* Los Angeles: University of California Press.

Holmes, S. (1994) 'Liberalism for a world of ethnic passions and decaying states', *Social Research,* 61(3): 599–610.

Holmes, S. (1995) *Passions and Constraint.* Chicago: University of Chicago Press.

Holmes, S. and Sunstein, C. (1999) *The Cost of Rights.* New York: W.W. Norton.

Hont, I. and Ignatieff, M. (1983) *Wealth & Virtue.* Cambridge: Cambridge University Press.

Hopfl, H. (1992) 'The making of the corporate acolyte: some thoughts on corporate leadership and the reality of organizational commitment', *Journal of Management Studies,* 29(13): 23–34.

House of Lords (1998) *Report of The Select Commitee on Public Service.* London: HMSO.

Hume, D. (1998) *Selected Essays.* Oxford: Oxford University Press.

Humphrey, K. (1998) *Shelf Life: Supermarkets and the Changing Cultures of Consumption.* Melbourne: Cambridge University Press.

Hunter, I. (1993) 'Subjectivity and government', *Economy & Society,* 22(1): 123–34.

Hunter, I. (1994a) *Re-Thinking the School.* Sydney: Allen & Unwin.

Hunter, I. (1994b) 'Metaphysics as a way of life', *Economy & Society,* 23(1): 93–117.

Hunter, I. (1998) 'Uncivil society', in M. Dean and B. Hindess (eds) *Governing Australia.* Sydney: Cambridge University Press.

Hunter, I. (1999) 'Is Metaphysics a Threat to Liberal Democracy?', paper presented to a colloquium on 'The End of Postmodernism?', Humanities Research Centre, Australian National University, August.

Hunter, I. (2001) *Rival Enlightenments.* Cambridge: Cambridge University Press.

Hunter, I. (2005) 'Security: the default setting of the Liberal State', accessed at http://www.apo.org.au/webboard/results. chtml?filename num=42404.

Hunter, I. (2006) 'History of theory', *Critical Inquiry,* 33: 78–112.

Hunter, I. and Saunders, D. (1995) 'Walks of life: Mauss and the human gymnasium', *Body & Society,* 1(2).

Jambet, C. (1992) 'The constitution of the subject and spiritual practice', in T. Armstrong (ed.) *Michel Foucault, Philosopher.* Brighton: Harvester Wheatsheaf.

Jessop, B. (1998) 'The rise of governance and the risks of failure: the case of economic development', *International Social Science Journal,* 155: 29–46.

Johnson, N. (1983) 'Management in government', in M. J. Earl (ed.) *Perspectives on Management.* Oxford: Oxford University Press.

Johnston, D. (1986) *The Rhetoric of Leviathan.* Princeton: Princeton University Press.

Jones, N. (2001) *The Control Freaks.* London: Politicos.

Jonsen, A. and Toulmin, S. (1988) *The Abuse of Casuistry.* Los Angeles: University of California Press.

Jordan, G. (1994) 'Re-inventing government: but will it work?', *Public Administration,* 72: 21–35.

Kallinikos, Y. (2004) 'The social foundations of the bureaucratic order', *Organization*, 11(1): 13–36.

Kaufman, H. (1977) *Red Tape: Its Origins, Uses and Abuses.* Washington, DC: The Brookings Institution.

Keat, R. (1990) 'Introduction', in R. Keat and N. Abercrombie (eds) *Enterprise Culture.* London: Routledge.

Kriegel, B. (1995) *The State and the Rule of Law,* trans. M. LePain and J. Cohen. Princeton: Princeton University Press.

Kundera, M. (1993) *Immortality.* London: Faber and Faber.

Larmore, C. (1987) *Patterns of Moral Complexity.* Cambridge: Cambridge University Press.

Lash, S. and Urry, J. (1994) *Economies of Signs and Space.* London: Sage.

Latham, M. (2001a) 'The new economy and the new politics', in P. Botsman and M. Latham (eds) *The Enabling State.* Annandale: Pluto Press.

Latham, M. (2001b) 'The moral foundations of government', in P. Botsman and M. Latham (eds) *The Enabling State.* Annandale: Pluto Press.

Latour, B. (2002) *La Fabrique du Droit: une ethnographie du Conseil d'État.* Paris: La Découverte.

Latour, B. (2004) 'Why has critique run out of steam? From matters of fact to matters of concern', *Critical Inquiry,* 30 (Winter): 225–48.

Latour, B. (2005) *Reassembling the Social.* Oxford: Oxford University Press.

Law, J. (1994) *Organizing Modernity.* Oxford: Blackwell.

Law, J. (2002) 'Economics as interference', in P. du Gay and M. Pryke (eds) *Cultural Economy.* London: Sage.

Leadbeater, C. (1999) *Living on Thin Air.* Harmondsworth: Penguin.

Le Grand, J. (2003) *Motivation, Agency, and Public Policy.* Oxford: Oxford University Press.

Leymonerie, C. (2006) 'La vitrine d'appareils ménagers. Reflet des structures commerciales dans la France des années 1950', *Réseaux,* 24 (135–6): 93–124.

Lestition, S. (1989) 'The teaching and practice of Jurisprudence in 18th Century Prussia: Königsberg's First Chancellor, R.F. von Sahme (1682–1753)', *Ius Commune,* 16: 27–80.

Levine, D. (2001) 'Know no limits: the destruction of self-knowledge in organizations', *Psychoanalytic Studies,* 3(2): 237–46.

Lévi-Strauss, C. (1987) *Introduction to the Work of Marcel Mauss,* trans. F. Baker. London: Routledge.

Lind, M. (2005) 'In defence of Mandarins', *Prospect,* 115 (October): 34–7.

Long, A.A. (2001) *Stoic Studies.* Los Angeles: University of California Press.

Long, A.A. and Sedley, D.N. (1987) *The Hellenistic Philosophers (Vol. 1).* Cambridge: Cambridge University Press.

Longstaff, S. (1994) 'What is ethics education and training?', in N. Preston (ed.) *Ethics for the Public Sector.* Sydney: The Federation Press.

Loughlin, M. (2004) *The Idea of Public Law.* Oxford: Oxford University Press.

Lowndes, V. and Skelcher, C. (1998) 'The dynamics of multi-organizational partnerships: an analysis of changing modes of governance', *Public Administration,* 76(2): 313–33.

Luhmann, N. (1980) *The Differentiation of Society*, trans. S. Holmes and C. Larmore. New York: Columbia University Press.

McFall, E. (2002) 'Advertising, persuasion and the culture/economy dualism', in P. du Gay and M. Pryke (eds) *Cultural Economy*. London: Sage.

McFall, E. and du Gay, P. (2002) 'Consuming advertising, consuming cultural history', in S. Miles et al. (eds) *The Changing Consumer*. London: Taylor Francis Routledge.

McFarquhar, H. (1987) 'Legal Personality', in H.McFarquhar *General Principles of Law*. London: Longman.

Macpherson, C.B. (1964) *The Political Theory of Possessive Individualism*. Oxford: Oxford University Press.

Marshall, T.H. (1977) 'A Note on status', in P. du Gay, J. Evans and P. Redman (eds) (2000) *Identity: A Reader*, London: Sage (originally printed in T.H. Marshall (1977) *Class, Citizenship and Social Development*. Chicago: University of Chicago Press).

Mauss, M. (1973) 'Techniques of the body', *Economy & Society*, 2(5): 70–87.

Mauss, M. (1979) *Sociology and Psychology*, trans. B. Brewster. London: Routledge & Kegan Paul.

Mauss, M. (1985) 'A category of the human mind: the notion of person, the notion of self', in P. du Gay, J. Evans and P. Redman (eds) (2000) *Identity: A Reader*. London: Sage (originally printed in M. Carrithers, S. Collins and S. Lukes (eds) (1985) *The Category of the Person*. Cambridge: Cambridge University Press).

Miller, D. (1995) 'Consumption and the vanguard of history', in D. Miller (ed.) *Acknowledging Consumption*. London: Routledge.

Miller, D. (2005) 'What is "best value"? Bureaucracy, virtualism and local governance', in P. du Gay (ed.) *The Values of Bureaucracy*. Oxford: Oxford University Press.

Minson, J. (1993) *Questions of Conduct*. Basingstoke: Macmillan.

Minson, J. (1998) 'Ethics in the Service of the State', in M. Dean and B. Hindess (eds) *Governing Australia*. Sydney: Cambridge University Press.

Minson, J. (2004) 'Human Imperfection: Civil Prudence and Psychoanalysis', paper presented to the Centre for the History of European Discourses Seminar Series, University of Queensland, December.

'Miraculous Mandarins', *Analysis*, BBC Radio 4, 25 July 2002.

Moe, R. (1994) 'The "Re-Inventing Government" exercise: misinterpreting the problem, misjudging the consequences', *Public Administration Review*, 54(2): 111–22.

Mulgan, G. (1994) *Politics in an Anti-Political Age*. Cambridge: Polity Press.

Mulgan, G. (1998) *Connexity*. London: Vintage.

Mulgan, G. and Wilkinson, H. (1992) 'The enabling (and disabling) state', in P. Ekins and M. Nett (eds) *Real Life Economics*. London: Routledge.

Munro, R. (1998) 'Belonging on the move: market rhetoric and the future as obligatory passage', *Sociological Review*, 46(2): 208–43.

National Performance Review (NPR) (1993) *From Red Tape to Results: Creating a Government That Works Better and Costs Less*. Washington, DC: US Government Printing Office.

Niskanen, W. (1971) *Bureaucracy and Representative Government*. Chicago: Aldine-Atherton.

Nussbaum, M. (1994) *The Therapy of Desire.* Princeton: Princeton University Press.

Oakeshott, M. (1975) *Hobbes and Civil Association.* Indianapolis: Liberty Fund.

*The Observer* (1999) 'Blair poised for Whitehall purge', 1 August, p. 2.

Oestreich, G. (1982) *Neostoicism and the Early Modern State.* Cambridge: Cambridge University Press.

Ogbonna, E. and Wilkinson, B. (1990) 'Corporate strategy and corporate culture: the view from the checkout', *Personnel Review,* 19(4): 9–15.

Oliver, D. (2003) *Constitutional Reform in the UK.* Oxford: Oxford University Press.

Orren, K. (1994) 'The work of government: rediscovering the discourse of office in Marbury v. Madison', *Studies in American Political Development*, 8(1): 60–80.

Osborne, D. and Gaebler, T. (1992) *Re-Inventing Government.* Reading, MA: Addison-Wesley.

Osborne, D. and Plastrik, P. (1997) *Banishing Bureaucracy: The Five Strategies for Reinventing Government.* Reading, MA: Addison-Wesley.

Osborne, T. (1998) *Aspects of Enlightenment.* London: UCL Press.

Painter, M. (2000) 'Contracting, the enterprise culture and public sector ethics', in R.A. Chapman (ed.) *Ethics in Public Service for the New Millenium.* Aldershot: Ashgate.

Parker, R. (1993) *The Administrative Vocation.* Sydney: Hale and Iremonger.

Paton, R. (2003) *Managing and Measuring Social Enterprises.* London: Sage.

Pattison, S. (1997) *The Faith of the Managers.* London: Cassell.

Peters, B.G. (1993) 'Managing the hollow state', in K.A. Eliassen and J. Kooiman (eds) *Managing Public Organizations.* London: Sage.

Peters, B.G. (2000a) 'Governance and comparative politics', in J. Pierre (ed.) *Debating Governance.* Oxford: Oxford University Press.

Peters, B.G. (2000b) 'Is democracy a substitute for ethics? Administrative reform and accountability', in R.A. Chapman (ed.) *Ethics in Public Service for the New Millenium.* Aldershot: Ashgate.

Peters, B.G. (2003) 'Dismantling and rebuilding the Weberian state', in J. Hayward and A. Menon (eds) *Governing Europe.* Oxford: Oxford University Press.

Peters, T. (1987) *Thriving on Chaos.* Basingstoke: Macmillan.

Peters, T. (1992) *Liberation Management.* Basingstoke: Macmillan.

Peters, T. (1994) *The Pursuit of Wow!* New York: Random House.

Pierre, J. (2000) 'Introduction: understanding governance', in J. Pierre (ed.) *Debating Governance.* Oxford: Oxford University Press.

Plant, R. (2003) 'A Public Service Ethic and Political Accountability', *Parliamentary Affairs*, 56: 560–79.

Plowden, W. (1994) 'Public interests the public services serve: efficiency and other values', *Australian Journal of Public Administration*, 53(3): 304–12.

Pocock, J.D. (1985) *Virtue, Commerce and History.* Cambridge: Cambridge University Press.

Pollitt, C. and Bouckaert, G. (2000) *Public Management Reform.* Oxford: Oxford University Press.

Pollock, A. and Dunnigan, M. (1998) 'Public health and the private finance initiative', *Journal of Public Health Medicine*, 20(1): 1–2.

Popper, K. (1944/1985) 'Piecemeal social engineering', in D. Miller (ed.) *Popper Selections*. Princeton: Princeton University Press.

Power, M. (1997) *The Audit Society*. Oxford: Oxford University Press.

Pufendorf, S. (1691/2003) *On the Whole Duty of Man, According to the Law of Nature*, trans. Andrew Tooke. Indianapolis: Liberty Fund.

Quinlan, M. (1994) 'Changing patterns in Government business', *Public Policy and Administration*, 9(1): 27–34.

Quinlan, M. (2004) 'Lessons for Governmental process', in W.G. Runciman (ed.) *Hutton and Butler: Lifting the Lid on the Workings of Power*. Oxford: British Academy/Oxford University Press.

Rhodes, R. (1994) 'The hollowing out of the state: the changing nature of public service in Britain', *Political Quarterly*, 65(2): 138–51.

Rhodes, R. (1996) 'The New Governance: governing without government', *Political Studies*, XLIV: 652–67.

Rhodes, R. (1997) 'From Marketisation to Diplomacy: it's the mix that matters', *Australian Journal of Public Administration*, 56(2): 40–53.

Rhodes, R. (1999) 'Foreword', in G. Stoker (ed.) *The New Management of British Local Governance*. Basingstoke: Macmillan.

Rhodes, R. (2000a) 'Governance and public administration', in J. Pierre (ed.) *Understanding Governance*. Oxford: Oxford University Press.

Rhodes, R. (2000b) 'New Labour's Civil Service: summing up joining up', *The Political Quarterly*, 71(2): 151–66.

Rohr, J. (1989) *Ethics for Bureaucrats*, 2nd edn. New York: Marcel Dekker.

Rohr, J. (1998) *Public Service, Ethics and Constitutional Practice*. Lawrence, KS: University of Kansas Press.

Rorty, A.O. (1988) *Mind In Action*. Boston: Beacon Press.

Rorty, R. (1989) *Contingency, Irony and Solidarity*. Cambridge: Cambridge University Press.

Rose, N. (1996) 'Identity, geneaology, history', in S. Hall and P. du Gay (eds) *Questions of Cultural Identity*. London: Sage.

Rose, N. (1999) 'Inventiveness in Politics', *Economy & Society*, 28(3): 467–96.

Rosenau, J.N. (1992) 'Governance, order and change in world politics', in J.N. Rosenau and E.-O Czempiel (eds) *Governance without Government: Order and Change in World Politics*. Cambridge: Cambridge University Press.

Runciman, D. (1999) *Pluralism and the Personality of the State*. Cambridge: Cambridge University Press.

Runciman, D. (2002) 'The garden, the park and the meadow', *London Review of Books*, 24(11), June.

Runciman, D. (2005) 'Institutional hypocrisy', *London Review of Books*, 27(8), April: 21.

Ryan, A. (1996) 'Hobbes's political philosophy', in T. Sorrell (ed.) *The Cambridge Companion to Hobbes*. Cambridge: Cambridge University Press.

Sabl, A. (2002) *Ruling Passions*. Princeton: Princeton University Press.

Saunders, D. (1991) *Authorship and Copyright*. London: Routledge.

Saunders, D. (1997) *The Anti-Lawyers*. London: Routledge.

Saunders, D. (2002) '"Within the orbit of this life" – Samuel Pufendorf and the autonomy of law', *Cardozo Law Review*, 23(6): 2173–98.

Saunders, D. (2005) 'The Moment of Theory in Critical Legal Studies', paper presented to the 'History of Theory' Seminar, Centre for the History of European Discourses, University of Queensland, 3 November.

Sayer, A. (1997) 'The dialectic of culture and economy', in R. Lee and J. Wills (eds) *Geographies of Economies*. London: Edward Arnold.

Schaefer, D. and Schaefer, R. (1992) 'Editors Introduction: Sir Henry Taylor and the study of public administration', in D. Schaefer and R. Schaefer (eds) *The Statesman by Sir Henry Taylor*. Westport, CT: Praeger.

Schmitt, C. (1986) *Political Romanticism*. Cambridge, MA: MIT Press.

Schneewind, J.B. (1990) *The Invention of Autonomy*. Cambridge: Cambridge University Press.

Schotter, A. (1981) *The Economic Theory of Institutions*. Cambridge: Cambridge University Press.

Scott, A. (1996) 'Bureaucratic revolutions and free market utopias', *Economy & Society*, 25(1): 89–110.

Seth, A. and Randall, G. (1999) *The Grocers*. London: Kogan Page.

Shields, R. (1992) *Lifestyle Shopping: The Subject of Consumption*. London: Routledge.

Skelcher, C. (2000) 'Changing images of the state: overloaded, hollowed-out, congested', *Public Policy and Administration*, 15(3): 3–19.

Skinner, Q. (1989) 'The state', in T. Ball, J. Farr and R.L. Hanson (eds) *Political Innovation and Conceptual Change*. Cambridge: Cambridge University Press.

Skinner, Q. (2002) *Visions of Politics Volume III Hobbes and Civil Science*. Cambridge: Cambridge University Press.

Slater, D. (2002) 'Capturing markets from the economists', in P. du Gay and M. Pryke (eds) *Cultural Economy: Cultural Analysis and Commercial Life*. London: Sage.

Stoker, G. (1998) 'Governance as theory: five propositions', *International Social Science Journal*, 155: 17–28.

Stoker, G. (2000a) 'The challenge of urban governance', in J. Pierre (ed.) *Debating Governance*. Oxford: Oxford University Press.

Stoker, G. (2000b) 'The three projects of New Labour', *Renewal*, 8(3): 7–15.

Strathern, M. (ed.) (2001) *Audit Cultures*. London: Routledge.

Strathern, M. (2006) 'A community of critics? Thoughts on new knowledge', *Journal of the Royal Anthropological Institute*, 12: 191–209.

Strauss, A. (1977) *Mirrors and Masks: the Search for Identity*. London: Martin Robertson.

Sturdy, A. (2001) 'Servicing societies? – colonisation, control, contradiction and contestation', in A. Sturdy et al. (eds) *Customer Service: Empowerment and Entrapment*. Basingstoke: Palgrave.

Tawney, R.H. (1926) *Religion and the Rise of Capitalism*. New York: Harcourt, Brace and World.

Taylor, S. (2002) 'Attacking the cultural turn: misrepresentations of the service encounter', *Sociological Research Online*, 7(1), URL (consulted March 10, 2005): http://www. socresonline.org.uk/7/1/taylor.html

*The Times* (1957) 21 January, p. XVI.

Thompson, D. (1987) *Political Ethics and Public Office*. Cambridge, MA: Harvard University Press.

Towsey, R. (1964) *Self-Service Retailing: Its Profitable Application to All Trades*. London: Iliffe Books.

Treasury Taskforce on Private Finance (1997) *Partnerships for Prosperity – The Private Finance Initiative*. London: HMSO.

Tuck, R. (1993) *Philosophy and Government 1572–1651*. Cambridge: Cambridge University Press.

Tully, J. (1988) 'Governing conduct', in E. Leites (ed.) *Conscience and Casuistry in Early Modern Europe*. Cambridge: Cambridge University Press.

Turner, C. (1992) *Modernity and Politics in the Work of Max Weber*. London: Routledge.

Uhr, J. (1994) 'Managing the process of ethics training', in N. Preston (ed.) *Ethics for the Public Sector*. Sydney: The Federation Press.

Uhr, J. (1999) 'Institutions of integrity', *Public Integrity*, Winter: 94–106.

Uhr, J. (2001) 'Public service ethics in Australia', in T.L. Cooper (ed.) *Handbook of Administrative Ethics*. New York: Marcel Dekker.

Unger, R.M. (1986) *The Critical Legal Studies Movement*. Boston: Harvard University Press.

Walker, D. (2004) 'Leviathan lite', in A. Gamble and T. Wright (eds) *Restating the State?* Oxford: Blackwell.

Walzer, M. (1980) *Just and Unjust Wars*. Harmondsworth: Penguin.

Walzer, M. (1984) 'Liberalism and the art of separation', *Political Theory*, 12(3): 315–30.

Weber, M. (1930) *The Protestant Ethic and the Spirit of Capitalism*. London: Harper Collins.

Weber, M. (1948) 'Religious rejections of the world and their directions', in H.H. Gertz and C.Wright Mills (eds) *From Max Weber*. London: Routledge.

Weber, M. (1978) *Economy and Society Vols I & II*. Berkeley: University of California Press.

Weber, M. (1989) 'Science as a vocation', in P. Lassman and I. Velody (eds) *Max Weber's Science As A Vocation*. London: Unwin, Hyman.

Weber, M. (1994a) 'Parliament and government in Germany under a new political order', in P. Lassman and R. Speirs (eds) *Weber: Political Writings*. Cambridge: Cambridge University Press.

Weber, M. (1994b) 'The profession and vocation of politics', in P. Lassman and R. Speirs (eds) *Weber: Political Writings*. Cambridge: Cambridge University Press.

Weinrib, E. (1988) 'Legal formalism: on the immanent rationality of law', *Yale Law Journal*, 97(6): 949–1016.

Wilkinson, H. (1998) 'The family way', in I. Hargreaves and I. Christie (eds) *Tomorrow's Politics*. London: Demos.

Wilson, R. (2004) 'Issues of evidence: discussion', in W.G. Runciman (ed.) *Hutton and Butler: Lifting the Lid On the Workings of Power.* Oxford: British Academy/ Oxford University Press.

Wolter, U. (1997) 'The officium in medieval ecclesiastical law as a prototype of modern administration', in A. Padoa-Schioppa (ed.) *Legislation and Justice.* Oxford: Clarendon Press.

Zimmerman, M. (1955) *The Supermarket: A Revolution in Distribution.* London: McGraw-Hill.

## british trade journals and reports

*Mrs. Housewife and Her Grocer* (Alfred Bird and Co. Ltd, 1957).

*Self-Service and the Shop Worker* (USDAW, 1955).

*Self-Service and Supermarket (1964).*

*Shop Equipment News.*

*Shopping in Suburbia* (J. Walter Thompson Ltd, 1963).

*Shop Review (1955).*

## retail company literature and archive materials

The John Lewis Partnership, *The Gazette of the John Lewis Partnership* (1948–1965)

Marks & Spencer plc, http://www2.marksandspencer.com/thecompany/ whoweare/our_history/1932_1955.shtml

J. Sainsbury plc, http://www.j-sainsbury.co.uk/company/history.htm

*JS 100: The Story of Sainsbury's* (J. Sainsbury Ltd., London, 1969)

# Index